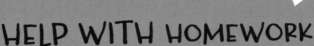

HELP WITH HOMEWORK
ADDING & SUBTRACTING

How to use this book with your child:

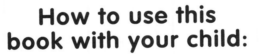
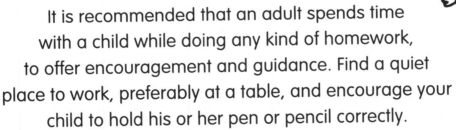

It is recommended that an adult spends time with a child while doing any kind of homework, to offer encouragement and guidance. Find a quiet place to work, preferably at a table, and encourage your child to hold his or her pen or pencil correctly.

Try to work at your child's pace and avoid spending too long on any one page or activity. Most of all, emphasise the fun element of what you are doing and enjoy this special and exciting time!

Don't forget to add a reward sticker to each page you complete!

Autumn
Publishing

Number bonds to 10

Do you remember your number bonds to 10? Refresh your memory by writing the missing numbers in the boxes.

7 + 3 = 10

8 + 2 = 10

9 + 1 = 10

4 + 6 = 10

5 + 5 = 10

Good job!

Number bonds to 20 and 100

Can you use what you know about number bonds to 10 to solve the following calculations?

[2] + 8 = 20

[ ] + 40 = 100

[ ] + 6 = 20

[ ] + 50 = 100

[ ] + 11 = 20

[ ] + 90 = 100

[ ] + 5 = 20

[ ] + 30 = 100

7 + [13] = 20

20 + [ ] = 100

Addition on the farm

Complete these farmyard sums by writing the missing numbers in the boxes.

$\boxed{5} + 7 = 12$ $\boxed{14} + 4 = 18$

$7 + \boxed{7} = 14$ $4 + 13 = \boxed{15}$

$\boxed{10} + 10 = 20$ $\boxed{} + 9 = 18$

Reward sticker!

12 + ☐ = 17   17 + 9 = ☐

☐ + 7 = 19   ☐ + 11 = 29

8 + ☐ = 21   18 + 12 = ☐

☐ + 7 = 25   ☐ + 8 = 27

Reward sticker!

Alien addition

Solve these space sums. Write the answers in the boxes.

15 + 3 = ☐

16 + 5 = ☐

11 + 3 = ☐

18 + 7 = ☐

15 + 9 = ☐

13 + 4 = ☐

Reward
sticker!

26 + 7 = ☐

23 + 9 = ☐

18 + 5 = ☐

91 + 8 = ☐

48 + 3 = ☐

35 + 6 = ☐

67 + 7 = ☐

55 + 6 = ☐

Reward sticker!

Missing numbers

Answer the addition sums below, using one of the numbers in the balloons for each answer.

34 + 6 =

83 + 7 =

77 + 3 =

78 + 4 =

53 + 9 =

23 + 6 =

45 + 7 =

88 + 5 =

13 + 9 =

22

82

90

29

62

52

93

40

80

Reward sticker!

Adding 10s

Work out these sums. (They will help you in the next task!)

5 + 8 = [ ]   6 + 3 = [ ]

2 + 6 = [ ]   5 + 1 = [ ]

7 + 5 = [ ]   8 + 3 = [ ]

Now, use the sums above to help you answer the questions below.
Hint: 4 + 3 = 7, so 40 + 30 = 70.
What do you notice about the answers?

50 + 80 = [ ]   60 + 30 = [ ]

20 + 60 = [ ]   50 + 10 = [ ]

70 + 50 = [ ]   80 + 30 = [ ]

Adding 100s

Work out these sums using what you learnt on the previous page.
Hint: **5 + 4 = 9**, so **50 + 40 = 90** and **500 + 400 = 900**.

300 + 200 =   Hint: 3 + 2 = 5

400 + 300 =

200 + 700 =

100 + 700 =

200 + 500 =

400 + 500 =

Reward
sticker!

Match the answers

Do the additions, then match each sum to the right answer on one of the anchors.

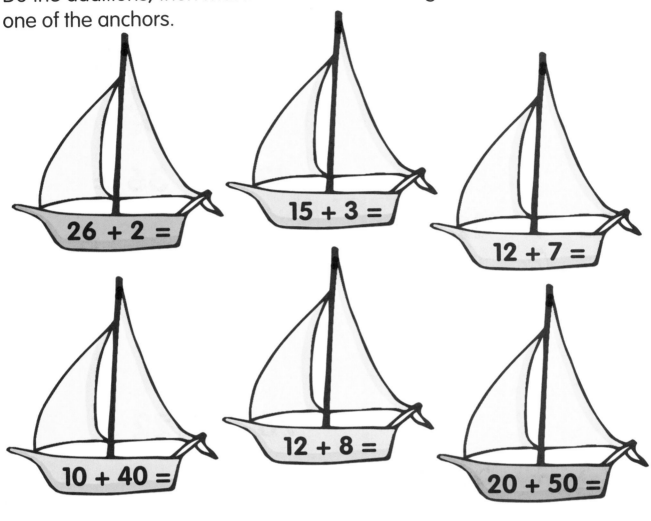

26 + 2 =

15 + 3 =

12 + 7 =

10 + 40 =

12 + 8 =

20 + 50 =

18

19

28

50

70

20

Double digits

Add the two-digit numbers together and write your answers in the boxes. If you need to, use a spare piece of paper to work them out.

35 + 22 =

43 + 36 =

25 + 42 =

65 + 24 =

52 + 34 =

76 + 22 =

23 + 51 =

43 + 16 =

67 + 20 =

37 + 51 =

Reward sticker!

It all adds up

Add the three-digit numbers to the two-digit numbers and write your answers in the boxes.

178 + 45 = ⬚

259 + 52 = ⬚

444 + 63 = ⬚

153 + 30 = ⬚

456 + 16 = ⬚

322 + 26 = ⬚

244 + 55 = ⬚

101 + 23 = ⬚

Reward sticker!

13

Test 1

Now take the addition test. Do the sums and write the answers in the boxes.

11 + 2 = ☐   16 + 7 = ☐

10 + 5 = ☐   3 + 12 = ☐

A boy has **5** sweets and a girl has **17** sweets. How many sweets do they have altogether?

☐

21 + 6 = ☐   20 + 8 = ☐

17 + 7 = ☐   12 + 6 = ☐

One alien has **18** eyes and another alien has **9** eyes. How many eyes do they have altogether?

☐

Reward sticker!

13 + 12 = ☐   20 + 16 = ☐

34 + 23 = ☐   42 + 16 = ☐

48 + 21 = ☐   57 + 22 = ☐

68 + 26 = ☐   45 + 37 = ☐

465 + 4 = ☐

353 + 6 = ☐

272 + 7 = ☐

756 + 7 = ☐

Fact families

A fact family describes a group of three numbers and the way that they relate to each other using addition and subtraction. **E.g.** Here is a fact family for the numbers **8**, **6** and **14**.

- 8 + 6 = 14
- 14 – 6 = 8
- 6 + 8 = 14
- 14 – 8 = 6

Complete the following fact families:

- 8 + 9 = 17
- ___ – ___ = ___
- ___ + ___ = ___
- ___ – ___ = ___

- 9 + 5 = 14
- ___ – ___ = ___
- ___ + ___ = ___
- ___ – ___ = ___

- 5 + 7 = 12
- ___ – ___ = ___
- ___ + ___ = ___
- ___ – ___ = ___

Here is a fact family for the numbers **13**, **7** and **20**.

- **13 + 7 = 20**
- **7 + 13 = 20**
- **20 − 7 = 13**
- **20 − 13 = 7**

Complete the following fact families:

- **8 + 5 = 13**
- **__ + __ = __**

- **__ − __ = __**
- **__ − __ = __**

- **13 + 3 = 16**
- **__ + __ = __**

- **__ − __ = __**
- **__ − __ = __**

- **11 + 4 = 15**
- **__ + __ = __**

- **__ − __ = __**
- **__ − __ = __**

Penguin subtraction

Work out the subtractions and write the answers on the penguins' tummies.

16 – 3 =

18 – 7 =

21 – 12 =

13 – 7 =

15 – 9 =

16 – 8 =

29 – 14 =

20 – 6 =

Reward sticker!

Missing numbers

Complete the subtractions by filling in the missing numbers.

13 − ☐ = 0   21 − ☐ = 14

☐ − 14 = 8   15 − 7 = ☐

27 − ☐ = 19   12 − ☐ = 9

☐ − 9 = 13   18 − 10 = ☐

15 − ☐ = 4   20 − ☐ = 10

Bubble subtractions

Complete the subtractions by filling in the missing numbers.

11 − ☐ = 5

☐ − 5 = 7

☐ − 7 = 6

☐ − 4 = 8

14 − ☐ = 9

☐ − 5 = 17

☐ − 7 = 16

Reward sticker!

Subtraction in space

Complete the subtractions by taking a one-digit number away from a two-digit number. Write your answers in the boxes.

79 − 6 = ☐   88 − 5 = ☐

99 − 8 = ☐   56 − 4 = ☐

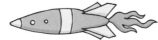

49 − 3 = ☐   37 − 5 = ☐

78 − 4 = ☐   29 − 8 = ☐

Reward sticker!

21

Magic calculations

Work out the subtractions and write the answers in the boxes.

49 – 5 =

37 – 6 =

55 – 3 =

28 – 6 =

67 – 4 =

23 – 9 =

76 – 8 =

54 – 5 =

Reward sticker!

Double digits

Complete the subtractions by taking a two-digit number away from another two-digit number. Write your answers in the boxes.

79 – 16 =

83 – 19 =

27 – 11 =

56 – 12 =

49 – 13 =

57 – 17 =

23 – 13 =

40 – 28 =

Reward sticker!

Fun with subtractions

Solve these problems and write the answers in the boxes.

Take **9** bananas away from this monkey. How many bananas are left?

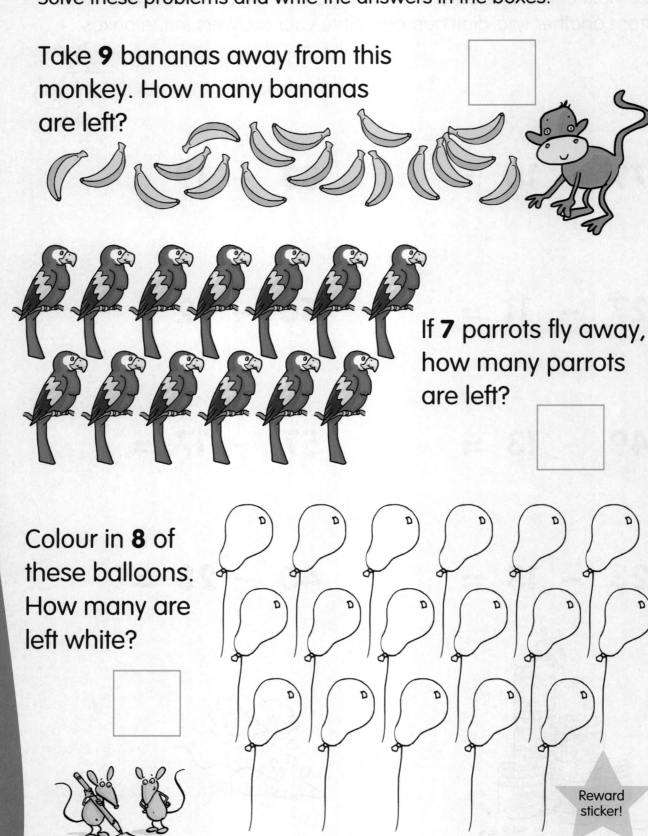

If **7** parrots fly away, how many parrots are left?

Colour in **8** of these balloons. How many are left white?

Reward sticker!

A rabbit eats **4** carrots. How many carrots are left?

Draw **11** lit candles on this cake.

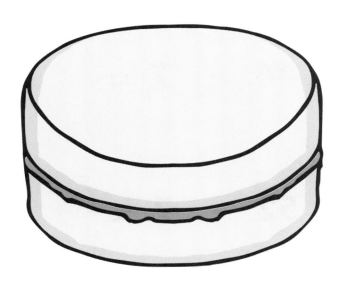

If Molly blows out **3** candles, how many lit candles are left?

Reward sticker!

Butterfly subtractions

Do the subtractions and write the answers in the boxes.

90 – 6 =

60 – 3 =

40 – 4 =

30 – 8 =

50 – 5 =

44 – 7 =

33 – 5 =

52 – 7 =

78 – 9 = ☐   63 – 6 = ☐

83 – 9 = ☐   14 – 12 = ☐

55 – 16 = ☐   77 – 17 = ☐

28 – 13 = ☐   84 – 18 = ☐

Reward sticker!

Super subtractions

Try taking a one-digit number away from a three-digit number. Write your answers in the boxes.

537 – 5 =

648 – 6 =

354 – 3 =

192 – 6 =

746 – 8 =

371 – 5 =

823 – 8 =

342 – 7 =

185 – 9 =

203 – 8 =

Reward sticker!

Test 2

Now take the subtraction test. Do the subtractions and write the answers in the boxes.

13 – 8 = ☐   **11 – 1 =** ☐

15 – 9 = ☐   **18 – 6 =** ☐

 A boy has **18** sweets and he eats **5**. How many sweets does he have left? ☐

14 – 12 = ☐   **17 – 8 =** ☐

22 – 10 = ☐   **24 – 5 =** ☐

 **25** rabbits are sitting in a field and **9** run away. How many rabbits are left? ☐

Reward sticker!

29 – 7 =

37 – 6 =

58 – 3 =

98 – 8 =

48 – 12 =

27 – 15 =

65 – 16 =

39 – 19 =

423 – 4 =

275 – 3 =

739 – 8 =

456 – 9 =

Reward sticker!

Answers:

Page 2: Number bonds to 10

7 + **3** = 10
8 + **2** = 10
9 + **1** = 10
4 + **6** = 10
5 + **5** = 10

Page 3: Number bonds to 20 and 100

12 + 8 = 20
14 + 6 = 20
9 + 11 = 20
15 + 5 = 20
7 + **13** = 20
60 + 40 = 100
50 + 50 = 100
10 + 90 = 100
70 + 30 = 100
20 + **80** = 100

Pages 4–5: Addition on the farm

5 + 7 = 12
14 + 4 = 18
7 + **7** = 14
4 + 13 = **17**
10 + 10 = 20
9 + 9 = 18
12 + **5** = 17
17 + 9 = **26**
12 + 7 = 19
18 + 11 = 29
8 + **13** = 21
18 + 12 = **30**
18 + 7 = 25
19 + 8 = 27

Pages 6–7: Alien addition

15 + 3 = **18**
16 + 5 = **21**
11 + 3 = **14**
18 + 7 = **25**
15 + 9 = **24**
13 + 4 = **17**
26 + 7 = **33**
23 + 9 = **32**
18 + 5 = **23**
91 + 8 = **99**

48 + 3 = **51**
35 + 6 = **41**
67 + 7 = **74**
55 + 6 = **61**

Page 8: Missing numbers

34 + 6 = **40**
83 + 7 = **90**
77 + 3 = **80**
78 + 4 = **82**
53 + 9 = **62**
23 + 6 = **29**
45 + 7 = **52**
88 + 5 = **93**
13 + 9 = **22**

Page 9: Adding 10s

5 + 8 = **13**
6 + 3 = **9**
2 + 6 = **8**
5 + 1 = **6**
7 + 5 = **12**
8 + 3 = **11**

50 + 80 = **130**
60 + 30 = **90**
20 + 60 = **80**
50 + 10 = **60**
70 + 50 = **120**
80 + 30 = **110**

Page 10: Adding 100s

300 + 200 = **500**
400 + 300 = **700**
200 + 700 = **900**
100 + 700 = **800**
200 + 500 = **700**
400 + 500 = **900**

Page 11: Match the answers

26 + 2 = **28**
15 + 3 = **18**
12 + 7 = **19**
10 + 40 = **50**
12 + 8 = **20**
20 + 50 = **70**

Page 12: Double digits

35 + 22 = **57**
43 + 36 = **79**
25 + 42 = **67**
65 + 24 = **89**
52 + 34 = **86**
76 + 22 = **98**
23 + 51 = **74**
43 + 16 = **59**
67 + 20 = **87**
37 + 51 = **88**

Page 13: It all adds up

178 + 45 = **223**
259 + 52 = **311**
444 + 63 = **507**
153 + 30 = **183**
456 + 16 = **472**
322 + 26 = **348**
244 + 55 = **299**
101 + 23 = **124**

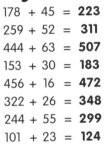

Pages 14–15: Test 1

11 + 2 = **13**
16 + 7 = **23**
10 + 5 = **15**
3 + 12 = **15**
22 sweets
21 + 6 = **27**
20 + 8 = **28**
17 + 7 = **24**
12 + 6 = **18**
27 eyes

13 + 12 = **25**
20 + 16 = **36**
34 + 23 = **57**
42 + 16 = **58**
48 + 21 = **69**
57 + 22 = **79**
68 + 26 = **94**
45 + 37 = **82**
465 + 4 = **469**
353 + 6 = **359**
272 + 7 = **279**
756 + 7 = **763**

Answers:

Pages 16–17: Fact families

8 + 9 = **17**	**9** + **8** = 17
17 – **9** = **8**	**17** – 8 = **9**
9 + 5 = **14**	**5** + **9** = 14
14 – **5** = **9**	**14** – 9 = **5**
5 + 7 = **12**	**7** + **5** = 12
12 – **7** = **5**	**12** – 5 = **7**
8 + 5 = **13**	**5** + **8** = 13
13 – **5** = **8**	**13** – 8 = **5**
13 + 3 = **16**	**3** + **13** = 16
16 – **3** = **13**	**16** – 13 = **3**
11 + 4 = **15**	**4** + **11** = 15
15 – **4** = **11**	**15** – **11** = **4**

Page 18: Penguin subtraction

16 – 3 = **13**
18 – 7 = **11**
21 – 12 = **9**
13 – 7 = **6**
15 – 9 = **6**
16 – 8 = **8**
29 – 14 = **15**
20 – 6 = **14**

Page 19: Missing numbers

13 – **13** = 0
21 – **7** = 14
22 – 14 = 8
15 – 7 = **8**
27 – **8** = 19
12 – **3** = 9
22 – 9 = 13
18 – 10 = **8**
15 – **11** = 4
20 – **10** = 10

Page 20: Bubble subtractions

11 – **6** = 5
12 – 5 = 7
13 – 7 = 6
12 – 4 = 8
14 – **5** = 9
22 – 5 = 17
23 – 7 = 16

Page 21: Subtraction in space

79 – 6 = **73**
88 – 5 = **83**
99 – 8 = **91**
56 – 4 = **52**
49 – 3 = **46**
37 – 5 = **32**
78 – 4 = **74**
29 – 8 = **21**

Page 22: Magic calculations

49 – 5 = **44**
37 – 6 = **31**
55 – 3 = **52**
28 – 6 = **22**
67 – 4 = **63**
23 – 9 = **14**
76 – 8 = **68**
54 – 5 = **49**

Page 23: Double digits

79 – 16 = **63**
83 – 19 = **64**
27 – 11 = **16**
56 – 12 = **44**
49 – 13 = **36**
57 – 17 = **40**
23 – 13 = **10**
40 – 28 = **12**

Pages 24–25: Fun with subtractions

9 bananas
6 parrots
9 balloons
17 carrots
8 candles

Pages 26–27: Butterfly subtractions

90 – 6 = **84**
60 – 3 = **57**
40 – 4 = **36**
30 – 8 = **22**
50 – 5 = **45**
44 – 7 = **37**
33 – 5 = **28**

52 – 7 = **45**
78 – 9 = **69**
63 – 6 = **57**
83 – 9 = **74**
14 – 12 = **2**
55 – 16 = **39**
77 – 17 = **60**
28 – 13 = **15**
84 – 18 = **66**

Page 28: Super subtractions

537 – 5 = **532**
648 – 6 = **642**
354 – 3 = **351**
192 – 6 = **186**
746 – 8 = **738**
371 – 5 = **366**
823 – 8 = **815**
342 – 7 = **335**
185 – 9 = **176**
203 – 8 = **195**

Page 29: Test 2

13 – 8 = **5**
11 – 1 = **10**
15 – 9 = **6**
18 – 6 = **12**
13 sweets
14 – 12 = **2**
17 – 8 = **9**
22 – 10 = **12**
24 – 5 = **19**
16 rabbits

Page 30: Test 3

29 – 7 = **22**
37 – 6 = **31**
58 – 3 = **55**
98 – 8 = **90**
48 – 12 = **36**
27 – 15 = **12**
65 – 16 = **49**
39 – 19 = **20**
423 – 4 = **419**
275 – 3 = **272**
739 – 8 = **731**
456 – 9 = **447**

Nelles Guides

... get you going.

AVAILABLE TITLES

Australia
Berlin and Potsdam
Brittany
California
Crete
Cyprus
Egypt
Florida
Hawaii
Hungary
India North
India South
Indonesia West
  (Sumatra, Java, Bali, Lombok)
Kenya
Mexico
Morocco
Nepal
New Zealand
Paris
Provence
Spain North
Spain South

Thailand
The Caribbean:
  Greater Antilles,
  Bermuda, Bahamas
The Caribbean:
  Lesser Antilles
Turkey

IN PREPARATION

Bali / Lombok
Cambodia / Laos
Canada East
China
Malaysia
Moscow / St. Petersburg
Munich
New York
Philippines
Rome

For your information:
Nelles Guides are also available in German, French and Dutch.

BRITTANY
©Nelles Verlag GmbH, München 45
  All rights reserved

First Edition 1993
ISBN 3-88618-389-0
Printed in Slovenia

Publisher:	Günter Nelles	**Cartography:**	Nelles Verlag GmbH
Chief Editor:	Dr. Heinz Vestner		Freytag & Berndt
Project Editor:	Catherine Bray	**DTP-Exposure:**	Nelles Verlag
Editor:	Angus McGeoch	**Color**	
Translation:	Michael Cunningham	**Separation:**	Priegnitz, Munich
	Simon Knight	**Printed by:**	Gorenjski Tisk

POPPLETON.

BRITTANY

First Edition
1993

TABLE OF CONTENTS

FEATURES

GUIDELINES

LIST OF MAPS

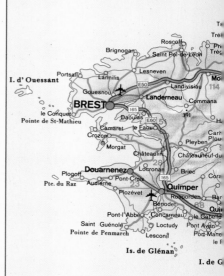

BRITTANY

0   20km   40km

HISTORY
AND CULTURE

THE CHARACTER OF BRITTANY

The unique character of Brittany is formed by the sea. It is a peninsula marked with coasts which have been carved by the waves to extend for almost 3000 km (1900 miles). The sea has had as much impact on Brittany's culture as on its history, for it is still responsible for the region's three main economic resources: commerce, fishing and tourism.

Brittany's maritime character may be the region's most obvious and most spectacular feature, but it is far from being the only one. There is water to be found everywhere – in rivers, canals, marshes, and in the rainstorms brought in by gales from the north west and the south west. There is also a gentleness and freshness which are bestowed by an ever-changing sky, and it is this that has prompted the notion that in Brittany "it is possible to see all four seasons in a single day". The blue of the open sea and the gray of the cliffs have their place, but it is green that dominates this rain-washed region of France.

Landscape

All along the coastline, dunes alternate with cliffs, while bays alternate with headlands made of dark granite or red sandstone rocks. It is a place where the winds and the waves rule supreme, and

Previous pages: A wedding photo outside a house in Plougrescant. A chaos of pink granite at Ploumanac'h. Women wearing Breton headdress at the pardon of Notre-Dame-de-Tronoën. Left: A house in the Change district of Nantes.

one that often produces quite dazzling landscapes: in Breton, it is called *Ar mor,* which means "the land of the sea".

As the windswept heathlands sweep up to the skyline, they are brightened first by wild flowers, clumps of yellow broom and spiky gorse, and then higher up by pink tufts of heather. Of the huge forest which once existed, Brittany has managed to preserve no more than a few localized patches – and the traditional name of the Breton hinterland, *Ar goat,* which means "the land of the forest".

Up on the plains, the land is divided up by screes, *talus* (high stone walls surrounding fields) and streams, while the hand of the Breton farmer is seen in various determined attempts to tame the wind, the exposed hills and the water. This is mixed woodland and pasture land in innumerable tiny parcels of property, and on turning a corner round a clump of trees one can still come across a dark stone house with its roof sweeping almost to the ground, or the faded elegance of a farm or country house.

In fact, the 20th century has drastically changed these landscapes with the introduction of modern agriculture and the appearance of *méjous*, long strips of land extending over huge expanses of the region; the urban areas, too, have been undergoing intensive industrialization since the 1960s.

However, like its ever-popular and lively traditions, Brittany's natural heritage seems to have escaped the ravages of the modern era; the irresistible charm which the area still possesses, allied to the beauty of its coastline, makes Brittany the second most important tourist region in France, which is no small boast.

A Meeting of Cultures

There is another feature of Brittany which is not geographical but cultural. This is the story of Brittany's linguistic heritage which encompasses strongly

held religious beliefs and political opinions. On the one side, we have the east of Brittany known as Upper Brittany (Haute Bretagne): here, the French language won the day early but it still lives side by side with the Gallo dialect which survives mainly in rural areas. On the other side is western Brittany known as Lower Brittany (Basse Bretagne): this is Breton-speaking Brittany where almost a third of the population still understands or speaks the Breton language. It is also where the most lively traditions are to be found.

THE ORIGINS OF BRITTANY

The first signs of habitation on the Armorican Peninsula go back to the Paleolithic (8000 B.C.) and Mesolithic (6000-3500 B.C.) periods, but the earliest remains of an established civilization date from Neolithic times (3500-1800 B.C.): These striking remains are called dol-

Above: The mysterious alignment of menhirs near Carnac.

mens and menhirs, and go under the collective name of megaliths.

Dolmens, which look like huge stone tables and are a potent reminder of the importance of the worship of the dead, are communal tombs usually consisting of a circular chamber and a corridor covered with flat stones. The stones used in the construction of these dolmens sometimes weigh several tons each, and the overall dimensions can be breathtaking. Particularly striking are the enormous constructions on the Île Gaignog (Finistère) and Carnac (Morbihan), and those at Locmariaquer (Morbihan), which are also known as the *Table des Marchands* (Merchants' Table), *Mané-Lud* and *Mané-Rutual*. Some dolmens are decorated with engravings of idols, symbols such as an axe or a crooked stick, or sacred animals like a serpent or ox horns against a background of geometric designs (curving lines, spirals and arcs). In terms of ornamentation, the dolmen on the Île de Gavrinis (Morbihan) is one of the most remarkable of its kind.

The significance of menhirs, which are vertical stones, has never been established, but they may well have marked the spot where sanctuaries once stood, and they were certainly involved in the same type of worship as dolmens. There are splendid lines of menhirs at Carnac-Erdeven, and they are also found in circles, for example at Er-Lannic near Larmor-Baden (Morbihan).

The Bronze Age (1800-600 B.C.) is notable for the use of individual tombs known as *tumuli* which have been found to contain large numbers of swords, axes and jewels, proof of a significant metal industry at the time. Objects discovered in tombs, dolmens and tumuli today form part of archaeological collections in museums at Carnac, Penmarc'h, Rennes and Vannes.

Celtic and Gallo-Roman Armorica

The first Celts settled in Armorica (itself a Celtic word meaning "which gives onto the sea") during the 4th and 3rd centuries B.C., and gave many of the towns and villages the names that have survived to the present day. In the 2nd century B.C., the region was shared among five Gallic tribes, including the Veneti and the Coriosoliti, who left behind some beautiful coins and ceramic pieces. The decorative motifs found their inspiration on the other side of the Channel, but the figure of a horse with a man's head which is found on the coins is purely Armorican.

When Julius Caesar initiated the Gallic Wars in 58 B.C., the Veneti held sway over their compatriots and controlled both the tin mines and the Atlantic trade. The following year, they placed themselves at the head of a league of Armorican peoples in an attempt to repel the Roman invasion. The decisive battle, which was fought at sea, saw the large, heavy vessels of the Veneti fleet set against the lighter, better equipped and numerically superior Roman ships. The

Veneti were routed and the result was the formation of the Gallo-Roman Armorica. The Roman occupation lasted for four centuries, but the spirit and culture of the Armorican peoples were never subdued.

Julius Caesar's policy was to clip the wings of any power that posed a threat to him and to profit from the natural riches of a new territory. The trading superiority of the Veneti was now at an end, but two towns benefited from the prosperity which the Romans brought. These were Condevicnum (modern Nantes), the capital of the Namnete tribe and strategically placed on a river estuary, and Condate (modern Rennes), the capital of the Riedone tribe and sited at a major crossroads. The most important and most profitable businesses were the mining of ore and trading in whatever could be extracted from the sea, namely shellfish, fish and salt.

The artistic heritage of this early period known as the High Empire (Haut-Empire) includes fine examples of ceramics, statuettes, pottery and goldsmiths' art, such as a golden dish used in sacrifices which was discovered in Rennes and is now on display in the medal-room of the Musée de Bretagne. It was also in the 2nd century that the carving on the Kervadel menhir was further embellished with the addition of several bas-reliefs showing both Roman deities and figures from local mythology.

The barbarian invasions which swept through Gaul during the Low Empire (Bas-Empire) in the 3rd century AD were to have the effect of gradually weakening Roman domination; in the meantime, the coasts of Armorica were being ravaged by Vikings who spread down from the North Sea through the Channel.

While the fading power of the Romans now made it possible for the main towns and cities to revert to their tribal names, the inhabitants of Nantes, Rennes and Vannes were still forced to barricade themselves behind the ramparts and to

fortify their ports. When the invasions ceased, the ports continued to flourish at the expense of the inand towns.This trend was to last to the present day.

The splendor of Roman civilization finally collapsed in the course of the 4th century. A number of magnificent villas from this era survive, and have been excavated at Carnac (Morbihan), Gorré-Bloué de Plouescat and Saint-Frégant (Finistère). There was further Germanic incursion at the beginning of the 5th century, but this was met head on by the Armoricans who rose up and successfully defended themselves against occupation.

From Armorica to Brittany (5th-7th Centuries)

The year 450 saw the arrival of the first Breton immigrants who had been forced out of Wales by the Angles and the Sax-

Above: Ancient columns. Right: A menhir Christianized by the addition of a cross, near Fougères.

ons, but it was not until the following century that the historian Gregory of Tours first used the word *Brittania*; this was of no small significance as it indicated the presence of a sizeable Breton colony established alongside Gallo-Roman Armorica. There were even Roman enclaves that still survived in Breton Armorica, which extended as far as what is now Côtes-d'Armor, Finistère and Morbihan in the west. The eastern part was conquered by the Merovingian King Clovis I (481-511) and became Gallo-Frankish Armorica: it comprised the dioceses of Rennes, Vannes and Nantes, and covered an area which corresponds to present-day Ille-et-Vilaine, to the east of Morbihan and to the north of Loire-Atlantique.

The most prominent individuals of the 6th and 7th centuries were religious figures, bishops of Gallo-Roman ancestry and Breton monks who were as keen to exploit the land as to spread the gospel. The Celtic and religious place names dating from this time include such words as *plou* (parish), *tré* (part of a parish) and *lan* (hermitage). The texts which recount the lives of the saints, and were written many centuries later, also hand down a "golden legend" of Breton civilization. They tell of saints, like St Maclou, who are said to have gone to Armorica with the first waves of Breton settlers in the 5th century and founded bishoprics in towns such as Saint-Malo (St Maclou), Saint-Brieuc (St Brioc), Saint-Pol-de-Léon (St Pol), Dol (St Samson), Tréguier (St Tugdual), Quimper (St Corentin) and Vannes (St Patern).

The Bretons never gave up their attempts to push eastwards, but they were held at bay by the Frankish armies, and the frequent struggles turned the region into a permanent battlefield. Inside the Frankish kingdom, the Carolingian dynasty succeeded the Merovingians with the accession to the throne of Pippin the Short (751-68), and it was around this

time that the March of Brittany was formed, bringing the *comtés* (counties) of Nantes, Rennes and Vannes into a coalition which could make a stand against the incursions and rebellions of lower Brittany. The Frankish aristocrats who led this coalition included Roland, Charlemagne's celebrated nephew (768-814).

FEUDAL BRITTANY

Nominoé and the First Kings of Brittany (9th Century)

For many people, Nominoé, Duke of Brittany from 824, was the founder of the Breton fatherland. Appointed *missus* of the last Carolingian Emperor (Charlemagne was the first to appoint *Missi Dominici*, his personal emissaries who were given considerable powers to govern and exact the obedience of the counts, then the local rulers), he was to remain a loyal servant of Frankish power until the death of Louis the Pious (840). With the death of Louis, attempts were made to maintain the unity of the Empire which stretched from the Pyrenees to the Baltic and from the Adriatic Sea to the Atlantic. In a series of skirmishes, his sons, Lothair I (Emperor of Occident 840-55), Charles II the Bald (King of western France 843-77) and Pippin I (King of The West 814-38), disputed the succession. Nominoé chose to give his support to Lothair who would have allowed him to maintain his own independence, but Lothair was defeated by his brothers and was forced to divide up the empire. This treaty handed western France, including Brittany, over to Charles II who promptly took up arms against the Duke of Brittany. In 845, Nominoé's armies inflicted a major defeat on Charles's troops, and the Breton leader soon conquered Rennes and Nantes, thereby placing under his control both Celtic Brittany and the counties of the old March that had been held by the Franks. It fell to his heir, Erispoé, who in his turn also defeated Charles the Bald, to begin the line of the Breton monarchy,

17

church of Saint-Philibert-de-Grand-Lieu is the most important Carolingian architectural relic of 9th century Brittany.

The 9th C. also saw the first Norman invasions. In 890 Alain, Count of Vannes, crushed the invaders, thus earning the title of Alain the Great. He also crowned himself Alain I of Brittany, but on his death in 907, the Normans renewed their attacks. The Benedictine monks, whose influence had been important for more than a century, were forced to flee.

The Dukes of Feudal Brittany (10th-12th Centuries)

The Norman influence on Brittany's history did not come to an end until Nantes, the main town of a small Norman state, was captured by Alain Barbetorte in 937. On being elected Duke of Brittany, Alain II set about rebuilding a country that had been drastically weakened and disorganised by long periods of invasion.

The monasteries began to re-assert their cultural influence and, until the 11th century, even increased in number. The Landévennec manuscripts contain wonderful examples of the Celtic art of illuminating, as practiced in the great monasteries.

The death of Alain Barbetorte (Crookbeard) in 952 was a signal for a resumption of the War of Succession with the House of Rennes, supported by the Counts of Blois, opposing the House of Nantes, and the Counts of Anjou. The Count of Rennes, Conan le Tort (Conan I) succeeded in re-establishing his nominal authority over the whole duchy, and this was sustained by his son Geoffroi who broke free from the heavy-handed patronage of the Counts of Blois and sought the protection of the Duke of Normandy; however, the supremacy of the House of Rennes fell away sharply under his successors. Alain III (1008-40) was continually forced to crush rebellions by peasants, and even more frequently by

having received the title and insignia of the King of Brittany when swearing his oath of allegiance to the King of the Franks. However, he was assassinated shortly afterwards at the instigation of his cousin and rival, Salomon; Salomon then reigned from 857 to 875 when he too was assassinated.

The second half of the 9th century found Bretons moving into all the key positions in the community, from bishops to counts and *missi,* while within the feudal system that was beginning to take shape, the big landowners became powerful local aristocrats. First the Merovingians, and then the Carolingians, had a strong influence chiefly in administrative matters, but also to some extent in the arts. What little has survived from this time includes remains of carved ornaments with a mixture of pagan and Christian imagery (on display in the Dobrée Museum in Nantes), while the abbey

Above: The arcaded belfry of the Church of St Sauveur. Right: Mont-Saint-Michel.

the powerful, vindictive nobles; some of them, including the Counts of Cornouaille (in the south west of what is now Finistère) and the nobles of Penthièvre (part of modern Côtes-d'Armor), continued to create problems for his successor, Conan II (1056-66). It was one of these seditious nobles, Hoël, Count of Cornouaille and the Duke's brother-in-law, who was to inherit the ducal crown on Conan's death. It was a case of history repeating itself, however, and Hoël (1066-84) was himself obliged to confront both the uprisings led by the Seigneurs of Penthièvre and the attempts by William the Conqueror, Duke of Normandy, to seize control of the Duchy of Brittany. Hoël's son, Alain IV (1084-1112), also known as Alain Fergent, reunited the counties of Cornouaille, Rennes and Nantes by inheritance and himself married a daughter of the Count of Anjou. This would have been more than sufficient to ensure his authority and independence if he had not chosen an ally more powerful than himself: Henry I of England (1100-35), Duke of Normandy. In 1112, Alain abdicated in favor of his son Conan III (1112-48) who was also Henry I's son-in-law. Brittany had been part of the kingdom of France since the 10th century but it had always been neglected by its masters and had in fact enjoyed de facto independence. However, the Treaty of Gisors (1113) put an end to the wars and passed Brittany to the Duke of Normandy.

Romanesque Art

The era of the great Romanesque buildings in Brittany occurred in the last quarter of the 11th century and in the 12th century, the most beautiful examples of this period being the apse and crypt of the Church of Saint-Croix in Quimperlé, both notable for the balance and form of the arcades and the beauty of the capitals surmounting the columns. Once again, the carved decoration reveals innumerable influences from a variety of sources (English, Aquitainian and Norman), yet transfigured by the characteristic styles of the Armorican Celts: an illustration of this is the frequency with which groups of ornaments include sea monsters with hair of sea-weed and all kinds of plant and animal motifs from under the sea. An even more ambitious structure is the church on the summit of Mont-Saint-Michel which was started in 1017 but not completed until 1144. Today we see a striking contrast between the sombre nave and the choir, which was rebuilt between 1446 and 1521 in the gothic *flamboyant* style, and which continues the tradition of the magnificent buildings of the Merveille dating from 1211-38. The church at Redon also retains its low, dark nave so characteristic of 11th-century Romanesque, in addition to a remarkable arcaded tower. There is a similar, elegant simplicity about the church at Loctudy, one of the most beautiful in Brittany.

The Century of the Plantagenets (12th Century)

In 1152, the future Henry II, grandson of Henry I of England and heir to the counties of Anjou and Maine through his father, married Alienor (Eleanor) of Aquitaine and, through her dowry, became the possessor of vast new lands. Two years later, in 1154, Henry II (1154-89) inherited the Duchy of Normandy and the crown of England through his mother. Brittany had never known a leader of such ability nor one who so yearned for power and extension of his territories; sadly, it was about to lose its independence and be dragged into the first Hundred Years' War of 1159-1299, contested by the Kings of England and the Dukes of Anjou on the one hand and the Kings of France on the other.

In 1166, the Duke of Brittany, Conan IV, who had been considering an alliance

Right: Medieval buildings in Locronan.

with King William of Scotland, reaped the harvest of contemplating treason. Henry II destroyed the castle at Fougères, had his own even-year-old son Geoffrey (Geoffroi) betrothed to Conan's daughter Constance, and encouraged Conan to abdicate in favor of his future son-in-law, thereby creating a regency that lasted until 1181. When Geoffroi (1181-86) ascended the throne, however, Henry's hold over Brittany was in no way relaxed; indeed, the region continued to be ruled as firmly as ever, albeit indirectly. It has to be conceded, nonetheless, that the new sovereign, whose only association with England was through his title and who was much closer to his French origins, gave Brittany something that it had never been able to achieve through centuries of chaos and internal strife: namely, political organization and an administrative structure which enabled the region to catch up economically and culturally. Geoffroi was much closer to the hearts of the Bretons, and made a name for himself as a benevolent monarch.

Geoffroi's heir was called Arthur after the famous character whose epic story had been celebrated throughout Brittany since the 9th century. This legend contained the germ of the Bretons' growing patriotic fervor, and vividly symbolised the people's courage, pride and faith.

BRITTANY IN THE MIDDLE AGES

The Legends of Brittany (12th-13th Centuries)

No region has been more successful in giving to world culture a range of myths of such supreme literary importance. There can be few people today who would claim not to know King Arthur, Merlin the sorcerer or the Knights of the Round Table, not to mention the tragic story of Tristan and Iseult! What, though, are the sources of these myths and how were they turned into literature?

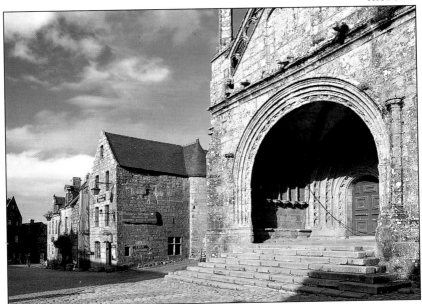

Despite centuries of internal struggles which left Brittany reduced in size and frequently in a state of chaos, a sense of identity, even of patriotism, slowly but surely began to take a hold from the time of Nominoé until the reign of Conan III. Although this sense was expressed within a marked cultural tradition that thrived under the dual influence of warriors and mystics, it is still not possible exactly to date the birth of the epic story of King Arthur, which appeared during the 9th century in *Historia Brittonum,* having been inspired by early fragments: it was not until 1135 that a 12th-century Benedictine of Armorican origin, Geoffroy of Monmouth, published a new Latin version entitled *Historia Regum Britanniae.* (History of the Kings of Britain)

Characters who were already making their appearance included Arthur, the son of King Uther Pendragon and the fair Igraine; Merlin the sorcerer, friend of Uther and then of his son Arthur; the treacherous Mordred; Hoël from Britanny, (or "little Britain") Arthur's ally and

friend and the future Lancelot; and Guanhumara, Arthur's wife, Lancelot's lover and the future Guinevere. A later work by Geoffroy of Monmouth, *Vita Merlini,* also introduced early personifications of the enchantress Vivienne (the Lady of the Lake) and Morgan le Fey. One way and another, the success of these books ensured that the Arthurian legend would give birth to a host of other literary versions. Around 1155, the poet Robert Wace (c 1110-75), a native of Jersey, wrote a French version for Eleanor of Aquitaine entitled *Geste des Bretons* (or *Le Roman de Brut*), and in it introduced the theme of the Round Table. The story of the quest for the Holy Grail made its first appearance in *Perceval ou Conte du Graal* (1180) by the writer of courtly novels, Chrétien de Troyes. Then came the romances of the Round Table, *Lancelot ou Le Chevalier à la Charrette* and *Yvain ou Le Chevalier au Lion.*

Within fifty years the vogue for Arthurian legends had swept through Europe. In another fifty years it reached its zenith

with the publication in 1230 of the entire cycle of legends under the title of *Lancelot en Prose* , also known as *Lancelot – Graal*. This anonymous work is in five parts *(l'Histoire du Saint-Graal, Merlin, Lancelot, la Quête du Graal* and *la Mort d'Arthur)* in which all the themes that had been explored earlier were brought together in a single cohesive narrative, with a harmonious blend of three styles: the epic, the courtly and the religious.

What came to be known as the "matter of Britain" (or Brittany) has been a rich source of fables and of symbolism which poets and novelists have drawn upon for centuries. It has its roots in the Celtic culture which is embedded in this mysterious region of France, and to an equal degree in the British Isles. Not only writers, but more recently film-makers have been inspired by these legends, notably Steven Spielberg in *The Fisher King* and the

British director John Boorman in his superb *Excalibur.*

If the forest of Paimpont could pass as the vestiges of the forest of Brocélande, it is around Douarnenez that memories of Tristan and Iseult still hang in the air. This myth, which is said to be based on events which took place in Brittany in the late 8th and early 9th centuries, has inspired the verse romances of Béroul (*Roman de Tristan* c.1150), Thomas (12th C.) and the *Lai du Chèvrefeuille* by Marie de France, whose *Fables et Lais* (1160-1170) were very popular in Brittany. The German version of this story, *Tristan* (1210) by Gottfried von Strassburg provided the material for Wagner's famous opera.

Brittany under the House of Capet (13th-14th Centuries)

The death of the Henry II, the English Plantagenet king, followed three years after that of his son, Geoffroi, Duke of Brittany. Then, when Richard the Lion-

Above: A haunting scene at Huelgoat.
Right: Hugues Capet and Henry II.

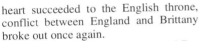

heart succeeded to the English throne, conflict between England and Brittany broke out once again.

Constance, Geoffroi's widow and Regent of the Duchy, was impsrisoned in 1197 and Arthur, the young Duke of Brittany, was placed under the protection of the King of France, Philippe Auguste (1180-1223), the founder of the House of Capet. Arthur was only thirteen years of age when John Lackland (1199-1216) succeeded his brother Richard the Lionheart as king of England and renewed hostilities against France, as he no longer recognized her sovereignty over his French territories.

Philippe Auguste chose Arthur to carry out the reprisals, and not only gave him full powers to govern Brittany but in 1202 also put him in charge of the fiefs of John Lackland whose treachery had led to the forfeiture of his lands. Hence his nickname. Sadly, the young Duke Arthur was to be assassinated the following year at the behest of the King of England. Philippe Auguste maintained his control

over Brittany by marrying the heiress to the duchy, Arthur's half-sister Alix, to a Capetian prince, Pierre de Dreux. Better known as Pierre de Mauclerc, Brittany's new governor (1213-50) was a powerful character. He fought hard to defend his rights, and also knew how to tame the nobles who were in a bellicose frame of mind and were already building an ever-increasing number of fortified castles; he was also independently minded and often attracted the fury of the Church, which was disputing the ownership of some of his goods and lands. Finally, he was an agile politician and moved from one ally to the next according to the needs and interests of the moment: he was first a vassal of the Kings of France, Philippe Auguste and Louis VIII (1223-26) until 1226, then he bowed the knee to Henry III of England (1216-72) until 1229, before returning to the French fold in 1234 under Louis IX (1226-70). He even added his own emblem, the ermine, to the Breton coat of arms as a mark of his years of government.

23

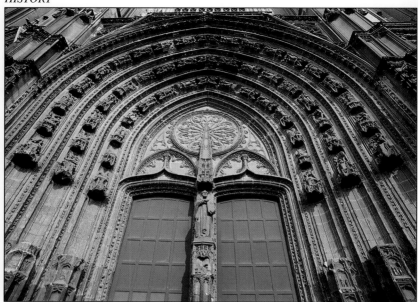

His son, Jean I (1237-1286) and grandson Arthur II (1305-12) remained loyal to the Kings of France, who were now beginning to assert increasing military superiority in the unending battles against the Kings of England. Jean I took advantage of this period of tranquility to discipline the nobles and establish his authority, something that was soon acknowledged to be a guarantee of internal peace; furthermore, he adopted a policy of taking over the numerous estates of the bankrupted nobility, thereby replacing the military actions that had previously been undertaken to expand the ducal domain. The duchy's administrative structure involved the setting up of eight *sénéchaussées* (seneschalsies or bailiwicks). When Jean I was not occupied with the affairs of state, he indulged in the luxuries that were appropriate to a cultured nobleman, wrote and composed courtly songs, acquired horses and for-

Above: The main door of the cathedral of Saint-Pierre in Nantes.

tified castles, and went hunting. At last Brittany's economy began to improve gradually, and during the 13th century the country enjoyed a long-awaited period of peace and prosperity.

The produce of the land was, with the exception of wine, largely consumed within the confines of Brittany itself, but fish and seafood were exported and new horizons opened up for sea trading. Fish-drying industries sprang up everywhere, and the Loire was now crossed in both directions by vessels trading in both Breton salt and wines from Anjou and Touraine. From ports on the south coast like Guérande, Breton fleets carried Bordeaux wine to England, while other ports like Saint-Malo which were too far off the wine routes developed another kind of commerce: piracy. The 13th century also saw the Breton language face yet another retreat; It now found itself driven back even further towards the Atlantic behind a zigzagging line running to the west of Saint-Brieuc, Ploërmel, Redon and Saint-Nazaire.

There was no let-up, however, in the hold that France had over the region. Under Jean II (1286-1305) and then Arthur II (1305-12), the clergy recognised for all practical purposes the authority of the monarchy who frequently, always with the connivance of the Pope, imposed "French" bishops on them. The Church was much more concerned with political rather than spiritual affairs, and was strongly criticized by the Breton nobility, but it is important to distinguish the Church from the Augustinian, Benedictine and Cistercian monastic institutions whose expansion in the 12th century and importance in the 13th century bear testimony to the deep religious fervor of the Breton people. At the same time, in 1303, Philippe le Bel (Philip the Fair – 1285-1314) was able to raise a tax on Brittany to finance his war in Flanders, and even, in 1308, to have the goods of the Knights Templar seized without fear of protestations. Finally, it was of Philip the Fair that Arthur II's second wife, Yolande de Dreux, demanded a guarantee that her son, Jean de Montfort, should ascend the throne in succession to Jean III, a son of Arthur II's first marriage. The seeds of discord had once again been sown, and Brittany was about to plunge into an exhausting war: the War of Succession.

GOTHIC BRITTANY
The War of Succession (14th Century)

Jean III (1312-41) died without an heir, and the succession was contested by Jean de Montfort, Jean III's half-brother, and Charles de Blois, a nephew of the King of France and the husband of Jean III's niece, Jeanne de Penthièvre. The two sides confronted one another for 24 years, and the alliances that were struck – Edward III of England supporting Jean de Montfort and Philippe VI of France supporting Charles de Blois – turned the Breton conflict into one of the major episodes of the second Hundred Years' War (1337-1453). When all the involved protagonists were made prisoner, their wives, Jeanne de Flandres and Jeanne de Penthièvre, continued the war. In 1362, however, the future Jean IV (1365-99), the son of Jean de Montfort, brought the exhausting struggle to its decisive phase, and Charles de Blois, who had already been defeated at Auray in 1364, perished in the ensuing battle. The following year, King Charles V of France (1364-80) handed the ducal crown to Jean IV de Montfort, but it was not long before the fires of conflict were to reignite. Jean IV rejoined the English camp, the deadly enemies of his master and, now exiled and branded a traitor, left the duchy vacant, whereupon Charles V confiscated it and reunited it under the French crown in 1378. In a final historic twist to this Breton episode, Jean IV returned to Brittany in 1379 with the support of the powerful nobles, including Jeanne de Penthièvre who had once been his bitterest enemy. Brittany had not taken kindly to being annexed, and the death of Charles V and the accession to the throne of Charles VI enabled Jean IV to re-assume the title in 1381. The Breton nobles wished to have no more dealings with the English, and Jean undertook not to ally himself with them again. So it was that the War of Succession came to an end.

It left part of Brittany utterly exhausted, disorganized and impoverished by the taxes that had been imposed to finance the Montfort and Blois armies. Paradoxically, however, the war had also had a positive influence on trade with England. The 14th century also saw an increase in the demand for salt, which ensured the independence of the Breton market and gave employment to a substantial sector of the Breton population. The rural economy found a new outlet in textiles, and the region produced cloth of all types for all purposes, from the roughest materials to the very finest, including the celebrated Morlaix linen.

**The Breton Fortified Castle
(13th-15th Century)**

The interminable wars of the 14th century and the troubles in the second half of the 15th century left their mark not only on Brittany in general, but on its architecture which no longer looked to the Loire for its inspiration and had developed a style of its own. The two facts coincided to stimulate the art of fortification, and fortified castles and towns grew up in many parts of the region, nowhere more so than along the old frontier of the Marches of Brittany from Mont-Saint-Michel to the area round Clisson south east of Nantes. An example of this is Fougères Castle (Île-et-Vilaine) which had been pulled down by Henry II, re-built at the end of the 13th century and had then undergone successive alterations until the

Above: The huge tower of the Chapel of St Nicodemus, near Pontivy. Right: Vitré Castle.

15th century. The outer wall is lapped by the River Nançon and the castle looks for all the world like an island defended by huge walls and thirteen towers. The external walls tell the story of architectural development starting with the modestly proportioned and square Cadran Tower (13th-century), moving on to the 13th-14th century Gobelin Towers and the 14th-century Mélusine Tower, already more imposing and rounded, and finishing with the huge U-shaped 15th-century Surienne and Raoul Towers which were specifically constructed for military purposes. That is not to say, however, that the castle lacks ornmentation: embrasures, merlons, machicolations, corbelling, windows and the trimmings of turrets are all picked out in a lighter colored stone; similarly, the pepper-pot roofs are covered with slate, a naturally beautiful material which changes color from blue to black according to the light.

The same slate-covered roofs are to be seen at Vitré Castle (Île-et-Vilaine). Rebuilt in the 13th and 14th centuries, this castle stands firmly on the top of a dark shale rock with the base of the towers built into the stone; two of these towers, bristling with machicolations and projections, guard the entrance to the triangular outer wall. To the right of the castle is a Romanesque porch with archstones of alternating colors, while an apsidiole close to the Oratory Tower is already in the Renaissance style.

Even more striking are the fortifications that go to make up Saint-Malo (Île-et-Vilaine) and its castle. The ramparts, which surrounded the town to protect it not only from pirates but also from enemy invasions, were started in the 12th century and were continually enlarged and altered up to the 15th century.The earliest elements of the castle are its small 14th C. dungeon keep and a larger keep dating from the 15th century. A chapel and a gallery were added in the 17th century, the golden age of the town.

The Heyday of the Duchy
(15th Century)

Despite a few skirmishes with the English and the lords of Penthièvre, the first half of the 15th century can generally be considered to have been the most peaceful and most prosperous period, for a very long time. Jean V (1399-1442) was a patron of the arts and also encouraged the building of chapels and cathedrals, and the duchy's economic expansion carried on apace. The textile industry continued to develop, and the Breton fleet replaced those of Normandy and Aquitaine as the leader in commercial traffic, which was rapidly increasing in volume. The new destinations for Breton shipping now included Holland, Flanders, Ireland and Scotland in the north, and Portugal and Madeira in the south. Brittany was now powerful as a result of this new prosperity and had become the second of the great French fiefs after Burgundy. It did not allow itself to be dominated by the central power and took measures to maintain the "freedoms, prerogatives and dignity of the duchy". It is true that the three Dukes of Brittany, François I (1442-50), Pierre II (1450-57) and Arthur III (1457-58), helped the French to drive the English out of Normandy and Aquitaine, and restored commercial and maritime links with those regions, but they also worked hard to consolidate ducal authority and aspired to genuine independence. François II (1458-88) had high hopes of realizing these ambitions when he formed an alliance with Charles the Bold, Duke of Burgundy, and Edward IV of England in 1468, but he was opposed by one of the most politically astute and enterprising of all French Kings, Louis XI (1461-83). In 1477, the most powerful of the rebellious subjects, Charles the Bold, was defeated at Nancy, and François, now isolated and threatened by the rapidly increasing strength of the new French state (swollen by the addition of Burgundy, Picardy, Maine, Anjou and Provence), went out in search of new alliances. One consequence was the marriage of the heir ap-

27

parent, Anne of Brittany, to the Archduke Maximilian of Austria, the future Emperor of the Holy Roman Empire. On Louis XI's death, François II joined those who were opposed to the heir to the French throne, but his armies were defeated in 1488 and he was obliged to swear allegiance by the Treaty of Le Verger and agree that his daughters could not marry without royal consent.

Gothic Religious Architecture

Religious art had reached unprecedented heights since the end of the 14th century thanks in part to certain dukes, like Jean V, who were passionate art lovers, but also to the affluence of a new social class, the merchant bourgeoisie. It was an age of great workshops and magnificent masterpieces. Until about 1460, Breton Gothic churches were charac-

Above: François I by Jean Clouet (1535). Anne of Brittany. Right: Rood screen in the Locamaria Chapel.

terized by simple spaces formed by large arches; it was a well balanced style, but one that would soon be enriched by the ornamental profusion of the Flamboyant style.

Examples include the Cathedral of Saint-Tugdual at Tréguier (Côtes-d'Armor), built between 1339 and 1469, and the Flamboyant Basilica of Notre-Dame at Le Folgoët (Finistère), built between 1422 and 1460; the Kreisker Chapel at Saint-Pol-de-Léon (Finistère) with its tall, pyramidal spire rising to 77 m (253 ft) is full of the spirit of the Normans and was widely emulated. It also contains a superb example of beautifully carved Kersanton granite, a gray-black and sometimes greenish volcanic stone, separating the choir from the nave. The five altars back onto the apse and are splendidly carved in the same stone. The abundance of the decoration is very striking, with flowers and leaves of stone apparently climbing all over the building from the gables to the trefoil arches and carved ridge ornaments of the roof. The church at Kernascléden (Morbihan), which was consecrated in 1453, is no less notable for its ornamentation: here, it takes the form of beautiful statues which decorate the wide porch, and the ridge ornaments with finials on either side of the belltower. Inside the church, there is a breathtaking assembly of 15th-century frescoes, including one of the few remaining examples in France of a *danse macabre* (dance of death). Other pictorial masterpieces of the period include paintings on the wainscotted vault of the church of Saint-Gonéry at Plougrescant (Côtes d'Armor) which show episodes from Genesis.

Rood screens, which are very characteristic of the religious ornamental art in Brittany, are usually carved in oak and other woods. The marvellous rood screen in the Chapelle Saint-Fiacre near Faouët (Morbihan) dates from 1480, and is a fine example of the elegant forms of the Flamboyant style; it contains a notable piece of goldsmith's work set off with red, blue, green and gold. The art of rood screen production continued to flourish in the 16th century with the admixture of Renaissance motifs, some of which can already be seen in the screen at Loc-Envel (Côtes d'Armor), an otherwise Gothic church. Perhaps the finest example is at Roche-Maurice (Finistère) which also has a Renaissance coffered ceiling.

Instances of medieval decoration are still to be found in numerous Breton towns like Tréguier, and this is even more marked in Dinan where the old town still boasts a number of houses with overhanging balconies and porches resting on wooden pillars.

THE 16TH CENTURY

The Duchy of Brittany becomes part of the Kingdom of France

On the death of François II in 1488, Charles VIII (1483-98) reasserted his

protectorate over Anne of Brittany (1488-1514), the heir apparent to the duchy. However, not only did Anne's guardian refuse the crown on her behalf, but in 1490 she herself took the step of becoming betrothed by proxy to the Archduke Maximilian of Austria. The French armies were soon besieging the town of Rennes where the Duchess had taken refuge, and for once the problem was resolved by a marriage: Charles VIII married Anne of Brittany at the Château de Langeais on 6 December 1491, and they passed all their rights over to one another. As a result, Queen Anne of France remained Duchess of Brittany.

When Anne's first husband died without an heir, she married his successor in 1499. He was the Duke of Orleans, who ascended the throne as Louis XII (1498-1515). Anne was able to negotiate for the freedom of Breton institutions and customs to be confirmed in the new marriage contract, and so the duchy survived .

Furthermore it was agreed that it would revert to the Queen's youngest son or his heirs. Unfortunately, however, History decided otherwise.

Anne's only child was a daughter, Claude, who was engaged to François of Angoulême, the son of her father's cousin. When Anne died in 1514, and Louis the following year, Claude's husband ascended the throne as François I (1515-1547). The same year, Queen Claude presented the Duchy of Brittany to her husband and from then on it was irretrievably bound to the Kingdom of France. She was to reverse that decision in her will by making her son, the Dauphin, Duke of Brittany in 1524, but the States (or legislature) of Brittany, under considerable pressure from François I, called for a "real and perpetual" union between Brittany and the Kingdom of France in exchange for the maintenance of their rights and privileges. This was agreed at the Act of Union which was signed at Nantes in 1532. When the Dauphin died young and his brother succeeded to the throne as Henry II, the title of Duke of Brittany fell into disuse. Henceforth, Brittany would be represented by its States, a periodic assembly of administrators forming a legislative body and, from 1554 onwards, sitting as a parliament in Nantes or Rennes.

The prosperity of Brittany, which had begun under Jean V, continued to develop during the 16th century. Sea trading was incontestably the most successful economic activity, extending as far as Brazil and sustaining highly successful business links with Spain, Bayonne, Bordeaux, La Rochelle and England. Brittany's deep-sea cod fishing fleets had been active in the waters of Newfoundland since 1514, but they were now followed by the navigator Jacques Cartier, a native of Saint-Malo, who explored the banks of the St Lawrence Estuary and in 1534-5 assumed possession of it in the name of François I.

Right: Josselin Castle by the River Oust.

16th-century Architecture

The popularity of the Gothic style which lasted into the 16th century co-existed with certain innovatory ideas introduced by a tentative Renaissance. Nantes Castle, in whose chapel Louis XII married Anne of Brittany, had been built over the remains of a fortified castle by François II, and later expanded by the Queen Duchess. It has characteristically 15th-century military installations including huge towers and tall curtain walls, but the fact that the castle was also a symbol of ducal power explains the trefoil arches over the lintels and ogee arches sculpted with the arms of Brittany above flat niches. The ducal crown in wrought iron is situated above the palace moat and its seven sculpted gargoyles on the curbstone, while the dormer windows of the Grand Logis, which were put in by Anne of Brittany, have ridge ornamentation in the Flamboyant style. Lastly, the Italian-style loggias in the Tour de la Couronne d'Or already show evidence of Renaissance influence, an infuence fully realized in the Petit Gouvernement, built during the reign of François I. The castle at Josselin (Morbihan) went from being a fortress to a country palace under Jean II, Lord of Rohan, in the 16th century. Delightful features include the false balustrades carved in granite that run along the façade of the palace and join the small columns of the dormer windows, themselves surmounted by finials.

The newer part of the Renaissance Châteaubriant Castle (Loire-Atlantique) was built by Jean de Laval, Count of Châteaubriant and the husband of one of François I's more celebrated mistresses, Françoise de Foix. Here, the elegant pavilions, the dormer windows decorated with carved coats of arms, the gallery, the staircase and the coffered ceiling were all inspired by the Italian styles and motifs which François I had imported into France. Much the same could be said in

favor of the castle at Kerjean – half-fortress, half-Renaissance palace – which stands isolated in the countryside south west of Roscoff (Finistère).

Nonetheless, the 16th century saw the end of the reign of the large castles. Now, country houses, elegant homes for the Breton gentry, sprang up all over the countryside, particularly in the Léon. Country houses soon outnumbered the castles, and they symbolized the wish of the small and middle nobility to settle down near their sources of income, be they agriculture, textiles or the sea. The merchant bourgeoisie, too, left behind some beautiful Renaissance houses in the middle of towns like Locronan (Finistère): these display a considerable style and elegance.

The Civil Wars

The second half of the 16th century saw the rest of France torn apart by religious wars, but Brittany was not seriously affected: Protestantism had been em-braced by only a handful of the leading families and Jean de Brosse, Governor of Brittany until 1582, opted for tolerance rather than persecution. However, under his successor, Philippe-Emmanuel de Vaudémont, Duke of Mercoeur and also related to the House of Guise, Brittany began to slip back into violence. The Duc de Guise, a claimant to the throne, was assassinated in 1588 on the orders of king Henry III. Henry was himself murdered in the following year, and this cast a slur on Brittany's loyalty to the French crown. When the Protestant Henri of Navarre became Henri IV of France (1589-1610), Mercoeur rebelled with the support of the majority of Bretons but the uprising was short-lived as Henri IV converted to Catholicism in 1593 thereby rallying old *Ligue* supporters (Catholics fanatically opposed to Protestantism) to his cause. Mercoeur was supported by the Spanish but lost his fortresses one by one and was forced to submit, and on 13 April 1598 in a town formerly controlled by the Ligue, Henri IV signed the famous Edict of

Nantes, the object of which was to quell the civil war which had now been raging for close on 30 years. For Brittany, the pain had lasted no more than ten years.

Popular Religious Art
(16th-17th Centuries)

Testimony to the great faith of the Breton people is shown in their Parish closes. These are the masterpieces of a popular art form that reached its zenith in the 16th century thanks largely to skills in sculpting Kersanton granite. A close is that area around a church or chapel which at one time contained the cemetery and which in Brittany had come to symbolize the life and togetherness of the parish. This plot of ground l usually contains a calvary or an ossuary and access to it is through a triumphal door, once known as the "door of death." As for the church itself, the

Above: Detail from the calvary at Plougastel-Daoulas. Right: The parish close at Saint-Thégonnec.

porch-belfry replaces the older type of open belfry, the tall pyramid-shaped spire remains or is replaced by a dome with a lantern light, and balustrades climb up towards the upper floors as at La Roche-Maurice (1589).

A calvary might take the form of a simple cross, a crucifixion scene or an elaborate and sumptuously ornate depiction of Christ's Passion; many consist of a simple plinth with carved friezes surmounted by a cross. An ossuary, on the other hand, is in the form of a reliquary and was used as a receptacle for human remains exhumed from the cemetery to make way for fresh corpses.

The most striking examples of closes are to be found in the Department of Finistère at Plougonven near Morlaix, Pleyben, Plougastel-Daoulas, Saint-Thégonnec and Guimiliau. The calvary at Guimiliau (1581-8) includes fifteen scenes from the life of Christ and almost two hundred characters altogether; it is probably the most impressive of the calvaries for its size and is also a very ac-

complished work of art, although the style could be mistaken for naïve were it not for the calvary's curious harmony.

The church at Lampaul-Guimiliau is notable for the brightly colored 17th-century reredoses and the 16th-century rood beam, while the interior decoration of the church at Plougastel-Daoulas is memorable for its oranges, greens, blues and violets. The calvary at Pleyben was built in 1555, further decorated during the 16th century and it then underwent alterations in the 18th century; the glories of the church include a Renaissance tower-belfry and an extraordinary support consisting of a cornice at the base of the vaults and painted and carved like panelling: the pictorial decoration is inspired by Celtic mythology as well as Christian imagery.

Pagan motifs are also to be seen at Lampaul-Guimiliau, Bodilis, Berven, Brasparts, Commana and Sizun: they take the shape of simple tie-beams in the form of alligator heads, serpent-women or mermaids, the horned god of Kernun-nos, the fairies Morgane and Dahut (daughter of Gradlon, the legendary King of Cornouaille) and so on. The other character traditionally seen in closes is the Ankou, the personification of death bearing a scythe, who is often sculpted in dark granite and is usually to be found perched over the ossuary where it appears to be lying in wait.

Reredoses flourished in the whole of Brittany mainly from the 17th century to the beginning of the 18th century. They are typically framed by marble columns or pilasters, and contain niches, statues and garlands of carved fruit and flowers, in addition to magnificent panels of carved wood painted with religious subjects. Artists now rediscovered their passion for bright, cheerful colors and for paler, more delicate hues, as well as an interest in stylized forms that retain some elements of naïveté. Typical subjects included fruit and flowers painted in voluptuous tones and angels exuding an air of innocent charm. An example is the early 18th-century *Ames du Purgatoire*

33

(Souls of Purgatory) reredos in Laz (Finistère) in which the flames resemble waving grass and the clouds are depicted as frothy, sinuous swirls. This is peasant baroque art refined by the Mannerist influences of the late 16th century and it is where the rural bourgeoisie's taste for ostentation mets the simple peasant's love of naïve and fabulous stories.

THE BRETON STATES AND PARLIAMENT

In 1631, Louis XIII (1610-43) gave Brittany a new governor, Cardinal Richelieu (1585-1642), who aimed to turn Brittany into a bridgehead to an ocean empire. The port of Saint-Malo was, until 1664, France's premier port for cod fishing and the trade in Canadian furs, and Nantes was Brittany's major port for internal trade thanks to its commanding position on the Loire. Brest was the only

Above: Louis XV (1723-74). Right: The warship Hercule, about 1680.

harbor whose potential had not yet been developed; it was planned that it should become a naval port, and in 1636 work began on the dockyard and the port.

The countryside underwent changes as well with the introduction from Normandy of the cider apple and the subsequent popularity of cider itself. The 17th century also saw the demise of vines as they became confined to the area round Nantes where they are still to be found to this day.

In 1662, Louis XIV appointed Jean-Baptiste Colbert (1619-83) Controller-General of Finances. The Sun King's grand ambitions were already in need of substantial funds, and new taxes were created in the form of a *papier timbré spécial* (stamp duty) on tobacco and pewter-ware. Up to 1675, Brittany had enjoyed a number of privileges including freedom from certain types of indirect taxation that had long been established elsewhere in France. Things were already beginning to stir in the two major cities, Nantes and Rennes, but soon the uprising began to spread; by June, the Revolt of the Papier Timbré had swept the countryside and by July it had taken hold of all of the interior of Lower Brittany. Rioting and violence were the order of the day. The rebellion was, however, swiftly and brutally repressed, and in the autumn, with all sedition stifled, there were many hangings in the countryside, and the States and Parliament of Brittany were now accorded even less power than ever. Louis XIV's reign was troubled no more.

The Great Age of Sailing Ships

Brittany was France's major maritime province from the end of the 17th century to the end of the 18th. The fleet's activities ranged from fishing to commerce, and from war to piracy, and Breton sailors were encountered everywhere: in the French Navy, the *Royale*, they accounted for 20% of the officers and 30% of other ranks.

Brest had already become the country's premier naval port. Meanwhile, Lorient had been built in 1666 and, as its name suggests, had become the port that traded with the East Indies. It was also the base of the *Compagnie Française des Indes*, a company with a virtual monopoly of France's foreign trade and which had been founded in 1719 by John Law (1671-1729), Controller-General of Finances during the regency of Philippe of Orléans (1715-23). France's two biggest commercial ports, however, were Nantes and Saint-Malo, and the Nantes fleets expanded their interests as far as the Indies and Guinea (West Africa) where they took on supplies of sugar and were active in the slave trade. The sailors of Saint-Malo were particularly celebrated for their fearlessness, whether they were trading in the Pacific, Peru or China or fighting in the Seven Years' War (1756-63), a colonial naval war which once again had the Kingdoms of France and England on opposing sides.

The great riches which the colonies were offering, not to mention the economic war that sprang up around them, opened up the way for the privateers but, unlike the pirates who worked independently, the privateers worked under license from their governments to destroy the shipping of enemy countries; accordingly, the privateers from Saint-Malo captured and destroyed English and Dutch vessels or held them to ransom. It may be that this belligerent strategy did not quite bring the advantages that the French government had been expecting – and English privateers were just as ruthless as their French counterparts – but, at all events, Saint-Malo derived considerable prosperity from these activities. Much of the myth is based on spectacular, yet isolated, victories such as the expedition carried out by that famous son of Saint-Malo, René Duguay-Trouin, who captured Rio de Janeiro and profited to the extent of approximately 1,500,000 livres.

Another activity linked to sea trading was smuggling, which reached its high point in the port of Roscoff. The government tolerated, and sometimes even approved of, this illegal trading with England and Ireland: far from impeding the spread of smuggling, the wars rendered this form of commerce more important than ever. Governments sought to hold the commercial stage, and what mattered more than anything was trade, whether it was conducted officially or secretively, accompanied by threats of violence.

Fishing had been almost entirely forgotten. Ships were still being constructed for deep-sea cod fishing, but this mainly took place in the Gulf of Saint-Brieuc and at Saint-Malo, both still of major importance in seafaring terms.

This picture of 18th-century Brittany concludes with the local shipyards, of which Nantes, Saint-Malo and Brest were the most important, dominating the French naval scene: Brittany's power

La Femme du Sans Culotte

fluctuated almost as unpredictably as the seas themselves, but the region was now approaching a point in history which would have serious consequences.

Brittany on the French Political Stage

The *Papier Timbré* Revolt of 1675 aroused a spirit of opposition among Bretons, but between 1661 and 1688 the region was gradually subjected to the law which prevailed in the rest of France, and its old privileges began to be eroded. Discontent was only just below the surface. In 1688, an Intendant (administrator) appointed by the King took up residence and, until 1789, he was to remain the sworn enemy of the Breton States and Parliament.

This was largely due to the fact that the Intendant controlled a burocracy with

Above: A 'sans-culotte' – a Republican woman at the time of the French Revolution. Right: The storming of the Bastille (14 July 1789).

wide powers which were slowly but surely short-circuiting those of the States, Parliament and even the bishops.

The Breton nobility had signed an Act of Union in 1718 as a way of indicating their wish to maintain the privileges of both Brittany and their class. The most committed opponents of the Intendant's powers, however, joined the Pontcallec Conspiracy which was led by the Marquis of the same name, an individual who combined a considerable unpopularity with an inability to rally more than fifteen conspirators to the cause: he died on the scaffold in 1720.

The Intendant exerted his authority successfully between 1715 and 1735, but the tide began to turn when the States succeeded in setting up an "Intermediary Commission", effectively a parallel administration which gradually restored some more financial independence to the States and thereby reduced the Intendant's authority.

There was a revival of discontent within the Breton Parliament when the Duke of Aiguillon was appointed Commander-in-Chief in 1753. Despite his success in military administration and in the laying of a road network, he only irritated the States by seeking funds to finance a new war against the English. The States joined forces with parliament, led by Caradeuc de La Chalotais, and from 1764 to 1768 he and Aiguillon fought out a political duel involving smears, accusations, anonymous letters and intrigues. La Chalotais was imprisoned in 1765 and later exiled, but Aiguillon was abandoned by the Court and left in 1768.

Greatly stimulated by this victory, the Bretons continued to make accusations about the Duke and succeeded in persuading other parliaments, including that of Paris, to support them. Louis XV's response was immediate: the Duke of Aiguillon was appointed Secretary of State for War and a member of the triumvirate for judicial reform, and promptly streng-

thened the King's control over Brittany which now found itself under the yoke of a new Intendant, Dupleix de Bacquencourt (1771-75).

The French Revolution and Events Leading up to it

The accession of Louis XVI (1774-92) to the throne meant both the abandoning of the programme of reforms and renewed opposition from a reconstituted Parliament. Confronted by the King's declining authority, the States reinforced their powerful position by controlling and managing virtually all taxes. Indeed, the last Intendant of Brittany, Bertrand de Molleville (1785-8) was little more than an impotent observer. However, although the fiscal advantages were good for the whole of Brittany, they clearly favored those members of the nobility who were members of the Bastion, a powerful political club. The burgeoning of new ideas and of the bourgeois class was not without incident and internal conflicts.

Furthermore, the economy was stagnating because the nobles, who still clung on to money and power, maintained a backward-looking policy which repressed ambition in commerce and industry and all innovation in agriculture. Rebellion was close at hand.

In the early days of the Revolution, Bretons were once again in the forefront of French political life. For instance, the Count of Kersaint, who hailed from Léon, chaired the Electoral Assembly in Paris; the deputies of the Third Estate founded the Club Breton, a predecessor to the Jacobin Club; and the people, now more optimistic than ever, drew up *cahiers de doléances,* books in which they set out their complaints. In July 1789, there were riots in Rennes just as there were in Paris, and the soldiers fraternized with the people, but revolutionary fervor rapidly waned, and it eventually died away in 1790 with the setting up of the Breton-Angevin Union at Pontivy.

In the countryside, people felt bewildered. Farmers were forced to sell

their produce in return for promissory notes issued by the Revolutionaries. If they refused, raiding parties from the towns, supported by the army, seized the food by force. Soon a "white" royalist movement arose in Brittany, against the Republican "blues."

"White" Brittany, that is to say the counter-revolutionaries, remained opposed to the privileges of the nobility but attached to religious values and to the clergy; in the main, it was supported by the popular masses, but it was led by aristocrats.

The abolition of the rights of the nobility and of tithes had put an end to the rural discontent of 1789-91 but in 1792 a counter-revolutionary uprising broke out in Fouesnant. In 1793 the revolt spread and a Royalist uprising known as the *Chouannerie* was born.

Above: The trial of the leader of the Chouans, Georges Cadoudal (1794). Right: Napoleon Bonaparte (1769-1821).

The Chouans and the Blues
(1793-1804)

The *chouans*, or Royalist insurgents, were settled in areas south and west of Ille-et-Vilaine, in Morbihan, and to the south of Loire-Atlantique near the Vendée. The various *chouan* groups had no proper plan of action, partly because they were separated by blue (i.e. Republican) zones, but they were at least led by men of considerable character, many of them officers from the *ancien régime*.

Their sporadic war included many bloody episodes, punctuated by defeats or periods of calm following the winning of certain concessions. 1793 saw the return of freedom of worship, together with a promise of amnesty and a reduction in taxes, and the revolt flickered out.

The battle fleet of the Revolution, facing the British at sea, suffered from a shortage of competent leaders, most of the aristocratic officers having emigrated as soon as the Revolution got under way. Apart from a handful of glorious episodes like the Battle of Ushant (1794) and the Battle of the Île de Groix (1795), the fleet was clearly either too weak or simply outclassed. Brittany did, however, provide Napoleon with soldier heroes, including Théophile-Malo Corret, also known as La Tour d'Auvergne-Corret, who was the "first Grenadier of the Armies of the Republic" and one of Napoleon's most famous generals.

In 1795 there was an attempt to land some counter-revolutionary *emigrés* at Carnac with the support of the English. They were defeated by General Hoche, and those who were unable to make it back to their ships were executed. Then, on the 18th Fructidor 1797 (in the Revolutionary calendar), the coup d'état under the leadership of the Comte de Barras against the Royalist and moderate majorities in the assemblies was followed by a policy of repression which caused hostilities to reignite in Brittany.

The most famous of the *chouan* leaders of this period was called Georges Cadoudal (1771-1804): his bravery and strategic acumen even gained the admiration of Napoleon who in 1799 had become First Consul (Consulate of 1799-1804).

In the meantime, though, the people had distanced themselves from the activities of the *chouans*. Things had degenerated badly, and instances of pillage and personal vendettas were inflicting considerable harm on *chouannerie* in general. Brittany had been ravaged by ten years of civil war and yearned again for peace. Abandoning armed action for conspiracy, Cadoudal planned to kidnap the First Consul in 1804, but he was discovered, arrested and beheaded.

In the same year, Napoleon Bonaparte became Emperor (First Empire 1804-14). His policy for bringing peace to France and his powerful personality were such that he was given a rousing reception when he visited Nantes in 1808, a sure sign of his huge popularity.

THE 19TH CENTURY

Brittany During the First Empire (1804-14)

The popularity of Napoleon I and the Empire was not to endure. Though calm returned to the province and there was once more confidence in a new prosperity – it was shortlived: Brittany soon became disenchanted. Since 1793, when war had been declared against England, conscription had been imposed in order to man the armies fighting Napoleon's campaigns. Furthermore, the continental blockade that the British had enforced in order to strangle the French economy, was particularly damaging to Brittany. Trading links, whether official or based on smuggling, had hitherto been able to survive in times of war, trade itself inevitably benefiting from the protection and tacit tolerance offered by both sides. When commerce between France and England began to decline as a result of the blockade, however, Breton interests

39

were now so closely linked to those of England that her own prosperity suffered in consequence. The war of the privateers was resumed briefly, mainly between 1803 and 1813, at the time of the celebrated Robert Surcouf (1773-1827), a native of Saint-Malo, but it did not last not long enough to counterbalance the losses that had been sustained during the war or caused by the drop in regular trading. All in all, Brittany remained desperately poor and weak for some time until 1815-20; agriculture was beginning to pick up, it is true, but the golden age of international trade was at an end. And with the loss of Santo Domingo (Haiti) around 1804, the profits that had once accrued to Nantes from the slave trade and cane sugar were drastically reduced.

Restoration and the July Monarchy (1814-48)

It was not until 1825 that trading climbed back to the level of commercial exchange which had obtained before the Revolution. Now that Nantes received no more profits from the Indies, coastal trade began to take over from ocean voyages. The period of the July Monarchy (1830-48) was punctuated by several events which impacted on the life and economy of Brittany. First of all, the restoration of *La Royale,* France's last great sailing fleet, enabled the naval ports of Brest and Lorient to see their way through the critical years without too much deprivation. Moreover, the economies based in river basins such as Nantes and Saint-Malo were now pinning their hopes on canals to regenerate their trading activities; as for the towns, they were simply waiting for the railways to arrive... The trouble was that these two aspirations were at odds with one another because the canals (the Blavet Canal (1804-26), the Nantes-

Right: An instrument panel in the Naval Museum, Brest.

Brest Canal (1806-42) and the Ille et Rance Canal (1805-43) had hardly been completed, when they began to lose out to competition from trains.

The only part of the economy to gain during this period was agriculture, which was able to take advantage of the advent of the railways and the stability of the 19th century's principal economic sectors, fishing and food-packing, both of which agriculture complemented. The increasing use of fertilizers and farm machines and new ways of improving the soil were beginning to have an effect, and the introduction of potato-growing in 1840 coincided with the development of forestry. It would take forty years for the countryside to be transformed, with the formerly unproductive heathland being taken over by cultivation. The emergence of a well-to-do class of peasants, who had clung on to many traditional festivals and costumes, gave a new lease of life to Breton folklore which was now beginning to make a name for itself beyond the province's borders and to attract the attention of painters and writers.

The Second Republic (1848-52) and the Second Empire (1852-70)

All the great technical advances in Europe reached Brittany late, if they got there at all, but the arrival of coal was something of a two-edged sword. On the one hand, the new steamships were ideally suited to coastal trading and also France's fleet of naval ironclads held supremacy over the English between 1855 and 1865; on the other hand, the new ships posed at least three new problems. For one thing, they needed substantially increased investment in a province where large fortunes were rapidly disappearing; for another, there was the difficulty of getting hold of coal (this was mainly imported from England); lastly, these ships were somewhat bigger than their predecessors and Breton ports needed to un-

dergo costly modernization in order to accommodate them. The first deep-water port, Saint-Nazaire, was opened in 1857. The big ship-yards were quick to move in and, being so close to Nantes, Saint-Nazaire rapidly became a major commercial competitor. Nantes ultimately lost its dominant position but was nonetheless able to survive as Brittany's second port. Much more disturbing was the up-and-coming, dynamic city of Le Havre which had had a rail link with Paris since 1847: The great French economic axis no longer passed through Brittany but ran between Le Havre, Paris and Lyon.

The other indicator of a failed industrial revolution was a decline of ironworks, mining and textiles: they were no longer able to compete with rival products in terms of quality and profitability. What is more, Nantes's sugar refineries, which had been getting their supplies of sugar-cane from Reunion Island following the loss of Santo Domingo, now faced a serious crisis with the arrival on the market of sugar-beet.

The End of the 19th Century (1870-1900)

Despite all the setbacks, Nantes managed to maintain its development, with commerce making commendable progress following the opening of the Martinière Canal in 1892 and its upgrading in 1903. The modernization of infrastructures came too late for certain ports such as Saint-Malo: it was too near Le Havre, and although its deep-water dock had been opened as recently as 1855, Saint-Malo could not cherish any great commercial ambitions. All that remained was fishing. Cod fishing was the great specialty of all the northern ports from Cancale through Saint-Malo to Paimpol, and the Breton fleets scoured the seas from Newfoundland to Iceland and as far as Greenland. As an industry, though, it was about to die out, largely because there was a drop in demand for cod; but there was another reason, and that was that the seamen were becoming dissatisfied with the harsh working conditions, and were

beginning to be seduced by the attractions of merchant shipping. Deep-sea fishing was gradually replaced by coastal fishing, and the south coast of the province began specialising in sardines. In response to this, a large canning industry grew up between Douarnenez and Le Croisic.

One way and another during the 19th century, Brittany lost its position as France's leading maritime province, simply because commerce fell victim to the gradual advance of modern methods, and was in consequence no longer able to act as the driving force of the economy. This left Breton sailors high and dry, but they now turned their unequalled experience to a whole range of activities, whether serving in the the French Navy or in the merchant navy or remaining

Above: Jules Verne (1829-1905). Honoré de Balzac (1799-1850). Right: Paysannes bretonnes (Breton peasant women) by Paul Gauguin (1894).

simple fishermen; and they have practiced their skills everywhere from the coasts of Brittany itself to the furthest oceans.

ART AND LITERATURE IN THE 19TH CENTURY

Breton Writers

In the course of the 19th century, Brittany exchanged maritime supremacy for artistic and intellectual glory. The first major figure to emerge was François René de Chateaubriand. Born in Saint-Malo, he was the acknowledged father of French Romanticism who inspired a whole generation of writers, from Victor Hugo to Lamartine. Before making his mark in the literary world of Paris, Chateaubriand had spent his childhood in Brittany and passed his early days walking the heaths. Subsequently, he took up arms against the Revolution and even knew exile, during which time he wrote *Le Génie du Christianisme.* (The Genius

of Chritianity). He settled in Paris in 1800 and between 1801 and 1805 published *Atala* and *René*. Between 1803 and 1828 he had a rather erratic career in politics, opposing Napoleon's imperial ambitions, then as diplomat and minister under Louis XVIII, counted among the ultra-conservatives.

In 1826, he published *Les Natchez* and *Aventures du dernier Abencérage* but he retired from politics in 1833 and devoted his time to editing his *Memoires d'Outre-Tombe* (Memoirs from Beyond the Grave) which were, not surprisingly, published after his death.

The most successful of all 19th-century writers came from Nantes: Jules Verne (1828-1905), the man who added a new dimension to French literature – science fiction. His works reveal little of his Breton childhood, except *Les Mirifiques Aventures de Maître Antifer,* which starts in Brittany.However, like many Bretons, Jules Verne never ceased to be drawn by distant horizons and long voyages, whether real or imaginary.

Less well known is the Count of Villiers de L'Île-Adam (1838-1889), born in Saint-Brieuc of an old aristocratic family. His contemporaries, including Baudelaire, acknowledged his originality, but he never achieved popular success.

Brittany as Inspiration

Brittany has been the inspiration for writers from other parts of France too. For Jules Michelet (1798-1874) the Atlantic Ocean was more than a backdrop for his *Histoire de France ;* it is one of the forces which has shaped the history of mankind. His writing is so full of life that it almost achieves the intensity of a novel.

Honoré de Balzac (1799-1850) was very familiar with the Gallo country of Upper Brittany between Nantes and Fougères, and *Les Chouans* (1829), his first great novel and the one which started the *Comédie Humaine* cycle, was set in the Brittany of 1799; his shrewd social obervation is always set against a background of dramatic events.

43

Above: A sad reminder of World War Two.

The last great "Breton" novel of the 19th century was written by Pierre Loti (1850-1923), a native of Normandy.

Pêcheur d'Islande (The Iceland Fisherman) is unquestionably his masterpiece and was published in 1886. As a naval officer, Loti knew both the charm and the violence of the sea, which appears as a fascinating and mysterious character .The novel is a hymn to the courage of Breton sailors.

Gauguin and the Pont-Aven School

In 1886, the painter Paul Gauguin (1848-1903) came to Brittany to seek an "atmosphere unlike the over-civilised places" he was used to. It was the ancient purety of Brittany that attracted Gauguin. But it was also the vivid colours and subtly picturesque quality of the landscape. Others to have rediscovered Brittany include the great landscape painter Camille Corot (1796-1875) who painted the marshes between Le Croisic and Guérande around 1850, Claude Monet (1840-1926) who spent some time working at Belle-Île, and Paul Signac (1863-1935) who painted at Portrieux where the rocks meet the sea.

Gauguin put Brittany on the map and ushered in modern art; he also gathered around him painters including Paul Sérusier, Emile Bernard and M. Maufray, and together they formed what would come to be known as the Pont-Aven School.

THE 20TH CENTURY

Aftermath of Two World Wars

The economic decline of the 19th century continued into the first half of the 20th century. It was Bretons, more than any other part of the French population, who migrated to the great industrial heartlands of the north. Quite simply, Bretons were abandoning a region in which economic decline had become synonymous with unemployment.

The 1914-18 war was soon to have a profound effect on the population of Brittany. Losses would eventually amount to 150,000 dead, or one in every six Breton soldiers, and before long the birth rate was affected, thus aggravating the impact of the world economic crisis. This continued in Brittany until 1935, although great efforts were made to modernize agriculture and ports were specially constructed to suit the new requirements of international trade, but they fell a long way short of encouraging the people to remain in the province. There was a brief let-up in 1937 and 1938 when major defence orders breathed new life into the naval shipyards, when seaside tourism began to develop, and the fishing industry began to be modernized, but once again this boom was cut short, this time by the 1939-45 war.

In May 1940, the Maginot line was breached and the German troops invaded France. On 15 June, General de Gaulle embarked from Brest in an attempt to reach England, and a few days later left Bordeaux for London from where he broadcast his celebrated appeal to the French people.

The response was huge, and many crossed the Channel from Brittany; Bretons also accounted for a quarter of the members of the first contingent of Free French Forces. During the Occupation, innumerable resistance networks were set up in Brittany, and the Liberation of France included many fierce battles of which Brest, Lorient and Saint-Malo bore the scars for many years to come.

Recovery

The year 1951 saw the setting up of the *Comité d'Etudes et de Liaison des Intérêts Bretons* (Committee for the Study and Coordination of Breton Interests), renamed the *Comité Régional d'Expansion Economique* (Regional Committee for Economic Expansion) in 1955. Its main aims were to break Brittany's isolation, to reverse the steep decline in population, develop manufacturing and service industries and to strengthen the maritime sectors.

With the aid of State funds two major road networks have been opened since 1968. Other advances include Brittany Ferries, which links Roscoff and Saint-Malo with Britain, and carries more than two million passengers every year together with freight worth approximately one thousand million francs; the superfast TGV (*Train à Grande Vitesse* - High Speed Train) *Atlantique* has been running between Paris, Rennes and Brest since 1989 and has included Lorient since 1991. Brittany has also been favored by a substantial rise in the number of regional, national and international airline connections, and, lastly, at Pleumeur-Bodou there is the National Space Telecommunications Station establishing worldwide links through its highly advanced satellite programme: together with France's national space studies center, this is one of the country's leading high-technology complexes.

As a result of huge investment programmes, commercial ports are now equipped to the most modern standards. The most important is at Saint-Nazaire which boasts a 3 km (1.8 mile) long bridge over the River Loire, the longest bridge in France; seaside resorts are springing up on either side of that city. Meanwhile,Concarneau, Douarnenez, Le Guilvinec, Lorient, and countless other ports still go in for fishing, though on a smaller scale.

As for agriculture, Brittany is the leading region in the production of cauliflower, artichokes, French beans, poultry, eggs, pig-meat and milk. All in all, the last fifty years have seen a spectacular transformation. What is more remarkable is that it has been achieved without sacrificing a precious heritage and a traditional way of life.

ILLE-ET-VILAINE

0   10km   20km

ILLE-ET-VILAINE

FOUGÈRES TO LA GUERCHE

RENNES

RENNES TO REDON

BROCÉLIANDE

THE HEATHLANDS OF COMBOURG

MONT-SAINT-MICHEL

THE EMERALD COAST

The department of **Ille-et-Vilaine** is a land of remarkable paradoxes. Though part of *Haute Bretagne* (High Brittany) the land is little more than gently undulating; it is scarcely a maritime region either with under 150 km (93 miles) of coastline out of Brittany's total littoral of some 3000 km (1900 miles). What is more, there are no parish closes, very few calvaries and *pardons* (annual pilgrimages seeking forgiveness for sins or fulfilling a vow), only a handful of famous menhirs – and the local inhabitants do not even speak Breton! And yet, it is undeniably Breton.

The sea does play a part in forming the character of the region, softening the climate many miles inland from the coast, fertilizing the fields with whiffs of sea wrack, and positively breathing life into the peoples of Argoat. Even though the traveller may penetrate deep into this land of woods, he is never more than 100 km (62 miles) from the coast.

FOUGÈRES TO LA GUERCHE

Throughout this part of Ille-et-Vilaine there runs, like a Breton Maginot Line, a

Previous pages: Waves bursting on to the rocks. A forest of masts in the marina at Perros-Guirec.

frontier which once bristled with impenetrable forests and fortresses. Relations between the Franks and the Bretons were invariably so strained that Rennes never complained about being cut off in this way. Between Antrain-sur-le-Couësnon and La Guerche-de-Bretagne, there are many small towns: Fougères which has the strongest castle, Vitré which has the most beautiful, and La Guerche which no longer has a castle at all – but they were all united by the same burning desire to defend themselves.

Fougères and the Surrounding Area

Fougères dominates a fertile, peaceful and quietly undulating landscape studded with small but solid granite towns with slate roofs. To the north, away from the main roads, lies the so-called "desert" which, with its rugged heathlands and distant views, preserves the memory of the great Forest of Glaine, the last refuge of the Druids. Nearby, the monotonous and barren slopes of Le Coglès, dotted here and there with an isolated farm, a little market town or a simple cross, are home to scattered herds of white, red and black of cattle.

By contrast, the Couësnon and Minette Valleys are more varied, well-watered and more wooded. Here, there are many

signposted walks taking in mills, country houses, beautiful farmhouses with slate roofs and façades of carved stones, and Romanesque or Gothic churches with ancient timbers. The area round **Antrain** also has a splendid range of walks; these include Villequartier Forest and its Druidic stones, Bonne-Fontaine Castle and the hill at Le Châtellier. From the top of this hill, on a clear day you can see 37 church steeples as well as Mont-Saint-Michel; in the foothills stand the splendid castles of La Vieuxville and La Folletière and also the quite magnificent **Rocher-Portail** Castle (on the D102).

There are many more opportunities for walking in the beautiful **Forest of Fougères** which is cut in two by the D177. At one time, it was inhabited by whole families of woodcutters, but its legends tell of Druids, fairies, mischievous spirits and *Chouans* -for it was in

Above: Cloudy sky above the imposing feudal castle of Fougères. Right: Outside a crêperie in Fougères.

these parts that the 19th-century Royalist insurgency was born. The forest also contains the Courcoulée Stone, the remains of a covered dolmen 7 m (23 ft) long and, near the Serpe crossroads, there is a megalithic alignment of 80 blocks of quartz rock. These are known as the Druids' Belt. Legend has it that another rock conceals a treasure hidden by fairies: The Fougères treasure is said to have lain in the forest for centuries, in the vast underground caves known as the Cellars of Landéan.

The town of **Fougères** boasts a pearl among medieval castles. Though believed to be impregnable it was nonetheless frequently captured. The **curtain wall** contains thirteen towers of all shapes and sizes, joined together by a high wall and surmounted by a riot of roofs, embrasures, chimneys, watch towers, turrets and machicolations, and is almost completely encircled by the River Nanson. The so-called **ville basse** (low town), which is built around the castle and is dominated by the tower of **Saint-**

Sulpice, has long been a center for the tanning and dyeing trades.The newer part of town is on a hill, some distance away, but still linked to the castle by a long fortified causeway.

There are some splendid walks along the foot of the curtain wall and up the steep roads by the castle. These roads are lined with extremely old houses which have somehow managed to survive a succession of catastrophes, from fires in the 18th century to bombing raids in 1944. St Leonard's Church, which was rebuilt between the 13th and 16th centuries and underwent alterations in the 19th century, looks onto a public garden, the Place aux Arbres. This has wonderful views over the fortress, and is a favorite haunt for photographers.

Vitré to La Guerche

Vitré Castle stands on a rocky spur and is surrounded by the old walled town. It is simpler in style than its counterpart at Fougères, but is no less imposing, elegant

and romantic. The town itself (on the D178) is marvelously preserved and restored and, as if arranged for a real-life architecture lesson, the streets (many of them pedestrianized) are lined with splendid examples of timber framing, Gothic façades, corbelling and sculpted pilasters. The most comprehensive and best preserved collection of buildings is to be found in **Rue de la Beaudrairie,** whose ancient ramparts were last invaded in the 18th century by an army of bourgeois merchants who decided to settle here and open their workshops and stalls. By contrast, the 15th-century Flamboyant church of **Notre-Dame** has changed little and still has the serrated designs on its façade and the outside pulpit from which the priests would harangue the townspeople.

Close to Châtillon-en-Vendelais, a small town noted for its plush (a velvet-like material) to the north of Vitré, lies the village of Montautour, at 194 m (636 ft) above sea level the highest inhabited spot in the department. It has been the destina-

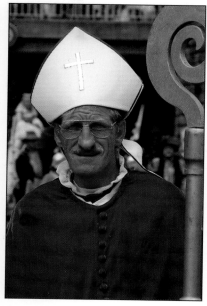

tion of an important pilgrimage since the 11th century. A traditional *pardon* is held there on the first weekend of July, and on the first Sunday of September there is a Buck-wheat Procession, which combines Catholicism with a pagan fertility rite and a secular *festnoz* (folk festival). To the east along the D29, the tiny village of Champeaux is remarkable for its lovely **Collegiate church of Sainte-Marie-Madeleine** which dates from the 15th, 16th and 18th centuries and is surrounded by the houses of the church's canons. It seems almost too beautiful and magnificent for such a small place, but not for the prosperous d'Espinay family who had it built and whose tombs adorn the interior. Their charming Renaissance castle is a few miles outside the village in the middle of the countryside. It is quite possible that the great letter-writer the Marquise de Sévigné visited it, as her

Above: A bishop carrying a cross and mitre at a pardon. Right: Quays along the River Vilaine in Rennes.

home, **Rochers-Sévigné Castle,** is not far away, a must for devotees of literary pilgrimages and formal French gardens.

At the eastern extremity of Île-et-Vilaine stands the small town of **La Guerche-de-Bretagne** (on the D178). This was once the fiefdom of the celebrated 14th-century French general, Bertrand du Guesclin. It has few architectural pretensions since its fortress was razed to the ground in the 18th century. The **Collegiate church of Notre-Dame,** which dates from the 13th century, had a galleried belfry added in the 19th century. However, the town's fairs and markets are justly famous. These include an enormous weekly pig market in the Place du Champ-de-Foire and another picturesque market in the Place de l'Hôtel-de-Ville; they have been held in the town every Tuesday since the 12th century. On the other side of **La Guerche forest** is the hamlet of Martigné-Ferchaud, on the banks of the Pool of La Forge and not far from Forge-la-Forêt. An ore that was brought up from beyond the Loire used to be smelted here in workshops that are still to be seen but now the forest consists of 75 hectares (185 acres) laid out for walks and including pools stocked for fishing. Much the most impressive monument in these parts is the immensely ancient and mysterious **Roche-aux-Fées** (Fairies' Rock). This megalithic structure comprises a score of huge blocks making a covered avenue 60 ft long and 12 ft high.

RENNES

Situated at a confluence of rivers and in a very good position to control the entire area, **Rennes** is the only Breton city which turned its back on the sea. Once the seat of the Breton Parliament and now host to the regional administration, Rennes has long vied with the city of Nantes for regional supremacy. Today it excels in the fields of communications

and medicine, and has first-class research facilities at its university. The town's cultural life is no less distinguished. In addition to the museums, the symphony orchestra and theater groups, there are two well known festivals. These are the *Transmusicales*, a rock festival, and *Tombées de la Nuit* (Nightfalls) which features many aspects of Breton artistic activity ranging from music to theater and from dance to marionettes.

Otherwise, Rennes has no great reputation to speak of. The town is often described as a large, gray, austere and inelegant place where people go to bed early. What is more, visitors also have to find their way through rings of bleak suburbs before they can see the town for what it truly is.

Then, all of a sudden, one is in the heart of the town wedged between the River Îlle and the River Vilaine, some of the latter having been covered over to provide car parking space. What is immediately striking about the city center is the extraordinary juxtaposition of styles and historical periods. A brief walk from the Saint-Sauveur church to the place du Palais in the eastern pedestrian precinct takes in everything from chaotic and brightly colored medieval fantasies to the strict and uniform rigor of classical façades. This amazing variety includes narrow alleys winding their way between pargeted walls, timber framing and corbelling, and then spacious, regular and well-paved streets. The reason for these extraordinary contrasts is the fire which swept through the city for a few days in December 1720, sparing only the district surrounding the cathedral. Everything had been built of wood but the architects who were brought in to reconstruct the town decided to use nothing but stone. They designed a four-square military layout with large open squares and arcades. However, on the outskirts of the new quarter, the tradition of half-timbered houses (sometimes camouflaged by stone façades) lived on in the poor shanties which were quickly built to provide accommodation for the homeless.

RENNES

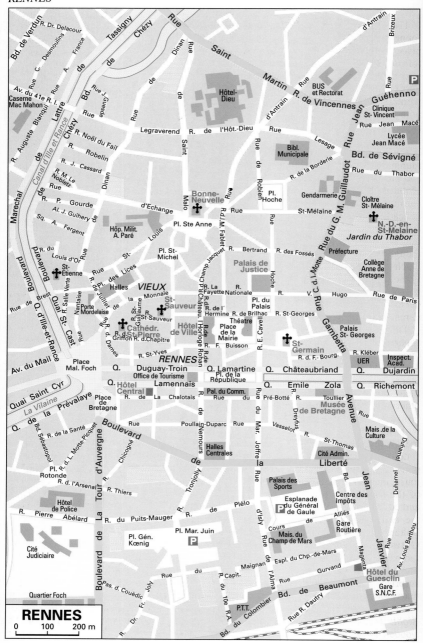

The classical part of Rennes is to be found around its two main squares. The place du Palais is dominated by the former Houses of Parliament of Brittany, now the **Palais de Justice** (Law Courts): The **Grande Chambre,** once the parliamentary debating chamber, is decorated with woodwork, a coffered ceiling, paintings and tapestries. The other square is in the south of Rennes. **Place de la Mairie** is the home of the town's 19th-century municipal theater which is now restored, and has been in use since the 1970s. The **Hotel de Ville** (Town Hall) is opposite, surmounted by its clocktower. A niche beneath the tower's pediment used to contain the statue of a woman kneeling at the feet of the King of France; this was thought to symbolize the union of the Duchy of Brittany and the kingdom of France. When this "shameful" figure was blown up in 1932 by separatists, the town decided simply to replace it with a tub of geraniums!

The **medieval quarter** has its own squares lined with houses of all types: tall ones, crooked ones, striped ones; some decorated with a chequerboard pattern, others in a herring-bone pattern; some of them tilting over like the Tower of Pisa, others perched above a ground floor of brown, flaking stone, and all surmounted with innumerable roguish-looking dormer windows standing guard over the slate roofs. A market is now held in the unusually long **Place des Lices** where jousts once took place; on opposite sides of the square there are also old houses and covered stalls designed in the style of the early 19th century architect, Louis Baltard. Close by are the **Mordelaise Gates,** almost the last remnant of the old ramparts.

All around, the streets are filled with surprises. One of the most famous is a marvelous house said to have belonged to

Right: Medieval houses with exposed wooden frames, Rennes.

du Guesclin which is now the no less celebrated Ty Coz restaurant. It is important not to miss the statues of angels, devils and archers apparently on sentry duty. Of particular interest are the splendid staircase in the Hôtel de Blossac and a 15th-century prison known as the Impasse Rallier-du-Baty.

The **Cathedral of Saint-Pierre** may have survived the great fire of 1720, but it sadly succumbed to old age forty years later. With the exception of two towers which stand either side of the façade, the exterior of the church is as it was in the 19th century, while the interior is decorated in a Rococo-bourgeois style very characteristic of the end of the century. By contrast, the Basilica of Saint-Sauveur is in a more orthodox form of early 18th-century Rococo.

Outside this small area, Rennes flaunts its charms much more extravagantly. These include the church of Sainte-Mélaine whose vaults are reputed to contain the legendary abbey treasure, and the **Thabor Garden** which used to belong to the church of Saint-Mélaine and nowadays consists of 10 hectares (25 acres) of botanical gardens, rose gardens and aviaries.

The Palais des Musées on the banks of the Vilaine comprises two museums: one is the **Musée de Bretagne** which tells the history of the region from neolithic times to the First World War; the other is the **Musée des Beaux-Arts** whose large and eclectic collections take in everything from Egyptian antiquities to contemporary art, and include works by Rubens, Philippe de Champaigne and the members of the Pont-Aven School. Smaller, but no less fascinating, is the **Ecomusée de La Bintinais** (Bintinais Ecological Museum) which depicts the living conditions and life style of peasants since the 16th century, in the setting of an agricultural theme-park.

The Country Round Rennes

Outside the city of Rennes, the countryside soon takes over , with a mixture of marsh, woodland and pasture. The shallow valleys shelter huge barns and many fine country houses. There is not a village, nor a hamlet in these parts that cannot boast its rustic manor house, its remains of a medieval castle, its Renaissance folly – or some romantic imitation of these. Some are open to visitors.

Needless to say, there are also large numbers of churches. Many of them are in the Flamboyant style, but there are some 19th-century restorations. These include Neo-gothic and Neo-romanesque churches, and even Neo-byzantine buildings with cupolas like that on the small church in the village of Corps-Nuds.

The countryside around Rennes is utterly rural and tranquil. The towns of **Châteaugiron** and **Nouvoitou** on the River Seiche became prosperous as early

Right: The most beautiful route from Rennes to Redon, along the Vilaine.

as the 16th century from the making of sailcloth, and the charming fortified castles and the fine merchants' houses bear witness to that. Amongst the most important are Artois Castle and the Manoir Boberil near Mordelles, and other splendid old houses at L'Hermitage and Bréal-sous-Montfort.

At **Saint-Aubin-du-Cormier**, there is an imposing church and the vestiges of an impregnable castle close to marshland where Duke François II of Brittany was defeated by the French in 1488. Just 500 years later, a cross was erected there in memory of the 6000 Bretons who died for the independence of Brittany.

RENNES TO REDON

The best route from Rennes to Redon does not follow a road but a river. This is the River Vilaine which runs through one of the prettiest valleys in the Argoat.

The Vilaine Route

Once past Rennes, the **Vilaine**, swollen by the waters of the Ille and of countless other rivers and streams, changes appearance dramatically. For one thing, it becomes navigable – modestly, it is true, and at a very gentle pace.

Also, the barges never exceed 100 tonnes whereas France's principal commercial rivers are comfortably able to handle ships three times that size. The Vilaine was long the favorite route of both thieves and merchants as they moved inland. However, from the 16th century onwards, there were worries about how the river could be kept adequately supplied with water, and this was eventually managed by means of locks and by diverting water courses, so as to keep the fisheries alive and the mills turning, some of which are still in operation.

The level changes by 16 m (52 ft) over 100 km (62 miles) and there are only twelve locks between Rennes and the

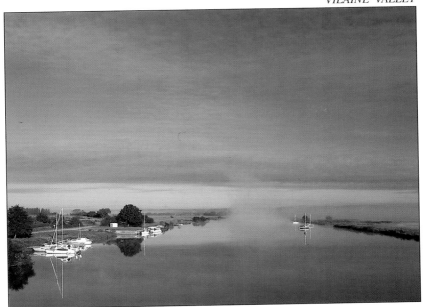

sea; compare this with 47 locks in the 90 km (56 mile) long Ille et Rance Canal to the north. The Vilaine lacks a gradient, and in the summer the water level is low, the river silts up, and below Redon the downward current is reversed by the incoming tide.

Even in Redon, which was equipped early on with a non-tidal dock, all sea traffic was banned at one time because ships were continually running aground. The Arzal Dam at the mouth of the Vilaine is supposed to have solved the problem since 1972 by controlling the flow of fresh and salt water. It has certainly been possible to reclaim thousands of hectares of land from the marshes, but recently there has been talk of getting rid of its lock, much to the displeasure of yachting enthusiasts who make up the majority of those using the river. The problem is that their comings and goings cause too much water to be lost.

Despite its liability to flood in winter, the **Vilaine valley** still has enormous charm. There is no road running along-

side the river, and navigation remains the only means of following its lively course through a kaleidoscope of ploughed fields, sheer cliffs, meadows dotted with reed-beds, manor houses deep in impenetrable woods, tiny ports with their old salt stores, fishermen's houses and mills. Tourism on the river is now well developed. In fact, there is almost too much to choose from, including a ten-hour trip as far as Messac involving the negotiation of ten locks, and bicycle rides to the towns on nearby hilltops which the river has passed by.

Rennes to Messac

Just outside Rennes on the D177 are the huge gardens of Blossac Castle laced with little streams and, on its peninsula, the Manor of Rivière-Kersan. To the south of Bruz, a Renaissance-style suburb entirely rebuilt after World War Two, lies the tranquil valley of **Le Boël,** whose red schist cliffs protect one of the last 17th-century mills to remain intact.

It stands as if anchored in the middle of the stream, and has now been turned into an attractive hotel. Further on, there is the village of Guichen, perched on the top of a hill and famous for its iron-bearing waters; Guichen in turn overlooks yet another mill, known as La Bouexière.

The D77 follows the river at this point before reaching Bourg-des-Comptes, which is less remarkable for its church in the Flamboyant style (rebuilt during the 19th century) than for the old world charm of the tiny port of Courbe, an ideal place for a brief stop. From there, it is possible to move on to **Sel-de-Bretagne** whose Museum of Rural Tradition contains carvings of long-dead kings and Druids, the work of a Breton sculptor. Other interesting towns in the vicinity include **Saint-Senoux,** where the stone front of the old Molière mill stands next

to the Byzantine cupolas of a rather modern church, and **Pléchâtel**, an old loyalist town with houses of alternating schists, sandstone and quartz that is fortunate enough to have both a rain water spring and a horizontal menhir.

Guipry-Messac and their twin ports are built on the last rocky outcrops encountered by the Vilaine. It was here that the tidal bore petered out in former times and any barges that tried to continue their journeys had to offload some of their cargoes as there was insufficient depth of water further upstream.

The Chapel of **Notre-Dame-de-Bon-Port** is a reminder of this maritime past, as are the large numbers of little white and blue boats moored in neat rows at the landing stages. Guipry-Messac is one of Brittany's main centers for river-based leisure activities.

The country round **Bain-de-Bretagne** to the east along the D177 is uninspiring, There are no old buildings to explore since the village was moved in the 19th century, to be closer to the main road.

Above: People fishing on the Vilaine at Redon. Right: The church of St Sauveur at Redon is a mixture of Romanesque and Gothic styles.

Grand-Fougeray to Redon

Amongst the many churches in this area that were altered during the 19th century is the one at **Grand-Fougeray**, which boasts a medieval dungeon as well asthe astonishingly elaborate decoration. Near **Langon** is a line of some 30 "young women" standing in Indian file; they were turned to stone for wishing to dance at the hour of vespers, and are still waiting for their punishment to be lifted. There are more neolithic remains a few miles away on the Cojoux and Quilly moors between **Saint-Just** and Sixt-sur-Aff: A signposted path leads to perforated rocks, vestiges of cromlechs and an ancient tumulus surmounted by standing stones.

Brain-sur-Vilaine marks the beginning of the marshland and of the country surrounding Redon with its schist standing stones arranged in the form of a fence. **Redon** itself stands at the junction of the Nantes-Brest Canal and the Vilaine. Redon has a tradition of bartering and holding markets, and every October it holds a famous chestnut fair, the *Foire Teillouse,* which coincides with a competition in traditional singing and cooking. The old town is always ablaze with flowers and contains more than its fair share of beautiful historic houses, the oldest of which date from the 15th century and are close to the church of **Saint-Sauveur.** This church has a rather gloomy nave with wood vaulting, and is curiously cut off from its Gothic belltower which was rebuilt on too small a scale after being burned down.

From the small island in the port, there is a splendid view over a long series of locks and passenger barges lying peacefully beside the quays.

Just 25 km (15 miles) to the south, near to Missilac and on the borders with Morbihan and Loire-Atlantique, lies **Bretesche Castle**. This magnificent 15th-century residence, which is surrounded by a moat and a small park, now serves as the clubhouse for the local Bretesche golf club.

BROCÉLIANDE TO THE HEATHLANDS OF COMBOURG

At one time, the **Forest of Brocéliande** covered an enormous area, and was a haunt of Druids long before literature converted it into the home of the Knights of the Round Table. There is also another legend from round these parts – that of Ponthus, the supposed founder of Paimpont who, in an attempt to impress the fair but indifferent Sydoine, spent several years murdering every knight that passed by.

This area had long been a kind of "other world" for the Celts, a meeting point between parallel universes, between life and death, between the real and unreal. It is hardly surprising that it then became home to the Holy Grail, to magicians and to fairies. There are those who say that, on a stormy night, it is still possible to hear King Arthur's armies

Right: Bretesche Castle, near La Roche-Bernard (Loire-Atlantique).

winding their way through the forest. There is not a single spot in the Forest of Brocéliande that does not have its own little mystery.

The forest, which has been slowly eroded over the centuries to serve the needs of blacksmiths, coalmining and the naval shipyards, eventually became the **Forest of Paimpont,** but today it covers an area of hardly more than 700 hectares (17,700 acres), and even that is under threat. The introduction of maritime pine has made it an easier prey than ever to fire, as the 1990 drought demonstrated, and there is even talk now of building a major road straight through the middle.

In **Paimpont** Merlin is everywhere: in the sunken roads, on the windswept hilltops, amongst the scorched heather and reeds, in the fourteen motionless, silent pools, and in the deep valleys littered with moss-covered rocks. His grave, which lies to the north, on the edge of the fields, is marked by two schist slabs and a holly tree. His palace, or rather Viviane's palace, is on the other side of the misty

Lake Comper (by the D773) in which there is always a reflection of **Comper Castle**. The castle now houses the *Centre de l'Imaginaire Arthurien*, a kind of center for Arthurian make-believe (tel: 97 22 79 96). No less magical places near here include the *Fontaine de Jouvence* (Fountain of Youth) and the beautiful pond known as the *Miroir aux Fées* (Fairies' Mirror): these are in the **Val Sans-Retour** (Valley of No Return), just 5 km (3 mi) off the winding, rocky path where Morgana lay in wait for unfaithful youths by the Mouille-Croûte fountain. Legend also has it that the **Fontaine de Barenton** had the power to unleash great storms if water was sprinkled over a step at its edge. No Christian saint was ever able to settle in this sacred clearing, but today priests frequently lead pilgrimages here to pray for an end to droughts. The icy, bubbling waters also provide a cure for rickets and madness. The nearby hamlet of **La Folle-Pensée** is thought to be built over the ruins of the priory of Eon de l'Etoile, a mystic and heretical "Robin Hood" of the 12th century.

Of great interest is the very beautiful **Trécesson Castle** which lies to the south west, just over the border with the department of Morbihan. This is a genuine manor house in red schist with 15th-century pointed turrets. Equally fascinating is the extraordinary church at **Tréhoren-teuc**. From 1945 to 1979, under the somewhat esoteric protection of magic numbers and zodiacal mysticism, a parish priest by the name of Gillard went to enormous lengths to change the church into a museum of the Holy Grail. This he attempted to achieve by installing stained glass windows, mosaics and Stations of the Cross. Those who are interested in such things can take part in *Contes et Légendes* (Stories and Legends) evenings and guided visits to the forest including a stop at an inn called the *Cour aux Etoiles.*

The Forest of Paimpont and the "mountains" of Bécherel are separated by

the **Meu country**. In this part of Brittany, there are many dry-stone walls and pollarded oaks bordering the fields. A large number of signposted paths have been created for the benefit of walkers. Finally, there is the village of **Monterfil** which comes to life once a year with a major competition of Breton music: this consists of three days of uninterrupted *fest-noz* with violins, Breton bagpipes – and as much grilled pork as you can eat!

On the very edge of the Meu country stands the village of **Montfort,** the home of the aristocratic family of the same name. It has managed to preserve much of its original character despite misguided modernization during the 19th century; sadly, the ramparts and the castle have not survived except for the **Papegaut Tower** which now houses the local **Ecological Museum**.

Nearby, the tiny village of **Saint-Méen-Le-Grand** has the honor of being the birthplace of the poet and song-writer, Théodore Botrel, and the singer Louison Bobet. **Montauban Castle** still has its drawbridge, although the moat which once surrounded it has now dried up, but there are many other castles in the neighborhood. They include those at Romillé, Lou-du-Lac (which is now used as a general stores and bar), and the very beautiful castles at **Landujan** and **La Chapelle-Chaussée.** Only the village of **Médréac** on the department border has menhirs of any interest.

Bécherel (on the D27), 176 m (577 ft) above sea level on its granite fold, was once a stronghold and important center in the Breton War of Succession, but soon afterwards opted for a lucrative trade in fine linen cloth. It now calls itself a "book capital," since it holds a second-hand book market on the first Sunday of every month and a book fair each spring. This delightful medieval town even has its own Versailles – **Caradeuc Castle** which still belongs to the family of a famous French attorney-general born in Rennes,

the Marquis de Caradeuc de La Chalotais (1701-85). Equally interesting is the 12th-century **Montmurant Castle** (and 14th-century entrance fort) where du Guesclin was knighted; the castle hosts a permanent exhibition in honor of the great French soldier. Nearby, at **Les Iffs**, is an exceptionally beautiful church which is mainly remarkable for the beauty and the striking blue of its Renaissance stained glass windows. There is also the little village of **Hédé** which stands between the Ille-et-Rance Canal and a pond. The stretch of canal taking in the eleven locks of the La Madeleine stairway is hugely popular: For those in boats, it is a marathon of incessantly opening and closing lock gates; for those on land, it is a most charming walk along the canal.

Another castle not to change hands over a long period of time is **La Bourbansais Castle** (on the N137). It has re-

Above: The nave of Dol-de-Bretagne Cathedral. Right: Mont-Saint-Michel.

mained in the same family for nearly twenty generations, and is now open to the public, having been expanded to include a zoo. Lastly, there is **Combourg** (on the D795), a must for anyone who wants to try to comprehend the Romantic spirit of the famous writer, René de Chateaubriand. He spent his youth in Combourg Castle, and never shook off his gloomy memories of its pointed towers and crenellated curtain walls.

MONT-SAINT-MICHEL AND THE EMERALD COAST

Ille-et-Vilaine has the smallest coastline of all the Breton departments, but what there is can still be breathtakingly beautiful. It runs from Mont-Saint-Michel Bay in the east to Saint-Malo and the Emerald Coast in the west.

The Country round Dol

As the traveler pushes north, the green, soft and rounded shapes of the Breton hinterland are replaced by the extraordinarily flat countryside round the town of Dol. This land is so uniformly and unremittingly flat that one cannot help thinking that the sea is no more than a few yards away, whereas in reality it is many miles distant. The sea has not always been far off. Seasoned wood, used in making furniture, and the remains of farms have been discovered in the silt at the edge of the bay, and this is thought to be evidence that the sea once engulfed the plain and has since retreated again.

The stretch of land that the sea has left behind is in two parts. One is the arable and wooded terrain to the south of Dol-de-Bretagne; the other is the marshland to the north which is frequently below sea level and is always in danger of flooding.

It is also really rather dreary with its four-square system of canals and dykes planted with poplars. The marshlands themselves are divided into two, with the

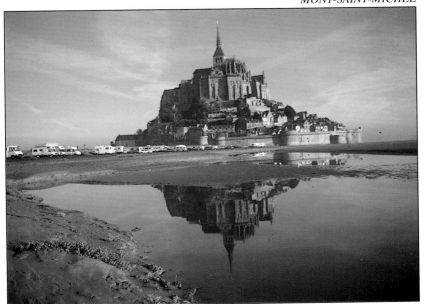

so-called "black marshes" full of damp meadows and the "white marshes", a chequer-board of long, narrow ploughed fields of gray, sandy soil.

Lastly, there are the polders which were reclaimed during the 19th century; these are salt meadows (*prés-salés*) where cows calmly ruminate in the company of the occasional seagull and the famous salt-meadow lambs.

The whole area is dominated by **Mont-Dol,** a granite mound some 65 m (213 ft) high boasting four springs and a site of sun-worshipping rites from the neolithic period until the end of the Iron Age. It is worth climbing to the top to visit the chapel built in 1857, to count the 60 church towers round about, and to catch a glimpse of the two spires of St Samson's Cathedral.

The center of **Dol-de-Bretagne** (on the N176) is dominated by **St Samson's Cathedral** which is surrounded by some beautiful old houses. No bishop has his seat at this unusual church. Its proportions are wrong, being too long at almost 100 meters (330 ft), and too tall (20 m or 66 ft); one of its sides is very austere while the other is Gothic and elaborately decorated. Just 2 km (1.25 miles) further on is the famous pink granite **Champ Dolent** (Field of Pain) menhir which is said to have played a part in stopping a fratricidal struggle many years ago. It is 9 m (29.5 ft) high and is thought to be falling over, but if that is true, it is doing so extremely slowly!

Mont-Saint-Michel

To the north lies the miraculously beautiful **Mont-Saint-Michel Bay,** in the center of which stands the famous rock. Probably the best way of appreciating its magic is to approach it from the sea, and to do that it is worth getting a pair of stout boots and a guide, perhaps one of the few remaining fishermen who still ply their trade on the foreshore. There is something irresistibly, even dangerously, appealing about the bay, and about the way its tide swirls in and out of the labyrinth

of channels and can so easily ensnare the unwary. There is no better way of approaching **Mont-Saint-Michel** itself than to splash one's way up to it just as the pilgrims did in ancient times, and still do today.

Once inside the **ramparts**, you see the **Grande-Rue** twisting and turning as it climbs, round hotels, restaurants and souvenir shops. Not even the permanent crush of pedestrians can rob the place of its unique charm. There are flights of steps everywhere on Mont-Saint-Michel, and the Grand Degré is the first of many: It leads up to the fortified gatehouse of the **abbey**. At this point, the visitor leaves knick-knacks and postcards behind, and enters a totally new world. A dark covered passage is followed by a stairway of 90 steps known as the Abbey Steps which lead directly to the first terrace. From here, one proceeds to the **church**, a wonderfully airy and well-lit

Above: The cloister of Mont-Saint-Michel Abbey. Right: Carved rocks at Rothéneuf.

Gothic building. A tour of the church follows a standard route, and moves level by level from the abbey to the **La Merveille** Buildings. Much has been written about this extraordinary place, and there is no doubt that it is extremely difficult to find words to convey the combination of spirituality and military power – the beautiful **cloister** which seems to be suspended in mid-air, the breathtaking **refectory** filled with diffused light even though it does not appear to have any windows, the Romanesque walk, the large workroom which gives the appearance of being small because of its huge fireplaces, the labyrinth of stairways and dark corridors. One could go on for ever!

On leaving the church, it would be a pity to miss a walk along the watchpath which follows the ramparts. There are also many other places to visit, including the **Parish Church,** the **Archéoscope** (which tells the story of Mont-Saint-Michel), the curious Grévin Museum and the so-called House of Tiphaine, one of many buildings where du Guesclin stayed.

Before returning to the mainland, one of Mère Poulard's exquisite omelets is strongly recommended, although it is essential to book a table in advance. Lastly, as you leave, you should turn round and take one last look at the sublimely beautiful mount, particularly in the evening, when it looks just like some resplendent transatlantic liner lying at anchor. Sadly, the mud flats are encroaching on the seashore and the great stone ship is beginning to run aground. This is mainly the fault of the causeway which prevents the ebb tide from taking the sand out to sea again. However, without the causeway there would be no tourists!

From Cancale to Saint-Malo

Towards the west, the main road – first the D797 and then the D155 – runs along the edge of the bay. If the tide is out, it

can mean that the sea is anything from 3 to 10 km (2-6 miles) away, and what we have instead is an enormous, gray, wet, salty plain cluttered with oyster beds and fish-farms. The little villages along this road include Cherrueix, Le Vivier-sur-Mer and Saint-Benoît-des-Ondes, and their low, white fishermen's houses face straight out to sea. However, there are no fishing boats, and no ports either. Le Vivier goes in for mussels, though, and its little beach bristles with mussel-beds. **Cancale** is quite different: its rock is almost the size of a cliff and its port, **La Houle,** is a real port even if the beach has only a few mackerel boats and some tractors on it. These are used on the 375 hectares (926 acres) of oyster beds which are uncovered at low tide. It must surely have been more exciting when the local *bisquines* (fishing boats) used to set out for the sandbanks off the coast once a year to find seed-oysters; sadly, the banks have become polluted and the baby oysters have to be brought in from Belon. It is still possible to see the very last of

these fishing smacks – the *Cancalaise*, an old black boat with three crooked masts that was rebuilt a few years back. A visit to the **Musée de l'Huître** (Oyster Museum) is also an opportunity to put in an order for some oyster hampers for Christmas (tel 99 89 65 29).

The Emerald Coast starts at **Pointe du Grouin** a rock 40 m (131 ft) high buffeted by the north west winds. The coast itself is dotted with tiny islands, rocks ceaselessly battered by waves, coves both stormy and calm, and ruggesd cliffs interspersed with golden beaches.This wild scene is made somewhat tamer by the hundreds of holiday homes of all kinds, ranging from mock farmhouses surrounded by wallflowers to seaside follies dating from the beginning of this century.

The road to Saint-Malo passes by the rocky Pointe du Meinga and in sight of a mass of little islands called les Tintiaux, where winkles are gathered, before reaching **Rothéneuf** and its **sculpted rocks.** These are the work of a retired and paralyzed priest who, towards the end of

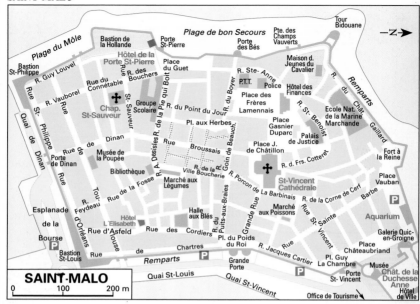

SAINT-MALO

0   100   200 m

the 19th century, carved over 300 grotesque figures representing sea monsters, chimeras, and hideous faces. From Pointe de la Varde, there is a splendid view over the Rance Estuary and the city of Saint-Malo.

Saint-Malo to Dinard

Saint-Malo lies on a peninsula which was an island a long time ago before sand began to accumulate on the Sillon (spit). **Paramé** and its ancient rival, Saint-Servan, are two pretty little towns nearby. After being largely destroyed during World War Two – the ramparts fortunately survived – and subsequently rebuilt brick by brick, the old privateers' city has now rediscovered its former charm. A walk along the **ramparts** is strongly recommended, as from here there is a splendid view over the sea, the

Right: The Noires breakwater, the Saint-Philippe Bastion and the ramparts at Saint-Malo.

Grand Jardin lighthouse, and the busy coming and going of innumerable sailing boats. Nearby is the **castle,** with its famous Quic-en-Groigne Tower, which has overlooked the Sillon since the 15th century. Further on, the Bidouane Tower stands on the top of the rocky Champs-Vauverts and looks out across to Grand Bé Island where the writer Chateaubriand is buried. Access to the Bon-Secours beach is through the Saint-Pierre Gate. The twin towers of the Grande Porte stand at the entrance to the inner harbour.

The tall houses atop the ramparts seem from a distance to be too identical, too regimented to be real, like toy soldiers on parade. From close up, however, they become more human, their slate roofs softened by golden lichen, and at sunset the tall, shining windows glitter with a myriad reflections. In the town center, a signposted route takes visitors to the most beautiful, and most historic, of Saint-Malo's buildings. These include the 12th-century **Saint-Vincent's Cathedral,** which is still standing after heavy

bombing during the last war and 25 years of restoration, and the *Bar de l'Univers* in Place Chateaubriand, the town's most famous and oldest bar, famous for the mementos covering its wooden walls. There are also reminders of the traditional historic and commercial links with Britain in an English shop, *Voisins et Compagnie* (6 and 14 Rue Broussais), tea rooms noted for their scones, *Tea Time,* (4 Grand-Rue), and English furniture mingling with ship's furniture in antique shops behind the church.

Saint-Servan faces Saint-Malo on its own peninsula, dominated by an 18th-century fort (where, since 1942, mushrooms have been grown in the cellars) and by the very beautiful and solitary **Solidor Tower.** This little town is hugely popular both for its spacious marina and for its enormous beach , marked off by a dyke which turns it into a giant swimming pool at low tide. Though called Saint-Servan-sur-Mer, the town in fact faces the estuary of the River Rance, which is barred by a 750-yard wide tidal

power-station. Above it, the mud-banks of low tide have been replaced by a large lake, almost a fjord, which winds its way inland, though unspoilt countryside to the Châtelier Lock, just short of Dinan. This charming waterway is lined on either side by meadows, dense woods, sleepy little towns with small beaches, tidal mills, farm, harbours and dozens of boats tied up in every creek and cove.

Opposite Saint-Malo across the estuary stand **Dinard** and two villages, Saint-Lunaire and Saint-Briac. This once fashionable seaside resort was "colonized" during the 19th century by the British, who turned it into a little Brighton, and later by the Americans. It has somehow managed to preserve a certain antiquated charm with its jumbled architecture which ranges from mock-Tudor manors to Hollywood-style villas. A marina and sea-water therapy center have been built as a concession to modern tastes, and the clientele has changed a lot since the days when one had to pay to go for a swim on the Ecluse beach.

69

Tourist Information

Information about the region: **Comité départemental du Tourisme d'Ille-et-Vilaine**, 1, rue Martenot, 35032 Rennes cedex, Tel: 99-790198.

BECHEREL
Castle

Château de Caraduec, Tel: 99-667776.

CANCALE
Accommodation / Restaurants

LUXURY: **Le Continental**, 4, quai de l'Administrateur-Thomas, Tel: 99-896016.

MODERATE: **Le Chatellier**, route de Saint-Malo, Tel: 99-898184.

L'Armada, 8, quai de l'Administrateur-Thomas, Tel: 99-896002, restaurant, moderate prices.

La Godille, rue Alfred-Baslé, Tel: 99-896565, inexpensive restaurant.

Museums

Musée des Arts et Traditions populaires, Tel: 99-897932. **Musée de l'Huître**, oyster museum, Tel: 99-896529.

Tourist Information / Leisure

Office de Tourisme, 44, rue du Port, Tel: 99-896372. **Boat Tours**, Association La Bisquine Cancalaise, in the town hall, Tel: 99-897787.

CESSON-SEVIGNE
(5 km east of Rennes)
Accommodation

MODERATE: **Germinal**, 9, cours de la Vilaine, Tel: 99-831101.

Castle

Château des Rochers-Sévigné, information, Tel: 99-967651.

COMBOURG
Accommodation

BUDGET: **Hôtel du Château**, place Châteaubriand, Tel: 99-730038.

Tourist Information / Castle

Office de Tourisme, Maison de la Lanterne, place Albert-Parent, Tel: 99-731393 in summer, otherwise Tel: 99-730018. **Château**, Tel: 99-732295.

CONCORET
Sightseeing

Château de Comper, castle, with the **Centre de l'Imaginaire Arthurien**, Tel: 97-227996.

DINARD
Accommodation

LUXURY: **La Reine Hortense**, 19, rue de la Malouine, Tel: 99-465431. *MODERATE:* **Hôtel des Dunes**, 5, av. Georges-Clémenceau, Tel: 99-461272. *BUDGET:* **Hôtel Printania**, 5, avenue Georges-V, Tel: 99-461307.

Festival

Festival du Film britannique, first week in October, Tel: 99-461265.

Tourist Information

Office de Tourisme, 2, boulevard Féart, Tel: 99-469412.

DOL-DE-BRETAGNE
Accommodation

BUDGET: **Le Logis de la Bresche Arthur**, 36, boulevard Derminiac, Tel: 99-480144.

Tourist Information

Office de Tourisme, 3, Grande-Rue, Tel: 99-481537 in summer, otherwise Tel: 99-480017.

FOUGERES
Accommodation

BUDGET: **Les Voyageurs**, 10, place Gambetta, Tel: 99-990820.

Tourist Information / Castle

Office de Tourisme, place Aristide-Briand, Tel: 99-941220. **Château**, Tel: 99-997959.

GRAND-FOUGERAY
Sightseeing

Tour du Guesclin, Tel: 99-084019.

LA GUERCHE-DE-BRETAGNE
Tourist Information

Office de Tourisme, place du Général-de-Gaulle, Tel: 99-963078.

HEDE
Accommodation / Restaurants

BUDGET: **Hostellerie du Vieux Moulin**, route de Saint-Malo, Tel: 99-454570, with restaurant.

La Vieille Auberge, route de Saint-Malo, Tel: 99-454625, inexpensive restaurant.

LES IFFS
Castle

Château de Montmuran, Tel: 99-458888.

LOUVIGNE-DU-DESERT
Accommodation

BUDGET: **Le Manoir**, 1, place Charles-de-Gaulle, Tel: 99-985340.

MONT-SAINT-MICHEL
Accommodation

MODERATE: **Mère Poulard**, Tel: 33-601401. *BUDGET:* **Le Mouton Blanc**, Tel: 33-601408.

Tourist Information / Leisure

Office de Tourisme, place Aristide-Briand, Tel: 33-601430.

Boat tours in the bay, departure from Le Vivier-sur-Mer, April–October, Tel: 99-488230.

MONTAUBAN-DE-BRETAGNE
Accommodation

BUDGET: **Le Relais de la Hucherais**, La Hucherais, Tel: 99-065431.

Castle

Château de Montauban, Tel: 99-064021.

MONTERFIL
Festival

Fête de la Musique gallèse, music festival, last weekend in June.

MONTFORT-SUR-MEU
Accommodation
BUDGET: **Le Relais de la Cane**, 2, rue de la Gare, Tel: 99-090007.
Museum
Écomusée du Pays de Montfort, Tour Papegaut, rue du Château, Tel: 99-093181.

NEANT-SUR-YVEL
Special Events
La Cour aux Étoiles, le Boschat, Tel: 97-930384.

NOYAL-SUR-VILAINE
Accommodation
BUDGET: **Les Forges**, 22, av. du Général-de-Gaulle, Tel: 99-005108, with restaurant.

FORÊT DE PAIMPONT
Accommodation
BUDGET: **Le Relais de Brocéliande**, Bourg, Tel: 99-078107.
Tourist Information
Office touristique de Brocéliande, in the town hall of Plélan, Tel: 99-068607.

PLEUGUENEUC
Castle
Château de la Bourbansais, Tel: 99-694007.

LA POINTE-DU-GROUIN
(5 km north of Cancale)
Accommodation
MODERATE: **Hôtel de la Pointe du Grouin**, Tel: 99-896055.

REDON
Accommodation / Restaurants
BUDGET: **Chandouineau**, 10, avenue de la Gare, Tel: 99-710204, with restaurant.
Le Moulin de Via, route de Gacilly, Tel: 99-710516, elegant restaurant.
Tourist Information / Festivals
Office de Tourisme, rue des États, Tel: 99-710604. *La Fête des Mariniers*, July 14 and 15. *La Fête de l'Abbaye*, middle of July–August.

RENNES
Accommodation / Restaurants
MODERATE: **Hôtel du Guesclin**, 5, place de la Gare, Tel: 99-314747. *BUDGET:* **Hôtel Central**, 6, rue Lanjuinais, Tel: 99-791236.
Auberge Saint-Sauveur, 6, rue Saint-Sauveur, Tel: 99-793256. **Le Corsaire**, 52, rue d'Antrain, Tel: 99-363369, both restaurants with tasty food, moderate prices.
Museums / Sightseeing
Musée de Bretagne and **Musée des Beaux-Arts**, 20, quai Emile-Zola, Tel: 99-285584/5. **Écomusée du Pays de Rennes**, la Bintinais, route de Châtillon, Tel: 99-513815.
Palais de Justice, open 10-11 am and 3-4 pm, closed Tue.
Festivals
Les Transmusicales, first week in December, Tel: 99-315533. *Festival des Tombées de la Nuit*, first week in July, Tel: 99-303801.
Sports
HORSERIDING: **Comité départemental des Sports équestres**, 1, pl. Pasteur, Tel: 99-364654. *GOLF:* **Golf de la Freslonnière**, Tel: 99-608409. *WATERSPORTS:* **Comité départemental de Voile**, 2, allée Port-Louis, Tel: 99-360416. *CANAL-TOURS:* **Comité de Promotion touristique des Canaux bretons A.B.R.I.**, 9, rue des Portes-Mordelaises, Tel: 99-315944.
Tourist Information
Office de Tourisme, pont de Nemours, Tel: 99-790198.

SAINT-MALO
Accommodation
LUXURY: **L'Elisabeth**, 2, rue des Cordiers, porte Saint-Louis, Tel: 99-562498. *MODERATE:* **Le Surcouf**, rue de la Plage, Rochebonne, Tel: 99-409220. *BUDGET:* **Hôtel de la Porte Saint-Pierre**, place du Guet, Tel: 99-409127.
Museum / Sightseeing
Château and **Musée de la Ville** (in the Grand-Donjon), place Châteaubriand, Tel: 99-407157. **Tour Quic-en-Groigne**, Tel: 99-408026.
Festivals / Events
Son et Lumière, July-August, Tel: 99-401830. *Festival de Musique sacrée*, middle of July-August, Tel: 99-565128. *Festival de la Francophonie*, first week in September, Tel: 99-404250.
Tourist Information
Office de Tourisme, esplanade Saint-Vincent, Tel: 99-666448.

SAINT-SERVAN
Accommodation
LUXURY: **Le Valmarin**, 7, rue Jean-XXIII, port de Solidor, Tel: 99-819476.
BUDGET: **La Rance**, 15, quai Sébastopol, Tel: 99-817863.
Museum / Sightseeing
Tour Solidor with the **Musée du Long Cours Cap-Hornier**.

TREMBLAY
Accommodation
MODERATE: **Le Roc Land**, "La Lande", Tel: 99-982046.

VITRE
Accommodation
BUDGET: **Le Minotel**, 47, rue de la Poterie, Tel: 99-751111. **Le Petit Billot**, 5, place du Général-Leclerc, Tel: 99-750210.
Tourist Information / Castle
Office de Tourisme, place Saint-Yves, Tel: 99-750446. **Château**, Tel: 99-750454.

CÔTES D'ARMOR

RANCE VALLEY
DINAN
EMERALD COAST AND
ARGUENON VALLEY
LAMBALLE AND PENTHIÈVRE
SAINT-BRIEUC TO PAIMPOL
RIVER TRÉGOR
PINK GRANITE COAST

Côtes d'Armor

When Bretons think of Armor (the sea-girt land), they think of the English Channel, a sea both revered and loathed, one that can change sharply from emerald to sapphire, express tenderness and rage, and look one moment like a river and the next like the open sea. When Bretons think of Argoat, on the other hand, they think of forests. The ghost of Brocéliande lives on, and the forests where she once roamed may be encountered quite unexpectedly in the heathlands, pasture lands and cornfields of Argoat, looking like so many little green islands. The Monts d'Arrée are the border between Argoat and the interior, but the heathlands run the whole length of the region. Armor also stands for fishing, with its quaint little ports, flourishing oyster beds and fleets of fishing boats. In its turn, the English Channel laps the pretty beaches of the Emerald Coast, although there are times when it becomes enraged and launches itself against the Goëlo cliffs or the strange rocks of the Pink Granite Coast.

The landscape varies from green, well-watered valleys near the River Rance to

Previous pages: Sunset over the Pink Granite Coast. Left: The Port Kamer Lighthouse.

fields growing vegetables around Tréguier. Also, as this land is granitic, it forms the base of the heathland of Menez-Bré. The people of the Côtes-d'Armor live between land and sea, always looking skywards for a sign of respite from a storm or rain for their crops.

RANCE VALLEY

The **Rance Valley** is a most green and tranquil part of Brittany. The waters of the two rivers on either side of the valley, the Arguenon in the west and the Rance in the east hasten down the valleys to be embraced by the English Channel. The Rance is a perfect example of an Armorican *ria* (a word of Spanish origin meaning a river estuary which cuts deep into the land), as it opens out into a magnificent estuary which seems far too big for such a minor watercourse. Even allowing for tributaries, it is scarcely believable that it is capable of carving such a deep channel and one that goes all the way from the little port of Dinan to Dinard and Saint-Malo in the neighboring *département* of Ille-et-Vilaine.

At its mouth, the River Rance presents two aspects to the world. At low tide there are vast expanses of mud, where fishermen come to inspect their lobster-pots; while at high tide it is a proud expanse of water. A walk along the estuary is a wonderful experience. The banks are dotted with quiet little villages, grand country houses, mysterious manors, romantic castles which are encircled by chestnut trees, mills and half-hidden churches – and even, just north of Dinan, a standing menhir in the outskirts of Saint-Samson-sur-Rance (by the D766).

The **Tiemblaye Menhir** rises to a height of over 7 m (23 ft) but, unlike the menhirs at Carnac, this one leans over at an angle of 30 degrees, making it possible to read the carving on the upper side. This can only be done at midday, however, when the light glancing off the stone makes the markings momentarily visible. There has always been fighting in these parts; and whether it was instigated by the Celts, the Romans , the English, or the *Chouans* the memories still linger on. A little way from the banks of the Rance, at Pleslin-Trivagou, there is the Carna Alignment – 65 quartz menhirs standing in five rows, and only 1 km (1.5 miles) from the charming Renaissance **Bois de la Motte Château** (on the D2). The village church also has baptismal fonts, stained glass windows and basins for holy water dating from the 12th to 18th centuries.

Nearby is the old Roman road, now prosaically renamed the D28 but following the same route. The hill on which **Haut Bécherel** stands appears to have been the most important site occupied by the Coriosolites, a Gallo-Roman community that lived at the time of Julius Caesar. Excavations at **Corseul** (on the D44) have revealed the existence of a town with streets and districts, occupying an area of 130 hectares (321 acres). A short distance away, at a place called Champ-Mulon, there are some thermal baths. Corseul has been the scene of excavations for over a century, and is a favourite haunt of archeologists.

On the top of the hill is a truly remarkable octagonal tower about 10 m (33 ft)

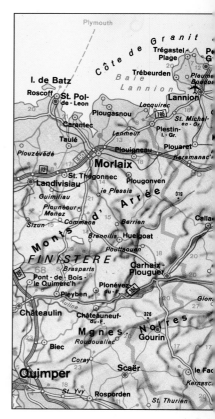

high. This was a **Temple of Mars** which probably formed part of a huge complex of fortifications built by the Romans in the 1st century A.D. to oversee and protect the western extremity of their empire. It is sited strategically where two important roads meet. In addition to a pretty church and a monumental Carolingian cross, there is a small **museum** in Courseul's town hall , displaying a large number of artifacts that have been discovered in the vicinity, including Roman sandals, engraved slabs of stone, coins, bracelets and small statues.

The site was had been abandoned and forgotten by the 5th century and was not inhabited until the 12th century when the viscounts of Dinan came to build a for-

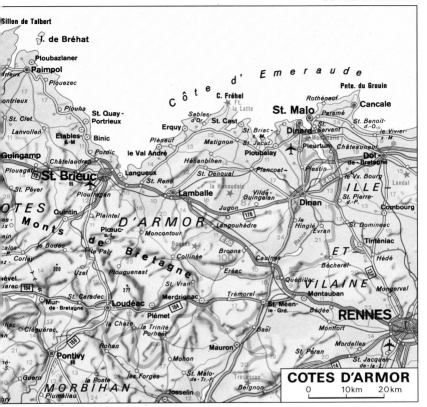

tified castle here on an oppidum, a kind of knoll. **Montafilan Château**, the property of Françoise de Dinan, the fiancée of Gilles de Bretagne and later governess of Anne of Brittany, was a wonderful building in its day but is now no more than a ruin. However, it is possible to walk peacefully through it along some still delightful paths.

The Rance Valley has for many centuries been dominated by Breton and French lords and their castles. The Hundred Years' War, the Breton War of Succession and the French Revolution left it scattered with fortresses, some of them built on the very banks of the Rance and the Arguenon. The period of the French Revolution was far and away the most bloody

in Breton history. The inhabitants of the Rance Valley were firmly opposed to the anti-clerical views which gained acceptance in Dinan: They stood unconditionally behind the Marquis de la Rouërie, the leader of the Chouan insurrection until 1793, the year of his death. As a result, throughout the valley, there was not a single manor house, not a single castle that was not involved in a conspiracy, an ambush or a killing.

The small, somber granite town of **Lehon** just outside Dinan has its own special claim to fame: the Saint-Magloire Abbey which was founded here by Nominoé. A priory was built here later on; its refectory and 13th-century church can still be visited.

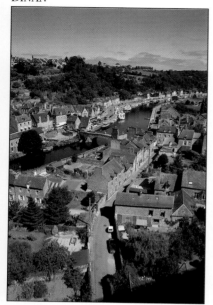

DINAN

Dinan stands on the edge of a steep plateau only a short distance from the mouth of the estuary. It is unquestionably one of the most beautiful medieval cities in Brittany, with numerous architectural jewels hidden away behind miles of ramparts and a splendid castle overlooking the Rance. Dinan sometimes gives the impression of being a corseted old lady who goes out of her way to ignore the passage of time, and fights off anyone who attempts to assail her mighty granite defenses.

Two centuries after its foundation by King Nominoé , the castle of the lords of Dinan, which was only built of wood, was attacked by William the Conqueror in 1065. He failed to capture it but the exploit was nevertheless celebrated in the Bayeux Tapestry. In 1359 the English army made an attempt on the fortifica-

Above: An aerial view of Dinan with the River Rance running through it.

tions but were met by a knight named Du Guesclin. He challenged the Duke of Canterbury to single combat, beat him and drove the English out once and for all. Ever since, Du Guesclin has been the hero of Dinan.

This is the kind of town that should be visited on foot. It is far and away the best way to appreciate the wooden façades, the balconies decorated with flowers, the old porches and the paved alleyways running down towards the river. The street names of the old town are better than any history lesson at recalling Dinan's past of artisans, merchants and gentry – names such as Place des Cordeliers (Cordeliers is a word used to describe Franciscan friars), Rue de l'Apport (a reference to currency exchange), Place des Merciers (Haberdashers' Square) and Rue de la Ferronnerie (Ironmongery Street). The town is also marvelously preserved, and there is a great sense of homogeneity about the buildings. Dinan is clearly of considerable historical importance, but it takes no less pride in its artistic heritage. For instance, the former **Couvent des Cordeliers** (Franciscan Monastery), built by Henri d'Avaugour in the 13th century, used to alternate with the Dominican Monastery in hosting the famous States of Brittany; it has since been turned into a private school but is still open to visitors during the school holidays. Then there is St Malo's Church which houses a beautiful English organ. The church was begun in the 15th century but was not finished until the 19th century, and is notable for an apse in the Flamboyant style, a Renaissance door, and an 18th-century pulpit. As for the organ, it was made by the famous English organ builder, Alfred Oldknow, and inaugurated in 1889; it was forgotten for a while before being revived by a group of enthusiasts. Place des Merciers leads into rue de l'Horloge in which there is a 60 m (197 ft) high **Beffroy** (clocktower), a gift to the town from the Duchess Anne in the 15th century.

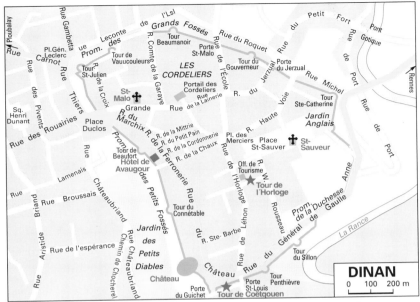

After passing a beautiful 15th-century house one comes into the **Place Saint-Sauveur,** formerly the butchers' market. The square is lined with a number of medieval houses including that of Auguste Pavie, the explorer (1847-1925), but is most remarkable for **St Saviour's Basilica,** an outstanding example of Gothic Flamboyant style. The entrance to this church is through a most unusual porch carved with mermaids, monsters, serpents and other infernal creatures. This remarkable mixture of Romanesque style with Byzantine influences was started in 1112 by order of Riwallon le Roux when he was about to depart for the Crusades, and is the oldest building in the town. The interior has a large number of 15th-and 16th-century chapels, a fine collection of statues, stained glass windows, altars and magnificent reredoses. The north transept contains the heart of Bernard du Guesclin, who died in 1380.

The maze of backstreets has a whole range of treasures including a small Renaissance town house, a fine rounded 15th-century porch and wooden framing and a masonic emblem above a doorway. Nor is there any shortage of historical associations. These include the birthplace of the writer Théodore Botrel in rue de la Mittrie, a statue of Mercoeur, governor of Brittany in the 16th century, in Grand'rue opposite the **Hôtel de Plouër,** and a memorial to the Bishops of Saint-Malo in the Hôtel Bazin. The most delightful views, however, are to be enjoyed along **rue du Jerzual** first thing in the morning. This street is a great favorite among the people of Dinan and is frequently restored. It is lined with the 15th-and 16th-century homes of craftsmen – potters, glass-blowers and weavers.

The Gothic Porte du Jerzual leads to the harbour, the scene of much activity in the days of sailing ships, and then on towards the **Jardin Anglais**. It was built on the site of the former Saint-Sauveur cemetery in 1852 and is the resting place of the town's leading figures; from a splendid terrace, there is also an outstanding view of the Rance. The English

Garden is the starting point for a tour of the **ramparts**, thought to be among the oldest in Brittany. They consist of fifteen towers and four gates, and were strengthened first by François II and then by Mercoeur; they also underwent restoration in the 18th century. The beautiful Promenade de la Duchesse Anne leads to the **castle**, also known as the Keep of Duchess Anne. It was constructed in the 14th century, and consists of a number of buildings and massive towers which were fortified by Mercoeur during the time of the League. Since 1908, the keep and Coëtquen Tower have served as a **museum** which recounts the history of the area. It houses numerous collections of artifacts from prehistory, the Gallo-Roman period and the Middle Ages, as well as sacred objects, headdresses and costumes. Most striking is a room of recumbent figures. Here, impor-

Above: An accordeon player on the terrace of a café in Dinan. Right: Moorlands and rocks at Cap Fréhel.

tant local dignitaries and members of local families lie beneath seven separate stones.

To the south-east of Dinan lies the **château of Beaumanoir**, with its proud flags and the manor farmhouses that form the parish of Champs-Géraux. South of Dinan, the visitor passes through a large number of peaceful villages abundantly adorned with flowers (including Saint-Juvat which has been awarded a prize for the best flower gardens in France), towards the **castle of Hac** (off the D39). This was built during the Hundred Years' War on the edge of a thickly wooded forest as a hunting lodge for the Dukes of Brittany. It is still in a perfect state of preservation, particularly the five beautiful towers, and exhibitions and concerts are regularly held there. The coat of arms of the Hingant du Hac family may be seen on tombstones in the tiny, thousand-year-old church at **Tréfumel**, which has a wonderful overhanging yew tree, itself many hundreds of years old. At Caulnes (by the D25), there is **Couëllan Château,** the property of the Saint-Pern family and notable for its long façade with bull's-eye windows, its gardens and its orangery. Yvignac Castle (north by the D62) owes its place in the history books to the fact that 400 *Chouans* settled there in 1795; even more interesting is the church of St Malo in the village, a fine example of the kind of Romanesque art that characterises so many old Breton churches. It was entirely restored at the end of the 19th century, but there is still an 11th-century door with somewhat enigmatic decorations (protected by a modern porch) and a 12th-century choir.

EMERALD COAST AND ARGUENON VALLEY

The word "emerald" captures perfectly the twinkling brilliance, the perfect scale and multiple facets of this stretch of Brittany's coastline. The **Emerald Coast**, which runs from the sandy beaches of Lancieux to the purple heathlands of Cap Fréhel, includes beaches, tapering headlands thrusting out into the open sea, huge bays which cut deep into the coastline, and long stretches of rocky coast pounded spectacularly and incessantly by the waves. According to its mood, it can be wild or languorous or utterly enchanting and is equally popular with holidaymakers who want the tranquillity of unspoilt countryside, and yachtsmen looking for a safe mooring.

The Emerald Coast's reputation for good hospitality goes back a long way. The British were building holiday homes in France as early as the 1850s, and it is still possible to detect a certain English air wafting around the coastal towns. Over the years, however, people have come to acknowledge an urgent need to diversify away from fishing, and as a result small resorts have sprung up everywhere to take advantage of the coast's pleasant climate. This area the begins at Jugon-les-Lacs on the **River Arguenon**.

Emerald Coast

It is very clear that the villages along the coast preceded the arrival of tourism. As elsewhere in Brittany, it was the Irish saints who were the first visitors from the north to land on these pleasant shores. An exception is **Lancieux**, a village 10 km (6 mi) west of Dinard. St Sieuc, a friend of St Brieuc, came here from England in the 11th century to found a monastery, although the belltower is all that now remains of the old church. There is, however, a very beautiful font in stone and two stained glass windows telling the life of St Sieuc. Lancieux, which stands on a peninsula, is very popular with fishing folk as it boasts a double ring of rocks which protects the longest of its sandy beaches, called Saint-Cieu. Bathing is extremely safe here, and there is also a wonderful view out to the Ébihen Islands and the headland near Saint-Jacut.

The **peninsula of Saint-Jacut** (by the D786) serves as a natural barrier between the bay at Lancieux and another bay into which the Arguenon flows, and is also one of the most characteristic headlands on the Emerald Coast. Its coastline is strictly determined by the movements of the tides – the land narrowing sharply when the water rushes towards the fore-shore, and broadening into huge mud flats at low tide. Low tide is the favorite time of day for fishermen, collectors of shells, and those who roll up their trouser legs and use a spoon net *(épuisette)* to catch shrimps.

According to geographers and ancient legends, this narrow strip of land jutting out towards the Ébihens has not always been a peninsula. It was certainly rela-tively isolated before the Middle Ages when some monks arrived and built a causeway, thereby permanently joining the village to the mainland.

Probably because the village of **Saint-Jacut-de-la-Mer** was once completely cut off from the mainland, it stands reso-lutely aloof from the rest of the world. The inhabitants, called Jaguens, have their own language called "Jegui," a vari-ant of Gallo and a form of French that was spoken before France was united under a single monarchy; even their his-tory, their legends, as retold by the folklorist Paul Sébillot (1846-1918), and their family names, are quite different. In short, the Jaguens are an independent people. The village was founded by an Irish monk in the 10th century and occu-pies a large part of the peninsula; in the winter, it is inhabited by only a few hundred people. They earn their liveli-hood mainly from mackerel fishing, but Saint-Jacut's reputation is based de-servedly on its eleven delightful beaches. There are no old stones to look at, and no historic remains.

The summer visitor has all the time in the world to amble gently from one fish-ing port to the next, and from the golden beaches to glistening mud flats, or to stride out to the Pointe du Chevet for a stunningly beautiful view over the Ebi-

hens. At low tide, it is even possible to walk across to Ebihen with its tower, the Tour Vauban, and find an empty spot on the beach. Within the village proper, little has changed in the past hundred years or so. The way the houses are arranged in groups, with their gables almost meting over the streets to protect them from the wind, is particularly attractive.

The **Quatre-Vaux** beach on the east side of the **peninsula of Saint-Cast** is another recommended port of call, its long sandy beach lined with rounded hil-locks offering superb views. The coast of the peninsula is marked by a series of jagged coves, weatherbeaten rocks, and majestic cliffs.

One last place to stop at before reach-ing the wide open spaces flanking the road to Cap Fréhel is **Saint-Cast-le-Guildo**, probably the best known resort on the entire Emerald Coast. This village is extremely commercialized but it is a delightful little spot for all that. It was founded in the 6th century by an Irish monk called Cadoc, and later divided into three separate settlements: Le Bourg, L'Isle and La Garde. Le Bourg is of little interest except for a modern church with a strange 16th-century round font and a fine stained glass window showing the Battle of Saint-Cast. The arrival in 1758 of several thousand English soldiers led to a widespread and violent uprising on the part of the inhabitants, and the ensu-ing battle, which was led by the Duke of Aiguillon, took place in the port. Not only was the battle won by the people of Saint-Cast, but it also forced the English to renounce all ideas of invading Brittany ever again. The event is recalled by an "English cemetery", and commemorative column surmounted by the Breton grey-hound crushing the English lion.

The fishermen's quarter, also known as Isle Saint-Cast, and its rocky headland are mainly important for wonderful views over La Frênaye Bay, La Latte Fort and Cap Fréhel from the viewing table

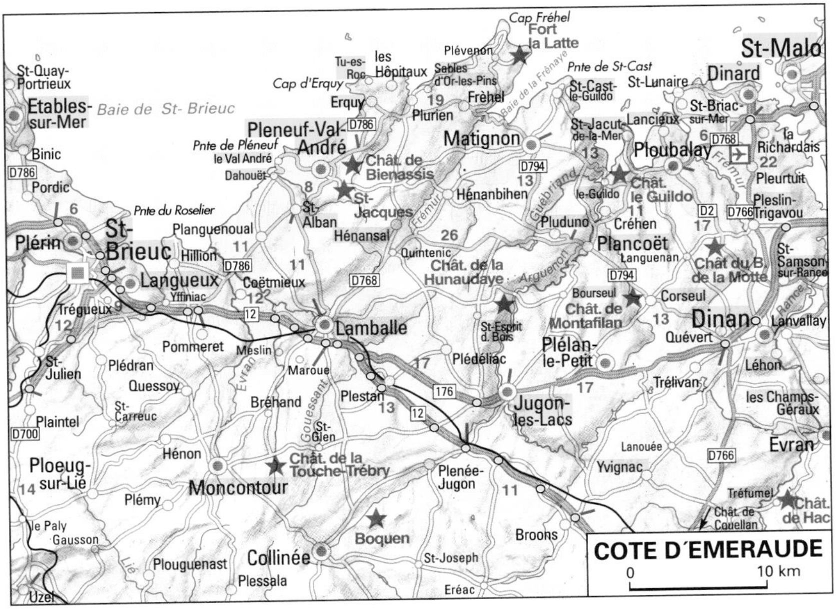
COTE D'EMERAUDE
0
10 km
Cap Fréhel
Fort la Latte
St-Malo
Dinard
St-Quay-Portrieux
Etables-sur-Mer
Baie de St- Brieuc
Binic
Pordic
Plérin
St-Brieuc
Langueux
Yffiniac
Trégueux
St-Julien
Plédran
Quessoy
St-Carreuc
Plaintel
Ploeuc-sur-Lié
Hénon
Plémy
Moncontour
le Paly
Gausson
Uzel
Plouguenast
Collinée
Plessala
Boquen
Chât. de la Touche-Trébry
Bréhand
Maroue
Plestan
St-Glen
Lamballe
Meslin
Pommeret
Coëtmieux
Hillion
Planguenoual
Pnte du Roselier
Dahouët
le Val André
Pnte de Pléneuf
Pleneuf-Val-André
Chât. de Bienassis
St-Jacques
St-Alban
Hénansal
Erquy
Cap d'Erquy
Tu-es-Roc
les Hôpitaux
Sables d'Or-les-Pins
Plévenon
Fréhel
Plurien
Matignon
Hénanbihen
Quintenic
Chât. de la Hunaudaye
St-Esprit d. Bois
Plédéliac
Jugon-les-Lacs
Plénée-Jugon
St-Joseph
Eréac
Broons
Yvignac
Lanouée
Plélan-le-Petit
Bourseul
Chât. de Montafilan
Plancoët
Languenan
Pluduno
Créhen
le-Guildo
Chât. le Guildo
St-Jacut-de-la-Mer
St-Cast-le-Guildo
Pnte de St-Cast
St-Lunaire
Lancieux
Ploubalay
St-Briac-sur-Mer
la Richardais
Pleurtuit
Pleslin-Trigavou
Chât du B. de la Motte
Corseul
Dinan
Lanvallay
Quévert
Léhon
Trélivan
les Champs-Géraux
Evran
Tréfumel
Chât. de Coüellan
Chât. de Hac
St-Samson-sur-Rance
Baie de la Frênaye
Arguenon
Frémur
Rance
Evran
Gouessant
Lié
D786
D700
D768
D794
D766
D2
12
176

next to the signal station. It is also the starting point for walks along the coastal path. The **Pointe de la Garde** is reached through Vieuxville wood and past the Moulin d'Anne , a windmill where the Duke of Aiguillon sheltered during the battle in 1758. From here there is a different view of the Ebihen Islands and some of the resort's seven beaches. The visitor walking south from Saint-Cast along the bay as far as Saint-Germain is recommended to stop at the *Moulin de la Mer* , a combined antique -shop and tea rooms (tel 96 41 09 19).

La Frênaye Bay is of quite outstanding beauty. It consists of a rectangular expanse of water encircled by cliffs and undulating countryside; it is sometimes extremely wild and, for some inexplicable reason, very few people go there. When the tide is in, the bay fills up with water quite dramatically, but low tide reveals enormous stretches of sand concealing crabs, molluscs and a huge variety of shrimps. Oyster farmers move in with their tractors as soon as the waters begin to recede and do not leave until the tide begins to turn. This is also where the salt-meadow sheep graze. on the dry grass, gambolling from one clump to another, while the sea-birds cry shrilly overhead. There are plenty of opportunities to appreciate local wildlife on walks around this impressive bay, which also boasts little fishing ports like Saint-Jean and Port-Nieux. Only slightly further afield is the tiny cove of Les Sévignés. Close by the cliff, the pale pink towers of **La Latte Fort** (by the D16a), the only fortress between the heath and the sea, stand defiantly challenging the savage power of the open sea. This stone stronghold, which was built in the 14th century on two precipices, is the property of the lords of Matignon and it is so spectacular in appearance that it has often been used as a background for films. The castle is accessible by two drawbridges which cross the deep moats. The keep, the walls and the watchtower are all worth a visit.

The Sévignés cove is dominated by **Cap Fréhel** (by the D16), a headland

which is particularly striking to the traveler approaching from Dinard or Saint-Malo. This cape is a stunning conglomeration of red, gray and black rocks, of schists and of sandstone grained with porphyry towering 72 m (236 ft) above the waters of the bay. From a bird sanctuary sited on the Fauconnière cliffs, there is an excellent view of large colonies of marine birds including the herring gull, the fulmar petrel, the kittiwake, the razor-billed auk and the shag, as well as rare flora such as lichens, white campion, sea-pinks and wild thyme. Reeds also grow abundantly throughout the whole area, and the 300 hectares (741 acres) of the Fréhel plateau are a classified nature reserve. From the end of the headland, there is a splendid view of the fractured rocks, and on a clear day it is possible to see all the way from Cotentin to Bréhat Island. More adventurous visitors may be

tempted to climb the 145 steps to the top of the lighthouse!

Arguenon Valley

A popular pastime in Arguenon Bay is to walk along the sand and play with the *pierres sonnantes* (ringing stones), round stones which emit a strange metallic sound when they are knocked together. The story goes that Gargantua, a native of these parts, had such a keen sense of smell that he could not stand the odors given off by the fish when the boats returned to port. One day, he unexpectedly flew into a great rage and swallowed a boat and its catch; unfortunately, the ballast stones proved too difficult to digest and he vomited them onto the village of Le Guildo. From Le Guildo, it is but a short step to the ruins of **Le Guildo Château,** which is said to be haunted by Gilles de Bretagne and the fair Françoise de Dinan. The castle stands opposite the port and is open to the public. It was built on the site of the house belonging to

Above: View of Cap Fréhel and its lighthouse. Right: An angler fishing off the jetty of a Breton port.

Chramme who rebelled against his father Lothair I (Emperor of the West), who then had him burnt to death in 560. In the 15th century, Gilles de Bretagne and Françoise de Dinan spent many happy years there together until Gilles took up arms for the King of England against his brother François; unfortunately, François had meanwhile allied himself with the King of France. Gilles stayed in prison for three years, and was finally smothered to death in his cell.

Finally, there is much to be said for a walk around the **port of Le Guildo**, ideally when the coastal vessels have just returned home with their long-awaited cargo of timber and are unloading in the Arguenon Estuary.

Like the Rance on its journey to the coast, the River Arguenon passes through lush countryside of velvety green , fed by bubbling, ice-blue streams. On this side of the river mouth, we are still in the *Poudouvre,* an area noted for its fine springs, the most outstanding of which is undoubtedly at **Plancoët** (on the D19).

This water, locally bottled and bearing the town's coat of arms on the label, has done more for the area's reputation than all the tourist offices put together. Indeed, throughout Europe Plancoët is synonymous with the very best in spring water. The Knights Templar were the first to take an interest in the Ruellan spring, whose waters were thought to have miraculous powers; it was located in a place then called Nazareth, which now forms the eastern part of the town. Later, in the 16th century, a granite statue of the Virgin Mary dating from the 13th century was discovered, and this is now on display in the church of Nazareth which was built in her honor.

The 19th-century Romantic author François René de Chateaubriand was confirmed in this church when he was seven years old, and the house belonging to his maternal grandmother where he spent his holidays is still standing in rue de l'Abbaye. From the square in front of the church, there is a view of the Brandefer knoll on top of which stands the

85

Roche de Véléda alluded to in Chateaubriand's *Martyrs*. Other references to Chateaubriand's life in the locality include **Monchoix Castle** at Pluduno (by the D794) where he spent some time, and the **manor of la Bouërtadaye** at Bourseul where his parents lived and from which he was able to get on to Véléda's rock by means of a footbridge. On the opposite bank of the Arguenon stands **La Hunaudaye Château**, now lost amongst the woods and marshes but once a fortress that provided accommodation for the Chouan regiments. Originally built by Pierre de Mauclerc to fight the Counts of Penthièvre, it was destroyed and then rebuilt by Pierre de Tournemine in 1378. It was partly destroyed yet again at the time of the French Revolution, but some impressive ruins remain. Lastly, **Jugon-les-Lacs** is a pretty little village full of old houses, the best known of which is the **Maison Sevoy**, built in 1634.

Above: A man gathering seaweed on the shore at low tide.

LAMBALLE AND PENTHIÈVRE

Cap Fréhel is the beginning of a long line of sunny beaches that take the Emerald Coast along as far as the River Trieux. The region of **Penthièvre** has more to offer historically than geographically. Its coast is a continuation of the Emerald Coast and is not very long, but its seaside resorts – Sables-d'Or-les-Pins, Erquy and Le Val André – are well known. The coast runs from Cap Fréhel to Saint-Brieuc, and the whole area includes Lamballe and the Mené heathlands, and goes as far south as the forests near Loudéac.

Penthièvre Coast

This section of the Emerald Coast drops down to sea level to embrace miles of golden, grassy dunes that extend as far as **Sables-d'Or-les-Pins**. This village deserves at least a brief visit, if only for its long sandy beach which was artificially laid near a pine forest at the turn of the 20th century; at the time, the resort had a brief period of great fame but it soon began to lose a lot of money. Although it was never properly completed, it nonetheless presents a charming picture of Norman façades, affluent granite villas and avenues which are really far too big for such a small town. In 1979, however, Sables-d'Or-les-Pins became important once more following an archaeological find. This came about when the remains of a Gallo-Roman villa were discovered as a result of tidal erosion of the clayey cliff. The objects found included three carved plates made of schist and bowls made of terracotta. Even more spectacular Roman remains are to be found at **Erquy** (by the D786), a seaside resort built on the site of a major Gallo-Roman port. Called *Reginae* in the *Tabula Peutingeriana* (a celebrated map of the Roman Empire) and *Nazado* according to Armorican tradition, it is one of a number of sunken towns. There are also signs of the Roman road from Rennes which passed near Corseul, but there is an even older hamlet called Tu-es-Roc (House of Rock) which points to habitation in prehistoric times.

A few kilometers away, in a place called Champ de César in a valley that runs down to the sea, there are two military entrenchments. The first of these, the Fossé Catuelan (Catuelan Trench), cuts across the **Cap d'Erquy** from north to south; the second one, the Fossé de Pleine Garenne (Rabbit Warren Trench), is more elaborate and consists of a double embankment. The town of Erquy is also a major center for scallops, and attracts an enormous number of visitors.

The cape with its reddish rocks is one of the most beautiful places in Brittany; it was scheduled as an area of outstanding beauty in 1978 and was subsequently bought by the Department of Côtes d'Armor in 1982. It has since become a paradise both for those who enjoy walking along the coastal path which takes in the jagged cliffs and the wild coves, and

for others who prefer the heathlands, the pine forests and the seashore. The resort itself is no less attractive: In addition to the seven beaches, the town is remarkable for the masses of flowers, the delightful houses and the pink sandstone, some of which was used to pave the Place de l'Etoile in Paris. Finally, anyone with a taste for freshly caught fish could do no better than eat at *La Marmite,* 21 Rue du Général-de-Gaulle.

The coast, which consists of a long string of beautiful beaches, is utterly enchanting as far as the port of Dahouët. In particular, Pointe de Pléneuf and the resort of Le Val André punctuate a charming journey that includes heathland, cliffs, fishing ports and old towns. The **port of Dahouët** was once used by the Vikings, but until the early years of the 20th century was better known for building the boats which went to the cod fisheries round Iceland. Even today, there is something very fetching about the small, traditional trawlers as they weave in and out of the sailing boats which have become so popular in recent years. **Val André,** now a major tourist center, was founded in 1882 and acquired a repuation for its fine beach. As in all the other resorts along the coast, walking is far and away the best way of exploring. Well signposted paths follow the coast round to **Pléneuf and Grande Guette Points** and even as far as the beach at Les Vallées. Just opposite Pointe de Pléneuf is **Verdelet Island** on which there is a bird sanctuary where seagulls, terns and cormorants roost contendly.

Penthièvre

Near to Le Val André stands the **castle of Bien-Assis**; it is approached by a long avenue almost a mile long. The grounds contain wide moats, a large courtyard, ramparts and dungeon dating from the 12th century, a 17th-century castle and some very beautiful formal French gar-

dens. Used as a prison during the League and the French Revolution, Bien-Assis Castle was also where the Jesuit missionary, Claude de Visdelou, was born in 1656.

Not far away is the **Chapelle Saint-Jacques** which was built in the 15th century on the route followed by pilgrims on their way to Santiago de Compostela in Spain. Legend has it that the building of the chapel was started with assistance from some fairies who helped carry the stones. On finding a magpie on the road – a sign of bad luck – they stopped working there and then, and that is why the work was never finished. It is more likely that a halt was called when Philip the Fair seized the Knights Templar's property. At all events, the chapel has a very beautiful porch, a gallery with openwork design, a 14th-century statue of the Virgin and

Above: The heathlands in flower, near Cap Fréhel. Right: A Breton man with his horse in the Argoat.

Child before a kneeling pilgrim, and a fine modern stained glass window.

The stained glass window at **Saint-Alban** dates from the 15th century; this, the first major Breton masterpiece in stained glass, shows Christ's Passion from the entry into Jerusalem.

The church at **Hénansal,** a very old town built on an outcrop of high ground, has some remarkable pieces in it. They include a 17th-century reredos-tabernacle and, following the plans of Morillon, the architect, two reredos bays which frame the stained glass window. The terracotta statues of St Sebastian and St Andrew come from La Poterie, a village noted for its pottery, a few kilometers from Lamballe. The material used in making them was extracted from the **Houssas heathlands** near the village; these moors boast an ecosystem containing several hundred varieties of plant species, and dozens of species of birds have also found refuge there. In an attempt to explain rural life in this region, the village of **Saint-Esprit-des-Bois** has opened a **farm-museum**

which includes a reconstruction of a traditional rural interior.

Lamballe

Lamballe is the capital of Penthièvre and has a population of a few thousand. The town is of considerable historical importance, but more recently it has acquired commercial skills more suited to this modern day and age. It is now a leading center specializing in animal foodstuffs, coach-building and leather; it holds major cattle markets, and has the second most important stud farm in France. This **stud farm** was set up in 1825 and is extremely well known, providing stallions for the breeding of thoroughbred horses, overseeing stock-rearing and organizing competitions. The buildings are themselves extremely attractive, and visits can be arranged to the stables, the carriage house, the harnessing room, the saddle room, the riding school and the blacksmith's workshop. Lamballe has always been a prosperous town, and this is quite clear from old houses lining **Place du Martray**, the private town houses elsewhere and numerous churches. In the 6th century, St Pol left England to found the commune of Lan-Pol which, five centuries later with the new name of Lamballe, was to become home to the House of Penthièvre and capital of the duchy. Indeed, the Penthièvre family acquired so much power and accumulated such great riches over the centuries that, at the time of the War of Succession, Jean V was obliged to lay siege to the town and demolish its fortifications. In 1626, César, Duke of Vendôme and Lord of Penthièvre, conspired against Richelieu, but his plans failed and his castle was razed to the ground. Behind the four-centered arch and small windows of the 14th-century **Maison du Bourreau** (Executioner's House) in place du Martray stands a museum devoted entirely to a history of the town. The **Musée du Vieux Lamballe et du Penthièvre** has on display huge collections of tools, costumes and objects. The

first floor is given over to another **museum** which houses the innumerable works of **Mathurin Méheut** (1882-1958), a local painter and designer. This museum contains 4000 works of art including pictures of seaweed gatherers, clog-makers, *pardons* and interiors of houses – an extraordinary ethnological history of the working practices and traditions of bygone days. Every year, the museum exhibits a few hundred pieces on a given theme. Only a short walk from the museums stands the octagonal tower of St John's Church which, since the 18th century, has housed the relics of St Amateur, a man utterly unknown elsewhere but greatly honored in Lamballe. The interior of the church is notable for the 17th-century high altar, enhanced by foliated scrolls and gold corbels, and an apse containing three reredoses.

St Martin's Church next to the stud farm has a pleasant 16th-century bell-

Above: A simple boundary post surmounted by a cross, in a field near Josselin.

tower and a porch with a carved wooden canopy of the same period. The town is dominated, however, by the **Collegiate Church of Notre-Dame-de-Grande-Puissance**, the last remaining vestige of the fortified town that was razed to the ground on Richelieu's orders. It was originally the chapel to the subsequently demolished castle but it later on became a church-fortress and then, in 1435, a collegiate church. The 12th-century door with covings resting on ten columns surmounted by sculpted foliage is particularly fine, as are a second door with a Gothic arch and a square 15th-century tower. However, the most outstanding pieces are a rood screen in the Flamboyant style, a gift from Marguerite de Clisson, the wife of the Constable of Clisson, which stands next to a beautifully worked Louis XIII organ chest.

Devotees of religious art will find another source of delight to the south of Lamballe – the Cistercian **Bouquen Abbey**, which was founded on the edge of the forest by twelve monks from Begard in 1137. One way and another, this abbey has had a troubled existence ever since it was built. All that remain now are some buildings set out in a rectangle. The abbey church has been splendidly restored and contains the memorial stone of Gilles de Bretagne who was assassinated at La Hardouinais Castle; it is now used by a religious order, the Little Sisters of Bethlehem.

In the area round Lamballe, there seem to be castles and manor houses at every turn. Probably the best way of discovering the most interesting buildings is to do a Chouan tour of the region.

La Touche-Trébry Castle near **Moncontour** (by the D6) stands opposite a pond and is a fine example of 16th-century architecture; two pavilions standing next to two towers conceal a large courtyard surrounded by a moat. The small town of Moncontour-de-Bretagne was the place where money used to be minted in the 14th century. Later on, it fell from favor but managed nonetheless to preserve considerable medieval charm. The most important building is **Saint Mathurin's Church** which dates from the 16th century; at the beginning of the 20th century, it was given an extraordinary belltower which goes surprisingly well with the rest of the church. The interior contains some of the best stained glass windows in Brittany, some of them dating from the time when the church was built. Other items include a marble and silver bust of St Mathurin, the original baptismal fonts, a high altar in polychrome marble and a statue of the Virgin attributed to Yves Corlay.

SAINT-BRIEUC TO PAIMPOL

The bay of Saint-Brieuc is a triangular piece of the English Channel and a kind of three-way maritime crossroads. The town itself, on the other hand, lies 5 km (3 mi) in from the coast and is something of a carousel displaying all the faces of the region. In front of Saint-Brieuc is the sea; behind lies the Argoat, a huge expanse of land taken up largely with agriculture, a whole separate world in which the dry heathlands merge imperceptibly with the forests and every corner seems to be marked by a doleful calvary; it is also a place where people really know the meaning of hard work. To the right stand the sparkling seaside resorts of Penthièvre and the jagged lines of Cap Fréhel; to the left stretch 50 km (31 mi) of coastline, the summits of the tall cliffs alternating with the pretty beaches.

Saint-Brieuc

Saint-Brieuc, the capital of the Department of Côtes-du-Nord, stands on a promontory between two waterways, the Gout and the Gouédic. It is also a modern urban conglomeration with predictable traffic jams. The city's appeal is not obvious. The famous old market town of Tro Breiz has now turned into a modern, industrial city with its working class districts, and the visitor may be sorely tempted to leave as soon as possible, but that would be a mistake. Saint-Brieuc may appear earnest and dull on the surface, but it would be wrong to underestimate a town that can produce the likes of Louis Guilloux (a 20th-century novelist), Tristan Corbière (a 19th-century poet), Alfred Jarry (the author of *Ubu Roi)* and Villiers de l'Isle-Adam (the 19th-century novelist and dramatist).

Historically, a Welsh chieftain called Fracan arrived on the coast of Saint-Brieuc in 465 and pitched his camp on the site of a village which still bears his name, Ploufragan. St Brieuc himself arrived later, although he too was still a Welsh chieftain by the name of Rigwal when he disembarked at the mouth of the Gout to establish his fief. After being converted by St Brivaël, he went on retreat to Hillion and made a gift of his castle to the monks. It was their monas-

tery that was the origin of the village of Saint-Brieuc which was later established as a bishopric by Nominoé in 848. The town grew steadily over the centuries, living quietly off fishing and commerce, although this tranquility was disturbed briefly during the time of the French Revolution when the Chouans went so far as to occupy the whole town in order to free their prisoners.

A new era was ushered in by the arrival of the railway and the construction of a wet dock in the port of Le Légué. Saint-Brieuc began to develop, and the inhabitants looked to activities that have since become traditional, like brush making, hosiery, steel manufacture and maritime trading. The old town is clustered round the cathedral, but very little remains of it. This central area round the place du Martray has been compared to Venice and used to be at a much lower level that it is today. It had originally been built over a

marsh and it formed a kind of channel which the waters poured into before stagnating; in fact, the situation was so bad at one time that people could only get about by using footbridges or even boats. As a result of drainage work in the 1930s, the whole area was demolished, and what is now place de la Grille was built on a raised spot over what was originally "Little Venice."

There are still some very lovely half-timbered houses in this district where Louis Guilloux was born; the most beautiful include the so-called Le Ribault house dating from the 15th century and the 16th-century town house belonging to the Dukes of Brittany. Nearby is the Fontaine Saint-Brieuc where the Welsh monk Brieuc (Brioch) built his first chapel; it stands under an ogival porch close to the Notre-Dame Chapel. From here, it is only a short walk through the pedestrian precinct comprising rue de la Charbonnerie, rue Saint-Guéno and rue Saint-Guillaume to the birthplace of Villiers de l'Isle-Adam and the Musée d'Histoire des

Above: A typically peaceful spot in Brittany.

Côtes-d'Armor which is housed in the former police barracks. The museum occupies two buildings. The larger of the two tells the story of the department's maritime, agricultural and industrial activities, gives an account of the ideas and customs of the area including family relationships, and includes collections of furniture, headdresses, costumes and objects. The smaller rooms are used for temporary exhibitions.

The original **Cathédrale St-Etienne** was built on piling over the marshland, and on the site of St Brieuc's former monastery. Today's cathedral dates from the 14th and 15th centuries, and has many of the characteristics of a church-fortress including a monumental porch framed by two massive towers, the Tour Brieuc and the Tour du Midi. Inside the church is the Chapel of the Annunciation, one of Yves Corlay's greatest works. The Baroque altar which he built in 1745 for the Chapel of the Sisters of the Cross, and which only escaped the ravages of the French Revolution because it was hidden beneath some hay, was presented to the cathedral in 1800. The nave is remarkable for the organ and the fine paneling of the organ chest suspended over the entrance to the church. This broad organ chest is decorated with small turrets, and is a splendid example of Renaissance style. The chapels close by are dedicated to the relics of St Stephen and the Virgin Mary; there is also a Stations of the Cross (1958) which extends all the way round the cathedral and is the work of students of the Ecole des Beaux-Arts in Rennes.

Inland from Saint-Brieuc

Saint-Brieuc can be said to be both an industrialized and an industrious city. Over the years, it has remorselessly spread over and beyond the rivers on either side and, through its ever-increasing prosperity, brought riches to the rest of the region. The whole countryside as

far as **Quintin** (by the D790) oozes affluence and charm, and consists of quiet country towns, farms and modern factories. The ironworks at Le Pas in the beautiful **Forêt de Lorge** on the D7 are a reminder that ore smelting was a profitable activity round here until very recently. They were built in 1828 and their raw materials were extracted from nearby mines. They were still employing a hundred or so workers until they were closed down in 1978. The earliest furnaces were established, however, a little further on in the large **Forêt de Quénécan** (by the D44 and the D767). Henri II of Rohan opened the first iron and steel works in Brittany during the 17th century, and he was swiftly followed by other aristocratic families in the region. The furnaces at Les Salles were well known as far afield as Belgium for two hundred years until they grew obsolete and were closed down for ever. The buildings are now used for completely different purposes, but they are still in an excellent state of preservation and stand in a delightful spot surrounded by woods and pools. The ruins of the castle belonging to the Rohan family stand on the banks of the pool, and **Bon-Repos Abbey**, which was also their property, is nearby. The abbey was built on the scarped approaches to the **Gorges de Daoulas** and, until the Revolution, its imposing buildings were an important center of religious worship in Brittany.

Quénécan Forest is thought to be a vestige of Brocéliande's mythical forest, although all that remains today is 3000 hectares (7413 acres) of wooded land inhabited by roe-deer and wild boar. In the middle of the forest, the small town of **Mur-de-Bretagne** (mur comes from the Breton *meur* which means "high") stands at 225 m (738 ft) above sea level and looks down over the valleys. It also boasts two lovely churches and a huge artificial lake close by. The **Lac de Guerlédan** was formed at the time that the

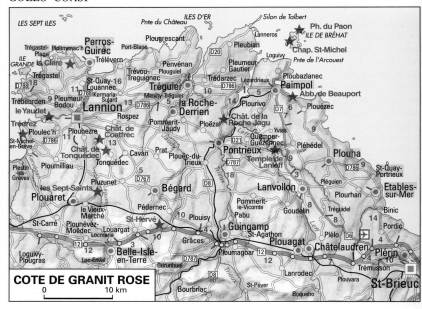

COTE DE GRANIT ROSE

0   10 km

hydro-electric dam of the same name was being built, and then the ancient valley was filled with water.

Goëlo Coast

The **Goëlo coast,** which runs from the beach at Les Rosaires to the ancient port of Paimpol, is as beautiful a piece of foreshore as one could hope to find anywhere. Whether one follows the main road (the D786) or the *Sentier des Douaniers* (Coastguard Path), the route is full of enchanting heathlands, woods and rocks. Examples include **Binic** which once built fishing boats that went to catch cod off Newfoundland, the holiday resort of **Etables-sur-Mer**, and **Saint-Quay-Portrieux** which is now a large modern port. For centuries, the churches and chapels have received offerings from the families of seafarers, and even today they bear witness to the fortitude of local people who have somehow managed to live through shipwrecks, the tragic disappearances of loved ones, and sea battles.

The coastline alternates continually between extraordinary softness and untamed wildness, and encompasses a whole jigsaw puzzle of coves, creeks and headlands. From one such beach, the Bonaparte beach at **Plouha,** over 135 airmen were able to escape under the very noses of the Germans. This was after a Resistance network had been set up in the locality and had hidden them in a small house in the cove at Cochat, codenamed "la maison d'Alphonse." Today, the house has its own monument on the beach and a commemorative plaque. Plouha is where the Breton-speaking part of the region begins. It stretches from here as far as the outskirts of Plouagat, and it was here that Alain Barbetorte (Crookbeard) fought the Normans in the 10th century. The Duke of Brittany crushed his enemies in 917 at Lancerf on the banks of the Trieux, and in a cottage garden in a nearby heath there is a Merovingian cross, thought to have been put up in 927. It is the oldest Christian monument in the region. One of Brittany's greatest enigmas is also to be found in these parts, the **Temple of Lanleff**, a ruined Romanesque church whose origins have given rise to much debate. Some believe that its circular form is that of a Gallo-Roman temple, others that it was a Merovingian baptistery or a church built by Templars. The nearby village of Yvias is notable for a two-story church which was probably built over an ancient tumulus.

Paimpol

Paimpol is squeezed into a hollow in its peninsula, and gazes out over the sea as far as the Bréhat Islands. Paimpol itself has good reason to smile on the elements, as they combine to give the town both prosperity from the sea and a fertile soil. The Trieux Estuary plunges deep into the landscape. Inland, it generously irrigates huge areas growing cabbages, carrots and lettuce; out to sea, it contains the oyster beds and is controlled by the oyster farmers. Théodore Botrel and the Pampolaise (a cliff near Paimpol referred to in one of Botrel's songs) made the town famous, but Pierre Loti's stories of deep-sea fishermen mean that it will now never be forgotten.

There have been no Iceland fishermen since 1935, and pleasure craft have taken the place of the fishing boats. Just the same, one cannot help feeling a little nostalgia for the old days as one passes along the narrow streets lined with beautiful Renaissance houses in place Martray and rue de la Vieille-Poissonnerie that once belonged to the town's shipbuilders.

The parish church is dominated by a statue of Notre-Dame-de-Bonne-Nouvelle which used to be carried in processions for the *pardon* of the Iceland fishermen. The great era of the Paimpol fleet started with Louis Morand, a fearless ship-owner who was convinced he could make his fortune in Icelandic waters and, with his ship the *L'Occasion,* initiated al-

most a hundred years of grand adventure and prosperity. The high point was reached in 1895 when no fewer than 95 ships weighed anchor and set off for the northern fisheries. The expeditions never lasted less than six months and life on board was harsh and dangerous, but it gave the fishermen's families a living. Wives would wait for the ships to return by the cross at Veuves de Ploubazlanec, from where they had a clear view out over the sea. To this day, in the cemetery at the north of the peninsula, it is possible to read simple and moving wooden boards painted black and containing long lists of those who were lost in Icelandic waters. Similarly, the south porch of the chapel at Perros-Hamon is inlaid with plaques commemorating the fishermen who went to Iceland and never returned. As for Louis Morand, he is buried in the cemetery of the chapel at Lanvignec together with other victims of the cholera epidemic which struck Paimpol in 1832.

The fishermen of yesteryear have not been forgotten. An example of this is the *Mad Atao*, a ketch from the lobster port of Camaret in south Finistère which was built in 1938 for dredging seaweed, and is now used as a floating museum. In collaboration with the Musée de la Mer, it tells the story of local maritime history and the saga of the Icelandic fisheries. There is also a festival every July commemorating the boats and the doughty men who sailed in them to Iceland and Newfoundland.

Paimpol's origins have been lost in the mists of time, but the town first emerged from obscurity in the 13th century when the **Abbey of Beauport** was founded on the orders of Alain d'Avaugour, Count of Goëlo. In its early years, it consisted of four large buildings arranged round an internal courtyard: the church, the chapter house, the cellar and the refectory. Before the French Revolution, the abbey had jurisdiction over thirteen parishes, but it ceased to be used as a church in 1790.

It is now open to the public, and the surrounding landscape and seascape make the church even more splendid than ever. Another member of the Goëlo family, Henri d'Avaugour, was responsible for yet another religious building in the area, the **Kermaria-an-Iskuit Chapel** which was built in 1240 on Henri's return from the Crusades to thank the Virgin Mary for protecting him. Access to this church, which has been perfectly restored, is by way of a porch decorated with wooden statues of the Apostles. The choir is illuminated by five large bays, and the north aisle contains some fine paintings including a superb *Danse Macabre*.

Bréhat Island

Boats for **Bréhat Island** depart from the landing stage at Pointe d'Arcouest,

Above: A small house in front of Beauport Abbey near Paimpol. Right: A house decked in flowers on Bréhat Island.

and the brilliant pink of the hydrangeas on the granite houses comes into view in little more than a quarter of an hour. This island of flowers, much favored by the Japanese-born painter Foujita, could easily pass for a resort in the Mediterranean. The gardeners of Bréhat have remarkable skill in growing flowers, and a profusion of geraniums, fuchsia, agapanthus, frangipani, mimosa and palm trees vie with equally abundant artichokes, potatoes and lettuce. Aided, it is true, by a propitious micro-climate, Bréhat is a miniature Garden of Eden 3 km (1.8 mi) long and 1 km (0.6 mi) wide; it is surrounded by rocks with names such as Lovrec, Logodec and Béniguet, and these expand Bréhat into a minor archipelago. The island is best visited on foot – or, at a pinch, on a bicycle – but never by car. From Paimpol, Bréhat is approached from the south. Although these islands are fairly small, they make up for it by being able to offer two worlds which are geographically quite different, linked by a bridge, the Pont-ar-Prat, built by Vauban.

In the south, the atmosphere is extraordinarily peaceful with people playing *boules* in the main square, gardens overflowing with flowers, the large pine forest at Goarevas, and pretty slate-roofed houses. Even the cemetery, flanked by a wonderful 12th-century church in the form of a Latin cross, avoids being too sad. The church, called **St. Michael's Chapel,** contains a Louis XIII high altar, an 18th-century lectern which was probably made in England, and a magnificent pulpit supported by a caryatid. The chapel was built on a relatively high point of the island, 26 m (85 ft) above sea level, and from it there is an opportunity to take in the whole of Bréhat and also to visit an old mill standing close to the church.

Towards the north, the island becomes much wilder before the heathlands eventually peter out in splashes of pink granite. This part of Bréhat is much more violent, secret and turbulent – and it is also the very stuff of legends. What is more, anyone foolish enough to set out alone to walk over the heath would almost immediately get lost, and might never be found. From the chasm where the **lighthouse of Paon** stands, there comes the roar of the foam as the waves crash into the two sheer cliffs. The Trieux Estuary starts just north of the southern tip of Bréhat. Here, the waters of the Trieux and the English Channel mingle and hurl themselves towards the lobster port of **Loguivy-de-la-Mer,** where Lenin stayed in the early years of the 20th century, reaching the shores of **Lézardrieux,** and a tide-mill at **Traou-Meur-en-Pleudaniel**.

TRÉGOR FROM GUINGAMP TO TRÉGUIER

The river **Trégor** flows into the sea on a stretch of sunny coastline of which Tréguier is the most commercially affluent town. By the time it has reached the sea, the Trégor has penetrated deep into the Argoat, negotiated the Monts d' Arrée and the Montagnes Noires, before turning into the Léguer Valley and almost encircling the town of Guingamp. The

sea seems to be light years away. Farmers in these parts think only of the soil: it is fertile, but extremely hard to work. As the visitor plunges into the Argoat, it can be very difficult to understand why everything is suddenly so different. The gray-stoned and gray-slated houses are subsiding slowly on their heavy foundations, the villages are empty, the young have upped and gone. All that is left are some dark shadows stumbling towards the parish closes, some statues of Christ by the side of the road, and heathlands where only creaking cart of the *Ankou* and some dancing *korrigans* remain. The woods, too, are still there – Coat-an-Hay and Coat-an-Noz, the day wood and the night wood – even their names exuding a sacred, pagan, Celtic atmosphere. However, now they are little more than small patches of wooded land, mementos from the days of Brocéliande. They are scat-

tered mostly behind Menez-Bré Hill which in turn casts a shadow over them that is no less mystical than the woods themselves. By following the Trégor's inland route, the traveler is committed to following a religious path marked by churches and saints with plenty of "reconverted" dolmens, "sanctified" Druid fountains and the somewhat un-Catholic legends which live on amongst the gorse.

Saint-Hervé (on the N12) seems quite unconcerned about the exorcists, sorcerers and the workers of spells that have plied their trade in the locality over the centuries. This chapel dedicated to the great healing saint looks down over the close-cropped grass at the top of Menez-Bré Hill. It stands on the very backbone of northern Brittany and offers a view which, for once, extends as far as the sea.
Loc-Envel (by the D13) boasts another lovely church which is well worth visiting if only for the rood screen in painted oak. Despite four centuries of weathering, it is still possible to make out elegant arabesque decorations, delicate festoons

Above: A pardon at Saint-Hervé. Right: An open-air theater in Guingamp.

and birds. The **Locmaria Chapel** in Belle-Isle-en-Terre, which dates from the same period, is nowadays used as a gallery. The recumbent marble figures of Lady Mond and her husband lie in the ossuary of the surrounding cemetery. As her name suggests, Lady Mond was not a saint, but it comes as something of a surprise to learn that she came from this part of the country. She was brought up Marie Le Manac'h, the daughter of a humble miller in Belle-Isle-en-Terre. In Paris she met and so charmed an extremely rich English lord that he asked her to marry him. When she was left a widow, she returned to the countryside to end her days in the castle on the outskirts of the town. The church at **Gurunhuel** (by the D54) may no longer be visited because it is in danger of collapsing, but the **calvary** with three crosses can still be seen. On two of the crosses are two thieves, and their souls are shown leaving their bodies through their mouths; one of the souls is being received by an angel, the other by a devil.

The 14th-century **Church of Notre-Dame de Bulat** at Bulat-Pestivien (by the D787) has an original fresco showing the son of a local lord being carried off by a monkey. After the child was safely returned by the Virgin Mary, the lord built this unusual place of worship for her. It is mainly notable for its wonderful porch and a number of grimacing, shouting figures including the *Ankou*. The calvary at **Kergrist-Moëlou** (by the D31) is unusually interesting. It has a particularly fine collection of small figures, and was restored at the time of the Revolution but in a very confusing manner. The result was a set of scenes from the gospels which are wonderful to look at but are very difficult to understand. Nonetheless, it is well worth going to the calvary to try to solve the puzzle, and also visiting the **church** built in the Flamboyant Gothic style and its parish close. One of the inhabitants of this altogether rather eccen-

tric village is a man who raises ducks, turkeys and geese, and produces some of the best *foie gras* and *confit* in all of Brittany. Lastly, there is the nearby **Gorges of Toul Goulic**, a bewildering mass of rocks created by a huge granite massif meeting a depression of schist.

The last town along the Trégor is **Guingamp** (on the D8) which overlooks Goëlo to the north, Penthièvre to the east and Cornouaille to the south. **The Basilica of Notre-Dame-de-Bon-Secours**, which is the pride of Guingamp, is a reminder that this peaceful little town once had a prominent past. The church was begun in the 13th century, and has accumulated styles over the years in a bizarre jumble of Romanesque, Gothic and Renaissance; a day would scarcely be sufficient to do justice to the details of the architecture, the bas-reliefs, the coving and the arches. The visitor will also be impressed by the hundreds of offerings, the fervor of the adoration for the Black Virgin, and the deep devotion of the pilgrims at prayer.

**Tréguier and the
Surrounding Country**

The coastline on either side of Tréguier has an altogether different look about it. Its nicknames – "wild peninsula" and "bay of hell" – put one in mind of waves smashing into the reefs and the unending roar of the water rushing through the reeds and the heather. They also suggest people losing their lives at sea, and waves bursting over shipwrecked vessels. In fact, the delightful town of **Tréguier** stands in the midst of perfect picture postcard countryside. The historic capital of the Trégor is situated in a plain of well tended fields growing cauliflower, beans and artichokes, and is well protected from the winds. The town is also locked into a strictly Catholic past, and although it also managed to produce the 19th-cen-

Above: The statue of Ernest Renan in place du Martray, Tréguier. Right: The old gates to the town of Tréguier.

tury freethinking philosopher Ernest Renan, Tréguier is devoutly attached to the **Cathedral of Saint-Tugdual**. Like so many other churches in Brittany, this outstandingly impressive cathedral is a striking mixture of Romanesque and Flamboyant Gothic, and visitors are almost certain to be greeted by the carillon of St Yves which is rung out by the church bells every quarter of an hour. St Yves was a noted defender of the needy; he is venerated throughout Brittany and his remains are kept in the cathedral. On the Sunday closest to 19 May every year, the anniversary of the saint's death, there is a huge *pardon* which attracts thousands of pilgrims. On this day, his skull, which is kept in a bright red reliquary, is carried in procession through the streets from the cathedral to Minihy-Tréguier, his birthplace. A visit to the cathedral is likely to take some time, as the nave, the choir, the ambulatory, the recumbent figures and the stalls all merit close attention. If, however, there is time to visit only one part of the church, that would unquestionably have to be the cloister. This unique construction was built in 1450 and is still one of the best preserved in Brittany. It contains numerous recumbent figures which have come from various ancient chapels in the region, a large number of small figures set just below the vaults, and a magnificent 17th-century calvary.

There is nothing showy about this quiet, bourgeois town by the River Jaudy. It is a fundamentally decent and worthy borough with wood-paneled houses lining streets running up towards the cathedral, and the remains of its clerical heritage scattered elsewhere in the town. In **place du Martray** there is a statue of Ernest Renan, as ever lost in thought and dominated by a representation of the goddess Pallas Athene, while the house in which the famous philosopher was born stands in the street which bears his name. Renan lived for fifteen years in this

pretty, half-timbered house; it still displays mementos, letters, manuscripts and furniture on the ground floor, and a video on the first floor tells the story of his life and work.

An atmosphere of a very different type awaits the visitor who ventures as far as the *Manufacture of Krampouez* (8 rue Saint-Yves); it sells crêpes and cider in a traditional setting. Only a short distance outside the town is **Roche-Jagu Castle**, a military fortress which stands on steep slopes on one side of the Trégor. Meanwhile, on the other side of the peninsula by the banks of the Jaudy is the old fortress of La Roche-Derrien; it has lost its castle and fortifications, but has proudly preserved its strategic position astride two quite different worlds – the Armor and the Argoat. There is yet another change of atmosphere on the **Côte des Ajoncs** (Gorse Coast) with its wild landscape, howling wind and crashing waves. This coastline is divided into two parts by the Jaudy Estuary and has two peninsulas which are remarkable for

having extraordinary contrasts of landscape. The parts that are turned towards the land are full of gentle charm, while those that face out to sea are of a more angry and inhospitable disposition. To defend itself from the relentless assaults of the sea, the Côte des Ajoncs offers huge granite walls which have been battered over the centuries by storms and lacerated by the powerful tides. The shoreline is also scattered with strange rock formations, grooved screes, chaotic, lunar massifs, sharp needles of rock, crevasses and reefs. This is a desolate, untamed world, and when there is a storm raging, the effects are so extraordinary that it is more reminiscent of a Hollywood film than real life.

Another of the great curiosities of this part of the world is the **Sillon de Talbert** (Talbert Spit) (by the D20), an extraordinary strip of land covered in shingle, that juts 3 km (inearly 2 miles) out from the mainland. More strange than beautiful it is ideal for walks and is a favorite spot for flying kites.

In **Pleubian** there is a marine research center, the *Centre d'Etudes et de Valorisation des Algues*, specializing in the study of seaweed, which is open to the public during the summer (tel 96 22 93 50). Meanwhile, from the aptly named Port-Béni (Blessed Port), there is a good view across the water to Enfer de Plougrescant Bay where there are still many reminders of storms and shipwrecks. Such gloomy associations are entirely at odds with the village itself and the tiny islands nearby.

The **St Gonéry Chapel** with its leaning spire gives the impression of having surrendered to the buffeting it has received from the wind. It is well worth visiting for the abundance of furniture, tombs, some 15th-century paintings and an alabaster statue of the Virgin Mary dating from the 16th century.

Near the **Pointe du Château**, the most northerly point in Brittany, is the lovely house which was photographed for the tourist publicity campaign *Bretagne Nouvelle Vague*. However, from here to Port-Blanc the sea carries all before it, and it therefore comes as something of a surprise, after passing the great chasm at Castel-Meur and the curious piles of stones at Porz-Scaff, to come across a quiet little seaside resort with lovely sandy beaches. **Port-Blanc** shelters behind a line of dunes and, because it is out of the way of the waves, it is quite unexpectedly peaceful. It is no more than a modest fishing village, but over the years the islands out in the bay have been the holiday homes of such luminaries as the writer Anatole le Braz, the poet and songwriter Théodore Botrel, the physiologist Alexis Carrel (Nobel Prize for Medicine 1913) and the aviator Charles Lindbergh. The **Port-Blanc Chapel**, whose roof comes all the way down to the ground, dominates the hamlet; it was rebuilt in the

Right: Rocks on the Pink Granite Coast, fashioned by the sea and the wind.

16th century, and is particularly to be admired for its wall-belfry, a fine stone stairway and a beautiful wooden chancel with openwork design.

THE PINK GRANITE COAST AND THE COUNTRY ROUND LANNION

The north west coast of the Côtes d'Armor includes the Côte de Granit Rose (Pink Granite Coast), a remarkable coast which is particularly impressive at sunset, the Côtes de Bruyères (Heather Coast) in the Bay of Lannion, and the castle fortresses on the banks of the River Léguer. This is an area of exceptional charm.

Pink Granite Coast

The Pink Granite Coast is about 20 km (12 mi) long, and has such a great reputation that it never fails to attract thousands of visitors every year. All the way from Perros-Guirec to Trébeurden, the scenery remains exactly the same. However, to see it at its best, the visitor should wait until the sun begins to sink into the sea and throws its last beams on to the cliffs; at that moment, the granite rocks seem to dissolve into pink for a moment, grow red again and finally wrap themselves in a huge incandescent blaze. This unique sunset can only be seen for a few moments along only a few miles of the coast, but it has endowed this stretch of the Breton foreshore with a magical aura which people come from all over the world to experience. Visitors can spend a whole day walking the length of the *Sentier des Douaniers* (Coastguard Path) at Ploumanac'h and the corniche roads, or scrambling round the rocks at Trégastel and on Île Renote, and still not have enough time to see many of the amazing shapes that the granite has somehow adopted. These forms include a giant tortoise, Napoleon's hat, a dead man's head and a thimble. The Pink Granite Coast

has been fashioned by the sea for centuries without number. However, the contributions from human beings make it even more challenging, when menhirs, dolmens and covered passages are added.

The town of **Perros-Guirec** (on the D788) was a very popular seaside resort back in the days when bathers wore striped swimming costumes; with its rocky promontory it still symbolizes summer holidays in Brittany. Perched overlooking the very fashionable beaches at Trestraou and Trestrignel, the town still welcomes as many as a quarter of a million holidaymakers every summer who divide their time between the sand and the casino. Its original name was Pen Roz ("top of the hill" in Breton), and the first hotel was built at the end of the 19th century. Now, its thalassotherapy centers (for salt water and sea air cures), luxury hotels and yacht marinas are always booked up well in advance. The resort is equally busy in summer and winter with people keen to enjoy the magnificent views from the road where the *Sémaphore* (Signal Station) stands, the Pointe du Château and the nearby Chemin de la Messe. The Church of Saint-Jacques looks every inch a haven in which to seek shelter from a storm; it is completely pink, and in its close stands a strange balustraded bell-tower crowned by a cupola with a pinnacle turret. This church, which was dedicated to St James the Greater and St Guirec, is a classified national monument and contains some fine examples of Romanesque and Gothic art. Interesting local shops include the *Savonnerie* (22 Rue du Général-Leclerc) which sells a wonderful range of multicolored and perfumed soaps.

However, to savor nature to the full, the best place to go is **Sept-Iles** by taking a boat from the little quay at Trestraou; Île aux Moines (Monks' Island) is far and away the most important of the seven, although it is a pity that the boat does not stop at the others too. Franciscan friars gave the island its name when they settled there in the 14th century to live in an arid, barren land and do penance; the

island also has a lighthouse and an 18th-century fort built by a Saint-Malo engineer who was a student of Vauban. The other islands, particularly Rouzic and Malban, form a private bird sanctuary.

The belltower of the **Chapel of Notre-Dame-de-la-Clarté** stands on the coast between Perros and Ploumanac'h and could be mistaken for a lighthouse. In fact it was built in 1445 by the Lord of Barac'h, who was lost in the fog at sea, off the Sept-Iles, and promised the Virgin a chapel if he returned safely. The chapel may well have been built on the site of a natural spring which had health-giving properties; at all events, it was made of granite from the large quarries nearby, and has an entrance with a wooden Renaissance cloister and a porch decorated with painted wooden statues. Inside, there is an unusual font made of granite and carved with Moorish faces, a beauti-

ful 17th-century reredos, granite statues, and offerings presented by seafaring families in the form of model boats. The chapel is considered to be one of the most important places of worship for the people of Trégor, and a *pardon* is held there on 15 August every year.

It is possible to return to **Ploumanac'h** by the main road, but a three-hour walk along the *Sentier des Douaniers* has the advantage of taking in the beach at Saint-Guirec. This beach has an astonishing collection of rocks shaped by the wind over hundreds of years. The municipal park at Pointe Squewel contains the most extraordinary of these rocks, some of them over 25 m (82 ft) high. They are quite unique anywhere in the world, and are the main focus of interest in this old fishing village which now also boasts a research unit that studies geological phenomena and local flora and fauna. The Traouiéros Valley presents a wilder side of this part of Brittany; its gorges contain remarkable rocks and give opportunities for collecting rare ferns and mosses.

Above: The rocks at Pointe Squernel, near Ploumanac'h. Right: Asterix in the Gallic village near Pleumeur-Bodou.

104

The rocks at **Trégastel** offer a big challenge to the imagination. You can spend hours making out strange animals, faces and objects that are formed by the huge rocks dotting the beaches of Coz-Pors and Grève Blanche, on the **peninsula of Renote.** In a rocky gorge the local council has opened a prehistoric museum and a marine aquarium containing all species found in Breton waters. These are overlooked by a cement statue of the *Père Eternel* built in 1869 by the parish priest. The village church was constructed in the 12th century and looks onto a lawn planted with flowers and containing the grave of the Breton author and Academician, Charles le Goffic; inside, there is a very beautiful carved pulpit, a stained glass window and a device once used for measuring grain. Nearby, on the way to the beach, is a tiny chapel dedicated to St Golgon, the saint who is prayed to when a horse goes sick.

The road that leads to **Île Grande** plunges the visitor straight into the tradition of Breton legends. The first en-counter with the region's mysterious past is at the dolmen and covered corridor at Kerguntuil which are rather curiously sited in the middle of a cultivated field. As long as the crops are not disturbed, visitors may walk into the corridor and look at the nine pairs of breasts drawn in the rock. There is a similar covered alley at the junction of the corniche road. It has been called the *Allée des Korrigans* and exudes an extraordinary feeling of the magic atmosphere of the whole area. Meanwhile, the Île d'Aval which is only 100 m (300 ft) away is well known in the legend of King Arthur. It is here that he decided, with his knights, to become immortal, and Morgana made them invisible so that they could then wait in peace for the liberation of the Celts and return to earth. It is also said that King Arthur got caught in the quicksands off Île Canton and that Morgana erected the Aval menhir in his honor. Despite its port and beaches equipped for the holiday trade, Île Grande has managed to preserve a slightly unreal charm, and this is some-

how nurtured by the sound of the winds as they sweep across the heaths and by the waves as they smash into the rocks. The village, on the other hand, is a quiet, peaceful place with its neat lines of houses and a pretty granite church.

A visit to **Pleumeur-Bodou** (by the D21) is a chance to move from the mists of history to the 21st century in the twinkling of an eye. However, although one's intention may be to visit the futuristic telecommunications center, the first thing one comes across in fact is a perfect example of the religious and spiritual turbulence that has beset Brittany for so long. It is the Christianized **menhir** at **Saint-Uzec**, whose Celtic rock is carved with a representation of Christ's Passion and surmounted by a crucifixion. Not far away, though, is the great white dome of the **Space Telecommunication Station,** looking more like a giant spacecraft that has just happened to fall into the heather;

Above: A boat lying at the quayside. Right: Waves crashing into the rocks.

the science-fiction atmosphere is enhanced by the presence round about of parabolic reflectors and antennae. It is also the top attraction with the 80,000 or so visitors who come every year and watch the *son et lumière* shows. A museum was opened on 1 July 1991 to explain the mysteries of hertzian waves, satellite technology, and how networks and underwater cables work.

The Pink Granite Coast ends at the chaotic, granite peninsula of Le Castel near **Trébeurden**. This seaside resort has a good half-dozen beaches, of which the best known, Tresmeur, is right next to the port. Even here, there is evidence of Celts having inhabited the area at one time, with the covered alley at Lan-Kerellec and the granite-like slabs of stone at Prajou-Menhir. Île Milliau, which is opposite Le Castel and is accessible on foot at low tide, is 350 m (1100 ft) wide and contains 23 hectares (56 acres) of open air botanical garden; of the 270 species of plant life that are grown there, some thrive in sea air while others are protected by specially constructed shelters. Lastly, among the rocks on the nearby Île Molène, there is a single *pebble* which weighs no less than three tons.

Côte des Bruyères

After coursing through its charming valley, the River Léguer comes out into a superb estuary which is very peaceful, being largely sheltered from the waves. This is where the **Côte des Bruyères** (Heather Coast) begins; it finishes on the borders of Finistère. Few people come here and it is virtually unknown to property developers; it thus lends itself perfectly to peaceful walks amongst the hills planted with pine trees, the charming small heaths and the deserted coves. The area lies halfway between the world of agriculture and the world of the sea. The ancient hamlet of **Le Yaudet** overlooks the estuary and offers a magnificent view

of the river running into the sea. Le Yaudet was built on a Gallo-Roman site, and vestiges of a military camp have been discovered there. From the top of a headland, there is a view of a large, flat stone with a radiant circle carved on it: this was probably a sacrificial slab dedicated to a fertility goddess. Hidden away in the middle of the village, the chapel has some delightful 15th-century doors and a 17th-century reredos. More important, however, is a sculpture of the Virgin lying on lace bedding with the Infant Jesus, while God the Father sits at their feet watching over them. A dove flying over the bed suggests that this sculpture depicts the Holy Trinity rather than the Nativity.

Side roads now lead to a small port on the Léguer, and the remains of the wall delineating a fishing ground near the cove at Pont-Roux. Next comes **Trédrez**, which can trace its history back to the time of St Yves, and its Church of Notre-Dame. The church was built in the 16th century and contains carved stringers, a fine baptistry in the Flamboyant style, and a statue of Christ from the 13th century. The **manor of Coat-Trédrez** is a reminder that the village was once upon a time inhabited by rich lords and their families. The Trédrez cliffs extend like a huge rocky wall as far as **Saint-Michel-en-Grève,** but it is possible to return to the village along the Roman road which ends in the main square. Trédrez has become a seaside resort and a favorite with those who are keen on sailing, but now it is also a major center for archaeological digs: So far, a number of prehistoric objects have been unearthed, and two Roman baths have been discovered at low tide.

Lannion

Lannion, Côtes d'Armor's second town, is perched on the edge of the mouth of the River Léguer, and is like one of those large country towns that are so quiet that they seem to have gone to sleep. Appearances can be deceptive,

though. Lannion has been able to preserve its historic heritage and has also kept up with the sweeping advances made in the fields of electronics and telecommunications. During the 1960s, the town was selected to host the research departments of the *Centre national d'études des télécommunications (CNET)* (National Centre for Telecommunications Studies), and since then it has moved rapidly from family-based craft work to highly skilled technology. Having been roused from its sleep, Lannion promptly doubled its population, developed its manufacturing and service industries and gained for itself the title of electronics capital of France. It was a revolution which made Lannion much more sophisticated and also greatly expanded the size of its suburbs, but it never succeeded in disfiguring the town. On the contrary, the economic boom made it possible for Lan-

Above: 16th- and 17th-century houses in Lannion, one with carved half-timbering, the other hung with slates.

nion to revitalize its architecture, restore its lovely old half-timbered houses, and create a pedestrian precinct in the town center.

Lann (Breton for "earth") was once a place of worship dedicated to St Ion, and then, in the Middle Ages, it was attached to the bishopric of Tréguier. Nothing remains of the original fortifications which were destroyed during the War of Succession, but **place du Général-Leclerc** in the middle of the town still proudly boasts fine corbelled 15th-and 16th-century houses with slate roofs, turrets and caryatids. As so often happens, the old pedestrian streets recall the professional activities of a bygone age and even the names of the former inhabitants.

It was the Duke of Aiguillon who was responsible for the building of the quay which extends the entire length of the estuary, and which is usually submerged at high tide – to the fury of stranded motorists. The Duke had been attracted by the curative qualities of Lannion's spring (it was particularly noted for calming the spirits and restoring peace to troubled households!), and came down to drink from it so frequently that it was decided to build a quay to make it more convenient for him. There may no longer be any people taking the cure there, but Lannion's spring is still there in the middle of a block belonging to *Électricité de France,* the French national electricity generating company.

Just round the corner from the quay is the **church of Saint-Jean-du-Baly**. It was built in 1519 on the site of the castle's chapel, and has a delightful sundial carved into the slate and a hollow pillar which gives access to where the rood screen used to be. Little else is of much interest except the organ which is used for a festival of sacred music every Friday in July and August.

Off rue de la Trinité is an enormous flight of 143 steps, all that remains of a monumental stairway which once had as many steps as there are days in the year. A climb to the top of these steps is strongly recommended, as from the top there is one of the best views over the town. It is also where **Brélévenez Church** stands. Three small columns overhanging the Romanesque porch add an interesting touch to the church's façade. Otherwise, all that remains of the 14th-century fortifications is a building made of granite stone mixed with green schist and consisting of an angle tower, huge buttresses and loopholes. At the foot of this building is the stele of Gabrielle le Yaudet, a fisherman's daughter who was cured by a miracle and died in Jerusalem after spending some months as a hermit on the Mount of Olives. Inside, there is a beautiful 15th-century stained glass window, a wooden 17th-century reredos presented to the church by the weavers of Crec'h Tanet, a 12th-century ambulatory, a painting of the Resurrection and a representation of the Virgin Mary giving a scapular to St Dominic. There are two tombstones in one of the walls in the north chapel; one of them is decorated with the Maltese Cross, the other with strange geometric lines.

Léguer Valley

The tall tower which dominates the CNET buildings and receives messages from the Pleumeur-Bodou satellites is about 2 km (1.25 mi) outside Lannion. The telecommunications center is not open to the public, but the land on either side of the Léguer Valley (between the D767 and the D11) is a wonderful storehouse of the regions history. The banks of the Léguer are dominated by the ruins of **Coatfrec Castle** which, with the support upstream of **Tonquédec Castle,** controlled access to the river during the 15th century. All that remains of Coatfrec Castle is a high tower and living quarters in a poor state of repair. Inland from here and close to the hamlet of Kerauzern is **Kergrist Castle**, notable for its elegant, well preserved foundations; the castle was built in the 16th century, but it has been altered many times since and formal French gardens have also been added.

The **Sept-Saints Chapel** was built on the Stiffel dolmen in the 18th century and illustrates the depth of Breton religious fervor. The church owes its name to Louis Massignon, an orientalist at the Collège de France who discovered that the Sept-Saints *pardon* in Brittany and a Muslim religious cult of the Seven Sleepers of Ephesus had the same origin. These seven saints were Christians persecuted by the Emperor Decius; they are also said to have been walled up in a cave in the 250 AD and did not wake up again until two centuries later. Nobody knows how they could have had anything to do with the *pardon* traditionally celebrated by the people of this part of Brittany. Nevertheless, it has long been popular, and with Massignon's encouragement it now brings together both Christians and Muslims on the last Sunday of July.

Tourist Information
Information about the region: **Comité départemental du Tourisme des Côtes-d'Armor**, 1, rue Chateaubriand, BP 620, 22011 Saint-Brieuc cedex, Tel: 96-627200.

ÎLE DE BREHAT
Accommodation
BUDGET: **Belle-Vue**, Le Port Clos, Tel: 96-200005. **Vieille Auberge**, Tel: 96-200024.
Tourist Information / Ferry Connections
Office de Tourisme, in the old town hall, Tel: 96-200415. **Ferry connections** from Saint-Quay-Portrieux, Tel: 96-200066, from Pointe de l'Arcouest, Tel: 96-208230.

CORSEUL / CREHEN
Castles
CORSEUL: Château Montafilan, Tel: 96-279017. **CRÉHEN: Château de Guildo**, Tel: 96-841312.

DINAN
Accommodation / Restaurant
MODERATE: **Avaugour**, 1, pl. du Champs-Clos, Tel: 96-390749. *BUDGET:* **La Porte de Saint-Malo**, 35, rue St-Malo, Tel: 96-391976. **Le Saint-Louis**, 9, rue de Lébon, Tel: 96-398950, inexpensive restaurant.
Special Events
Concours international de Harpe celtique, international Celtic harp competition, last weekend in June, Tel: 96-868494.
Tourist Information / Castle
Office de Tourisme, 6, rue de l'Horloge, Tel: 96-397540. **Château de la Duchesse Anne** and **Museum Tel: 96-394520.**

ERQUY
Accommodation
BUDGET: **Le Brigantin**, square de l'Hôtel-de-Ville, Tel: 96-723214.
Tourist Information / Castle
Office de Tourisme, boulevard de la Mer, Tel: 96-723012. **Château de Bienassis**, Tel: 98-722203.

EVRAN-LE-QUIOU
Castle
Château de Hac, Tel: 96-834306.

CAP FREHEL / PLEVENON
Sightseeing
Phare, lighthouse, Tel: 96-414003. **Fort La Latte**, Tel: 96-414031.

GUINGAMP
Accommodation / Restaurant
MODERATE: **Le Relais du Roi**, 42, place Centre, Tel: 96-437662. *BUDGET:* **Armor**, 44, boulevard Clémenceau, Tel: 96-437616. **La Chaumière**, 42, rue de la Trinité, Tel: 96-437247, inexpensive restaurant.

Tourist Information / Festivals
Office de Tourisme, place du Vally, Tel: 96-437389.
Fêtes de Saint-Loup, August 15-22. *Festival de la Danse bretonne*, last week in August.

CHÂTEAU DE LA HUNAUDAYE
Tourist Information / Castle
Information in the Castle, Tel: 96-341847.

LAMBALLE
Accommodation
MODERATE: **Angleterrre**, 29, bd. Jobert, Tel: 96-310510. *BUDGET:* **La Tour d'Argent**, 2, rue du Docteur-Lavergne, Tel: 96-310137.
Tourist Information / Museum Sightseeing
Office de Tourisme, 1, place du Martray, Tel: 96-310538. **Musée Mathurin Méheut**, Tel: 96-311999. **Haras national**, Tel: 96-310040.

LANNION
Accommodation
BUDGET: **Hôtel de la Porte de France**, 5, rue Jean-Savidan, Tel: 96-465481.
Tourist Information / Festival
Office de Tourisme, 1, quai d'Aiguillon, Tel: 96-370735.
Fête de Sa Majesté Mallarg, carnival, Saturday before Ash Wednesday until Ash Wednesday.

MONCONTOUR
Tourist Information
Office de Tourisme, in the town hall, rue Bel-Orient, Tel: 96-734105.

MÛR-DE-BRETAGNE
Accommodation
BUDGET: **Hôtellerie de l'Abbaye**, Abbaye de Bon Repos, Tel: 96-249898. **Auberge Grand Maison**, 1, rue Léon-le-Cerf, Tel: 96-285110.
Tourist Information
Office de Tourisme, place de l'Église, Tel: 96-285141.

PAIMPOL
Accommodation
MODERATE: **Relais des Pins**, le pont de Lézardrieux, Tel: 96-201105. *BUDGET:* **L'Origano**, 7 bis, rue du Quai, Tel: 96-220549.
Festivals
Fête du Chant marin et du Bâteau traditionnel, Fri-Sun before August 15. *Fête des Terre-nuevas et des Islandais*, July 15-21.
Tourist Information / Abbey
Office de Tourisme, rue Pierre-Feutren, Tel: 96-208316. **Abbaye de Beauport**, Tel: 96-208159.

PERROS-GUIREC
Accommodation
MODERATE: **Grand Hôtel de Trestraou**, bd. Joseph-le-Bihan, Tel: 96-232405. *BUDGET:* **Kerys**, 12, rue de Mal-Foch, Tel: 96-232216.

Tourist Information / Festivals

Office de Tourisme, 21, pl. de l'Hôtel-de-Ville, Tel: 96-232115.

Festival de Musique classique, second half of July, Tel: 96-232264. *Pardon de Notre-Dame-de-la-Clarté*, religious celebrations, August 15.

PLEDELIAC / PLEUMEUR-BOUDOU
Sightseeing

PLÉDÉLIAC: Ferme d'Antan, St-Esprit-des-Bois, Tel: 96-341467.

PLEUMEUR-BOUDOU: Satellite Station, Tel: 96-239999.

PLENEUF-VAL ANDRE
Tourist Information

Office de Tourisme, Arcades du Casino, rue Winston-Churchill, Tel: 96-722055.

PLEUBIAN
Special Events

Rassemblement national de Cerfs-volants, meeting of hanggliders, Whitsun weekend (3rd week in May), Tel: 96-229217.

PLOEZAL / PLOUBEZRE PLUDUNO
Castles

PLOÉZAL: Château de la Roche-Jagu, Tel: 96-956235.**PLOUBEZRÉ: Château Kergrist**, Tel: 96-389144. **PLUDUNO: Château Monchoix**, Tel: 96-841113.

PORT-BLANC
Accommodation

BUDGET: **Les Îles**, boulevard de la Mer, Tel: 96-926649.

QUINTIN
Tourist Information / Special Events

Office de Tourisme, place de 1830, Tel: 96-740151. *Nuits musicales*, middle of July and middle of August, Tel: 96-740151.

ROSTRENEN
Tourist Information

Office de Tourisme, town hall, Tel: 96-290035.

SABLES-D'OR-LES-PINS
Accommodation

MODERATE: **Manoir Saint-Michel**, la Carquois, route du cap Fréhel, Tel: 96-414887. *BUDGET:* **Au Bon Accueil**, allée des Acacias, Tel: 96-414219. **La Voile d'Or**, allée des Acacias, Tel: 96-414249, with good restaurant.

Tourist Information

Office de Tourisme, place des Fêtes, 22240 Fréhel, Tel: 96-415197.

SAINT-BRIEUC
Accommodation / Restaurant

MODERATE: **Le Griffon**, rue de Guernesey, Tel: 96-945762. *BUDGET:* **Ker Izel**, 20, rue de Gouët, Tel: 96-334629. **L'Amadeus**, 22, rue du Gouët, Tel: 96-339244, restaurant, good value.

Tourist Information / Festival

Office de Tourisme, 77, rue St-Guéno, Tel: 96-333250 or 96-334229.

Art Rock Festival, international, "serious" festival of rock music end of October, simultaneous with the *Festival international du Clip et de la Vidéo musicale*, Tel: 96-337750.

SAINT-CAST-LE-GUILDO
Accommodation

MODERATE: **Ar Vro**, 10, bd. de la Plage, Tel: 96-418501. *BUDGET:* **Esperance**, 5, boulevard du Ponchel, Tel: 96-418113.

Tourist Information

Office de Tourisme, Tel: 96-418152.

SAINT-JACUT-DE-LA-MER
Tourist Information

Office de Tourisme, rue du Châtelet, Tel: 96-277191.

SAINT-QUAY-PORTRIEUX
Tourist Information

Office de Tourisme, rue Jeanne-d'Arc, Tel: 96-704064.

SEPT-ÎLES
Excursion

Boat trips from the Bay of Trestrou, Tel: 96-232247.

TREBEURDEN
Accommodation

MODERATE: **Ti Al Lannec**, allée de Mezo-Guen, Tel: 96-235726. *BUDGET:* **Ker-An-Nod**, 2, Pors Termen, Tel: 96-235021.

Tourist Information

Office de Tourisme, place Crech-Hery, Tel: 96-235164.

TREBRY
Castle

Château de la Touche-Trébry, Tel: 96-427855.

TREGASTEL
Accommodation

MODERATE: **Le Bellevue,** 20, rue des Calculots, Tel: 96-238818. *BUDGET:* **Les Bains**, rue du Général-de-Gaulle, Tel: 96-238809.

Tourist Information

Office de Tourisme, place Sainte-Anne, Tel: 96-238867.

TREGUIER
Festivals / Special Events

Festival musical, middle of July–3rd week in August. *Pardon de Saint-Yves*, religious celebration in honor of the patron saint of lawyers, held at Whitsun.

Rencontre internationale de Musique ancienne, in **Lanvellec-Tréguier**, between October 20 and November 5, Tel: 96-351882.

Tourist Information

Office de Tourisme, town hall, Tel: 96-923019.

FINISTÈRE

LÉON

BREST

PENINSULAS OF CORNUAILLE

FROM THE MONTS D'ARRÉE

TO THE BLACK MOUNTAINS

QUIMPER AND LE BIGOUDEN

FOUESNANT AND AVEN

Finistère is possibly the most fascinating and most captivating *départment* in Brittany. Many writers and poets have come to dream on this furthermost point of France, the "end of the land" *(Pen-ar-Bed)* in a constant duel with the great ocean. It was from the ports of Finistère that the sailors and adventurers of the West have, over the centuries, set off in search of the far distant East or the New World.

Some of Armorica's most enchanting countryside is to be found in Finistère. It extends from the jagged, tempest-tossed coastline near the port of Locquirec in the north to Le Pouldu in the very south of the department. It is almost as if every beauty spot seems to be trying to outdo the others in mystery and harsh, savage beauty. There is also something positively awe-inspiring about such places as the Coast of *Aber*s (river mouths), the majestic straits of Brest, the rocks at Cap Sizun, the peaceful Bay of Audierne and the strange Bigouden country, not to mention the picturesque islands of Ouessant (Ushant), Molène, Sein and the Glénan archipelago.

Previous pages: A menhir on the bare moorland of the Crozon peninsula. Left: Pointe du Raz.

However, any account of Finistère's riches and great character would be incomplete without a reference to the hinterland, principally the moors and the beauty spots in the Arrée and Noires (Black) Mountains. This is the land of forgotten towns and isolated, mysterious villages, but it is also where the profound religious passions of the Breton people are given expression by numerous parish closes, the best known of which are at Saint-Thégonnec, Guimiliau, Lampaul-Guimiliau and Commana. There are also many magnificent churches such as the basilica at Le Folgoët, the church of St Herbot, and the cathedrals of Quimper and Saint-Pol-de-Léon. The secular architecture does not compare unfavorably. The visitor who is interested in this aspect of Brittany is strongly recommended to devote time to buildings lining the streets of Quimper, Locronan and Morlaix, and to seek out the region's innumerable castles and manors like those at Kerjean, Kérouzéré and Trémazan.

Finistère is a shadowy gemstone of schist and granite block; it is the sort of place that is best discovered slowly.

LÉON

The **region of Léon** extends from the Morlaix River (the Dossen Estuary) in

the west to the highest peaks of the Arrée Mountains and the Élorn Estuary in the north. In fact, its boundaries correspond to those of a former bishopric based in Saint-Pol-de-Léon. Today, it is better known as Finistère Nord, but it has remained quite distinct from neighboring Cornouaille and Finistère Sud. Its social and economic structures are not the same for one thing, and there is also a particular kind of Breton spoken there – *Breton Large,* considered to be the most classical form of the language. Above all, although the people have a different mentality, Léon is no less strongly committed to religious observance, strict morality and mysticism, and it has long been known as "the land of priests." Nonetheless, the people know how to marry a powerful Catholic tradition to business sense and a wish to keep up to date: Their skills in producing early fruit and vegetables and in stock-breeding mean that Léon's economic potential is enormous.

Morlaix

Morlaix lies at the bottom of a steep-sided valley, and was a flourishing city at the time of Breton independence. In those days, it was the third most important city in Brittany after Nantes and Rennes. Products from the interior were exported on the many cargo boats which used the port, and the town's prosperity was augmented by linen and paper manufacture,

raids during World War Two. Just the same, a walk around the town is an excellent way of discovering the alleyways and corbelled houses which contribute substantially to Morlaix's considerable charm.

The first port of call is **St Mélaine's Church**. This church in the Flamboyant Gothic style has a beautiful 17th-century organ, some very old furnishings and a statue of St Rose of Lima, the patron saint of the New World. Outside St Mélaine's Church, **rue Ange-de-Guernisac** is lined with corbelled houses in local stone; it crosses Place des Viarmes in the direction of Place des Jacobins where there is a 13th-century church part of which has been turned into a **municipal museum**. This museum gives a very detailed account of the town's history with the help of numerous drawings, plans and portraits. There is also a splendid collection of old statues, some Dutch, Flemish and Italian paintings of the 16th and 17th centuries and, in the main room, an exhibition of Breton furniture.

A short walk by the River Jarlot along the Allée de Poan-Ben leads to St Matthew's Church, although all that remains of the original church is the 16th-century tower. Nearby, in **rue du Mur** is the so-called Queen Anne's house, one of the last surviving "lantern houses": this kind of design incorporates a spiral staircase which is lit by a skylight called a lantern.

This tour of the old town concludes in the **Grand'Rue**, the façades of whose houses are decorated with a large number of statues. Perhaps the most striking is the house at number 9 which has statues of the Angel Gabriel, the Virgin Mary, St James, St Laurence, St Nicholas and St Barbara.

Two visits are recommended for those interested in the town's traditional industries. One is to the *Manufacture des Tabacs* on the quai de Léon, a successor to the old *Compagnie des Indes* (India Company). It still turns out 300 million

tanning, sea trade and shipbuilding, despite fierce competition from the British. Economic activity declined, however, as Brittany began to work more closely with France; today, Morlaix is a modest subprefecture (an administrative area within a department with limited powers) but is looking for new ways of finding a second economic wind.

Until the mid-19th century, the town had some fine examples of medieval architecture. Since then, however, Morlaix's character has been profoundly changed by the construction of a railway viaduct across the valley which cuts the town down the middle, the wholesale demolition of many buildings as part of a road-widening scheme, and bombing

cigars a year and 82 tonnes of tobacco for chewing and smoking. The other visit is to the *Brasserie des Deux-Rivière*s in place de la Madeleine. The local water has always been ideal for the making of beer, and throughout the 19th century Morlaix enjoyed an excellent reputation for brewing. In 1985, after a break of 65 years, this old tradition was revived with the introduction of a Breton beer called La Coreff. It is an all-malt beer brewed from barley malt, using hops from Alsace and Germany. This *bière artisanale* ("real ale") is neither filtered not pasteurized. A brewery tour is followed by a tasting.

Morlaix Bay

A trip around the outskirts of Morlaix is an introduction to that part of the Trégor which is in Finistère. To the north, along the D46, is a rugged coastline

Above: The pedestrian walkway along the railway viaduct in Morlaix. Right: A general view of the viaduct at Morlaix.

marked with peninsulas and coves, rough-cast, whitewashed houses and narrow valleys, all bathed in a bluish-green light that is so characteristic of the whole region. After passing through the charming little port of Dourduff and the village of Plouézoc'h, whose church has a delightful tower with openwork design, the visitor comes to the **Cairn de Barnenez** (Barnenez Tumulus). This is 7000 years old and is one of the most important tumuli in Europe; a number of digs have established that it was originally used as a funerary chamber.

The road continues through most attractive countryside and past a long line of small ports and large beaches, including Saint-Samson. After **Primel-Trégastel**, an exceptionally charming seaside resort, the road leads first to Plougasnou and then to **Saint-Jean-du-Doigt**, a village well known for its *pardon* on 24 June. The village of **Locquirec** is a well established holiday resort; it has nine beaches, including the Plage des Sables-Blancs (White Sand Beach).

Another route is along the left bank of the estuary and the Morlaix straits (by the D173) as far as the attractive port of **Carantec.** This resort has been popular with writers, painters and public figures ever since the middle of the 19th century. The **island of Callot** is accessible on foot at low tide, and there are equally pleasant walks to **Le Taureau Castle,** built in the 16th century, and the luxuriantly green Pointe de Pen-al-Lann.

As early as the 6th century, Saint-Pol-de-Léon (by the D58) has been the seat of the bishopric founded by the Welsh monk Pol, also called Aurelian. It was captured first by the Normans and then by the army of Henry II of England, and finally passed into the hands of the House of Rohan, viscounts (later princes) of Léon from the 6th century onwards. Today, Saint-Pol is a prosperous town and is a very important producer of cauliflowers and artichokes.

The town is dominated by two major religious monuments. The first of these is the **cathedral** which has undergone almost continuous restoration since the 6th century. It was made with limestone from Caen, and the design was strongly influenced by Norman styles. Even more remarkable is the **Chapel of Notre-Dame-du-Kreisker** (*kreisker* is Breton for "middle of the town"); its superb belfry, which is almost 80 m (260 ft) high, was once enthusiastically described by the military engineer Vauban as a "marvel of balance and boldness". The tower is also notable for the extraordinary lightness of its pinnacle turrets with openwork decoration and gargoyles.

Roscoff was once a haunt of privateers and smugglers, and the town's period charm is still captured in the old port, the narrow streets and the stone houses. However, it has also become a dynamic modern business center with a new fishing port, well established sea links with Britain and Ireland and two centers for thalassotherapy. The gentleness of the climate and its Mediterranean vegetation make Roscoff enormously attractive to people who enjoy walking. The splendid 16th-century **church of Notre-Dame-de-Kroaz-Baz** is a fine example of Flamboyant architecture, and it has a most unusual lantern turret belfry in the Renaissance style. In the narrow streets nearby are lovely old shipbuilders' houses with decorated façades and carved dormer windows.

For a day's outing, the **Île de Batz** is only 20 minutes by boat from Roscoff. The island is 4 km (2.5 mi) long and 1 km (0.6 mi) wide, and it is possible to walk all the way round it in three hours.

"Pagan" Country

Léon's religious capital may have been Saint-Pol, but it was the more central town of **Lesneven** that became its administrative capital. It takes its name from Count Even who defeated Norman pirates in 937 and established the *Lez an Even*, the court of Even. Nothing remains

today of the old fortified town, not even the ramparts or the castle. What is mainly interesting these days is the cloister attached to the Maison d'Accueil, an Ursuline convent whose chapel houses the **Museum of Léon.** Its seven rooms offer a brief history of the town and of the achievements of its inhabitants.

The D125 which goes north from Lesneven to the coast is flanked by the **"Pagan" country** which comprises the ancient parishes of Guissény, Kerlouan and Plouénour-Trez.

Mystery surrounds the meaning of the word *pagan* although the Latin *paganus* has given the French words *païen* (pagan) and *paysan* (peasant). One explanation goes thus: When the deeply Christian Irish arrived on the coasts of Léon in the 5th century, they brandished a sword in one hand and held a crucifix in the other. The inhabitants of Léon were

Above: The nave of the cathedral in Saint-Pol-de-Léon. Right: A farmer tending his vegetable crop.

Christians but were by comparison more lukewarm in their devotion, and the Irish called them pagans, meaning that they did not believe in God. According to another, simpler explanation, *pagan* could be interpreted as the inhabitant of a *pagus*, a district of a Gallo-Roman city.

At all events, in olden times the people from these parts always enjoyed a deplorable reputation. They were frequently accused of looting shipwrecks. Other horrifying descriptions of what they got up to appear in *Tableau de la France* by the 19th-century French historian Jules Michelet, and include their propensity for using their teeth to sever the fingers of drowning women in order to remove their rings. Another story talks of them attaching lanterns to the horns of a cow to lure ships onto the rocks. Some of these stories may be more fanciful than true, but there is no question that the inhabitants of this coast, just like the people living on all other coasts, looked upon a shipwreck as a wonderful piece of good fortune. To their way of thinking, shipwrecked vessels were there to be pillaged from top to bottom, irrespective of interdictions from the local lord and the disapproval of the Church.

The Breton writer Yves Le Gallo paid due homage to this part of Brittany when he wrote of the arresting beauty of the coastline, and the way the countryside, the dunes, the sand and the reefs combine to make a unique land. He also spoke of how flat yet impressive the landscape was, so that the feeblest sunbeam piercing the clouds seemed to cause the surface of the sea to explode with light.

Just 2 km (1.25 mi) outside Lesneven lies **Le Folgoët**, the objective of one of Brittany's most important pilgrimages, which, on the first Sunday in September every year, attracts thousands of the faithful. According to legend, there was a simple-minded man named Salaün in the 14th century who begged for bread in the locality and otherwise lived out of doors in the wood. He only knew two words of Latin, *Ave Maria,* and he said them over and over again all day long. He also submitted himself to strange penances, such as sitting naked in the freezing waters of a spring while he sang Breton songs dedicated to the Virgin Mary. He was called *Ar Fol-goat*, Fool of the Woods. When he died in 1358, a sweet-smelling lily was discovered on his grave, and on its petals the words *Ave Maria* were written in gold. The flower remained in full bloom for six whole weeks. After the lily faded, the tomb was opened up and the flower was found to be growing out of Salaün's mouth; it was then decided to build a chapel dedicated to Our Lady over the spring of the saintly simpleton.

Thanks to gifts made by inhabitants of the area, the chapel was later replaced by a magnificent **basilica** in the Flamboyant Gothic style which may be visited today. It was constructed between 1422 and 1460, and achieves a curious harmony through the two dissimilar towers which stand on either side of the façade. The

north tower has a powerful, noble appearance and supports a tall, thin spire which stands on a base of elaborate stonework. The south tower is smaller in every way; it is also incomplete, and appears by comparison to be a symbol of humility. The spandrel is decorated with a representation of the Adoration of the Magi, and shows the Virgin Mary naked in bed with a sheet covering only half of her body. Inside the church, there is an outstanding rood screen carved in stone, the only one in Brittany made of Kersanton granite. There are also many very beautiful statues of the saints.

There is a huge number of castles and manors in Léon, mostly lost in the countryside of Upper Léon and standing at the end of avenues of huge trees or hiding in a rural hollow. The most illustrious of these Léon houses is **Kerjean Castle** (to the east near the D788), half fortified castle, half manor. It was built around 1540 by a rich canon, Hamon Barbier, for his nephew Louis. Kerjean was originally designed in the manner of the current vogue for Renaissance castles, but in the end it departed considerably from this style through the use of local materials and the influence of Breton styles. Kerjean is therefore a long way from the *châteaux* of Touraine and Île de France and the frivolous, carefree society that lived there. For one thing, Léon is a much more serious-minded place; for another, this castle was built as the home of socially reticent country gentlemen and their families. A fire in 1710 unfortunately destroyed many of the central apartments. Today, Kerjean Castle is the property of the French State and is the most beautiful house in Léon. Of particular interest are a vast park, apartments flanked by two wings and surmounted by a large portico, a chapel and fine collections of Breton furniture.

There is much to admire in the village of Goulven, and in its bay which has been turned into a bird sanctuary. The nearby seaside resort of **Brignogan** is a delightful spot with mountainous heaps of rocks on either side of it; to the north is the Christianized menhir of Maen-Marz (Stone of Wonder). The coastal D10 road also takes in a number of charming little villages. Of these, **Guissény** is the most interesting with a superb 17th-century altarpiece in the Chapel of the Immaculate Conception. It depicts an idyllic vision of Paradise.

Coast of Abers

Aber is Breton for a river mouths or deep estuary, many of which indent the the region's coastline, and some of them, like the Aber Benoît and the **Aber Wrac'h** and the Aber Ildut, are bordered with landscapes of quite unusual beauty. The Breton writer Yves Le Gallo described the Abers thus: *The abers are made up of sandy beaches with fine shingle, banks of sand and mud, colonies of birds and trails of seaweed. The banks of the rivers are teeming with an ever-changing scene of estuarine life, and the abers then carry it gently upstream into the placid landscapes. Seen from the higher ground upstream, these rivers become swollen with water coming in from the ocean. They then unfold towards the west in beautiful streams of cold liquid light which broaden as they reach the estuary, and are caught by the swell of the open sea. And these truly magnificent sights are repeated again and again, at dawn and at dusk, at low tide and at high tide.* **Plouguerneau** was reconstructed on the site of the lost city of Tolente, said to be the former capital of Armorica. It is also the starting point for a tour of this prodigiously varied coast. It is an astonishing succession of headlands, dunes, mud flats, rocks and reefs, but there is something almost ambivalent about this Coast of Abers in the way it is sometimes submerged under water and sometimes completely revealed. It is dominated by one of the highest lighthouses in Europe, the **Phare de l'Île Vierge** (Virgin Island Lighthouse), and there are magnificent views from Landéda on the **Baie des Anges**, the Sainte-Marguerite peninsula, Lannilis and **Keroüartz Castle.** There are also many ports along the coast which are worth visiting. They include Saint-Pabu, Portsall, Kersaint, Argenton, Porspoder, Lanildut, and **Trémazan** with its delightful chapel and somber feudal castle. This journey concludes at Pointe de Corsen, the most westerly point on the French mainland.

St Mathieu Point / Ouessant Island

Just outside Brest, the D789 runs along a stretch of coastline which contains a charming mixture of headlands, cliffs and fine sandy beaches, like the resort of Trez-Hir. It also has unforgettable views of the straits of Brest and the Plougastel

Right: The ruins of the abbey church and the lighthouse at Pointe Saint-Mathieu.

peninsula. Situated at the westernmost tip is **Pointe Saint-Mathieu**, a rocky headland 30 m (98 ft) high and crowned by the ruins of an abbey church. It is named after the Apostle Matthew because, according to legend, his remains were brought here from Ethiopia by local sailors. In the course of the voyage, they were caught in a storm but survived thanks to a miracle, and they decided there and then to name the nearest headland after the saint. The view from St Mathieu Point is certainly impressive. The Vieux-Moines (Old Monks) reefs are just below, the Chaussée-des-Pierres-Noires (Causeway of Black Stones) reefs are not far away, and slightly further out to sea are the islands of Molène and Ouessant (Ushant). On the left is the entrance to the Brest Channel, the Camaret peninsula, the Tas-de-Pois rocks and, far in the distance, Pointe du Raz and Sein Island. Michelet gives a description of the area in his *Tableau de la France: There can be nothing more sinister or more formidable that the Brest coast. It is*

the furthest extremity, the tip, the prow of the old world. There, the two old enemies are face to face: the land and the sea, humankind and nature. Look at the sea when it is growing angry and hurling enormous waves at St Mathieu Point! The spray carries all the way to the church where the mothers and sisters are at prayer. And even when the sea has called a truce and is silent, is there anyone who can walk along this funereal coast without saying or thinking silently 'Tristis usque ad mortem' (*Sad even unto death*)?

The **island of Ouessant**, known to all English-speaking seafarers as Ushant, is 7 km (4.3 mi) long and 4 km (2.5 mi) wide, and lies 20 km (12 mi) off the coast. With its sister island, Molène, it is the only island in these parts still inhabited today. It has been called "the island of terror" and has always been feared by seafarers. Indeed, sailors have a popular saying that goes:

Qui voit Molène,
voit sa peine,

Qui voit Ouessant,
Voit son sang.

Roughly: "If you can see Molène, you're in trouble; and if you can see Ushant, you've had it!"

The island is a very peculiar shape, being in the form of a crab's claw, the middle of which has been eroded by the sea. It also has cliffs rising to anything between 30 m and 65 m (98-213 ft) in height, and it is surrounded by fantastic rocks and encircled by currents that are among the fastest in Europe (13 kph or 8 mph). The violence, frequency and duration of the storms that lash the island, the non-stop winds and the mists make Ushant a savage, heartless place – and also the source of myths and legends.

It has been inhabited since prehistoric times, and was converted to Christianity by the Saint Pol Aurelian who came from Britain. He also founded a hermitage

Above: The stairwell of a lighthouse. Paintings on a ship's bow. Right: Ships tied up in Brest Harbor.

where the modern town of **Lampaul**, the island's capital, now stands. Through-out history, the waters surrounding Ushant have been the scene of innumerable battles between the English and French navies. The island sadly leapt into prominence at the end of the 19th century when luxurious ocean liner, the *Drummond Castle,* bound for Plymouth, ran aground on the Pierres-Vertes (Green Stones) reefs while taking the most dangerous route back home.

Today, the island has 1400 inhabitants. The men no longer go far afield, as they did in the old days when they sailed round the world in merchant vessels or joined the French Navy. As for the women, or the "girls of the rain" as they were called long ago, they do not have to work quite as hard as they used to while they awaited the return of their menfolk. Ushant has now opened up to mainland France and in particular to tourism, and the economy has thus been transformed. Meanwhile, the traditional breeding of *prés-salés* (salt-meadow lamb) continues

but on a small scale, but other types of farming have almost died out.

The island has now had an Armorican protection order placed on it, and is becoming an important bird sanctuary. There is now a colony of gray seals, and the island is visited by any number of migratory birds. Visitors may also learn about traditional Ushant styles of living at the **Maisons des Techniques et Traditions,** a kind of folk museum in the hamlet of Niou-Huella.

To conclude, nothing can take the place of walks or bicycle rides to appreciate Lampaul's charm and character, particularly the delightful houses with their blue and green shutters, the wonderful **lighthouses** at **Créac'h** and **Le Stiff,** the cliffs – and the views the cliffs offer of the mainland.

BREST

In his book *Le Livre de l'Emeraude,* the French-born writer André Suarès writes about Brest as follows: *Brest is a severe and hard-faced town that wears a frown on its brow at evening twilight. On a damp, warm autumn's evening when the sun has gone down over the Brest Channel, like a fiery orange over a bank of jade ... the whole city looks like some mortar gun made of stone, aiming its shells out over the ocean.* That rather poetic description underlines the impression of cold austerity that characterizes **Brest**, a city whose port has for so long been dedicated to military activities. The Romans established a fortified camp here as early as the 3rd century, and although the town began to expand in the 13th century, the following century brought with it over 50 years of English occupation. Brest had to wait for Richelieu, and then Colbert (the French Navy Minister in the 17th century), before its naval dockyard was built, and it was this that then stood in the way of the city becoming a commercial center. Indeed, at the beginning of the industrial era, Brest was already a jealously guarded fief of the military. As a result, it was not able to become a bridgehead for transatlantic trade and thereby become rich like Nantes, Saint-Malo and Morlaix. As a German submarine base during World War Two, the city underwent what the 20th-century poet, Jacques Prévert, referred to as a "storm of iron, steel and blood" from the Allied forces. No fewer than 165 bombing raids and a siege lasting 43 days reduced the city to rubble. Today, Brest is a city of neat, four-square lines of concrete buildings.

A walk around the city can nonetheless reveal one or two picturesque places For instance, the Saint-Martin quarter with its narrow streets and stone houses is one of the few parts to survive from earlier times. By contrast, Place de la Liberté symbolizes the present era. The Town Hall, a monumental building in reinforced concrete, looks on to one of the city's main thoroughfares, **rue de Siam,** named after a visit by the Ambassador of Siam to Brest in 1686. It was once a narrow, shaded street winding its way this way and that so as to keep out the biting sea winds. When the city center was rebuilt, it changed out of all recognition and all its bends and corners were rigorously straightened out. The **Cours Dajot** is a promenade that was built in the 18th century by prisoners from a local jail; from it, there is a splendid view of the Brest roadstead, the River Elorn widening into the Brest Channel, and, in between the two, the peak of Ménez-Hom. Over the centuries, the innumerable rivers that have poured into the straits have carved a channel through the rock The amazing result is a roadstead of 15,000 hectares (60 square miles) 20 m (66 ft) deep, and only connected to the open sea by a narrow channel 6 km (3.75 mi) long and 2 km (1.25 mi) wide. Not far from the Cours Dajot is the **Municipal Museum** which contains paintings by the Pont-Aven School, and at the very end of the Cours is the **castle** built in the 15th and 16th centuries. All that remain of it

are the dungeon and the Penfeld Gate. The River Penfeld, 3 km (1.8 mi) long and never more than 80 m (262 ft) wide, resembles a fjord, and its entire length is lined by port buildings, stores and yards, wharves bristling with enormous cranes, and slipways where ships used to be launched. The river is also crossed by the **Pont de Recouvrance,** the largest lift bridge in Europe; the bridge leads to the **Motte-Tanguy Tower** and the Musée du Vieux Brest.

The French Navy and its dockyard in Brest still provide jobs for 85,000 people living locally, but the city itself has diversified its economic activities in recent years. Now, the spread of new technology and an active policy aimed at scientific and technical development are placing Brest at the forefront of modern industry. An instance of this is **Océanopolis,** a scientific and technical research center dedicated to a study of the sea, and a symbol of the city's new image. It covers 5000 square metres (1.24 acres), and is constructed of glass and steel within a framework of concrete made in the form of a crustacean. Beneath its shell is hidden a huge panoply of Breton marine life. Yachtsmen also go there to study oceanography and meteorology.

Léon's Parish Closes

The **parish closes of Léon** are the most original, and possibly the most beautiful, examples of religious architecture in Brittany. They are to be found in a small area either side of the River Elorn (by the D712 and N12). The majestic constructions of the calvaries, their variety of form, and the intensity and expressiveness of the carving have a profoundly moving effect on people seeing them for the first time.

It is of course true that there are parish closes all over Brittany; it is just that those in Léon are the most elaborate and the most striking. This was due to a pe-

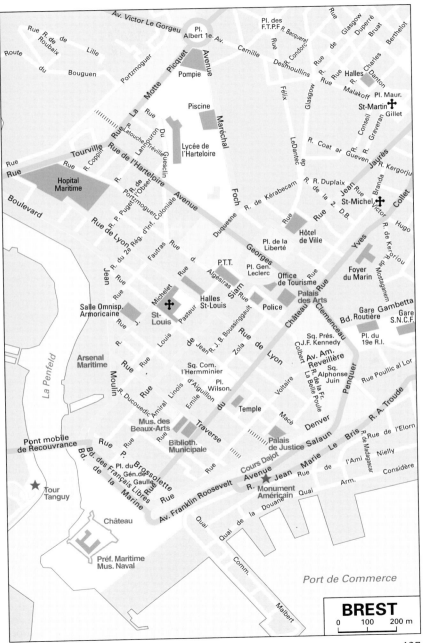

Av. Victor Le Gorgeu
Pl. des F.T.P.F
Pl. Albert 1e. Av.
Rue R. de de Roubaix
Route du Bouguen
Lille
Portzmoguer
La Motte Picquet
Avenue
Camille
Desmoullins
Rue
R. Becquerel
R. Condorc.
Rue de Glasgow
Duperré
Bruat
Berthelot
Pompie
Piscine
Rue
Félix
Glasgow
Rue
Rue Halles
R.
Charles Danton
Malakoff
Pl. Maur.
St-Martin ✝ Gillet
Maréchal
Latouche Tréville
Lanterprion
Du Guesclin
Lycée de l'Harteloire
LeDantec
Conseil
Graveran
R. Coat ar Gueven
Jaurès
R. Kergorju
Tourville
Rue de l'Harteloire
Rue
Rue R. Coppr.
R. de Portzmoguer
R. P. Puget
Rue d'Inf. Coloniale
Avenue
R. de Kérabecam
R. R. Duplaix
Jean
Rue
Branda
Victor
Rue
Collet
St-Michel ✝
Hugo
Hopital Maritime
Boulevard
Rue de Lyon
R. du 2e Rég. d'Inf.
Foch
Duquesne
R. de la 2. D.B.
Rue
Rue
R. de Kériou
Yves
Georges
Pl. de la Liberté
Hôtel de Ville
Fautras
Rue d.
P.T.T.
Pl. Gen. Leclerc
Office de Tourisme
Foyer du Marin
Jean
Rue
Rue
Michelet
Algésiras
Halles St-Louis
Siam
Rue
Police
Palais des Arts
Clemenceau
Gare Gambetta
Bd. Routière
Gare S.N.C.F.
Salle Omnisp. Armoricaine
St-Louis ✝
Pasteur
Rue
Château
Rue
Pl. du 19e R.I.
Arsenal Maritime
R.
Louis
de Jean R. J. B. Boussinggault
Rue
Zola
de Lyon
Sq. Prés. J.F. Kennedy
Av. Am. Reveillère
Colbert
Sq. Alphonse Juin
Moulin
Rue
R. Ducouedic Amiral Linois
Sq. Com. l'Hermminier
Pl. d'Aiguillon
Wilson.
Emile
du
Voltaire
R. de la Fr.
La Belle Poule
Rue Poullic al Lor
Penguer
La Penfeld
Mus. des Beaux-Arts
Rue
Rue
Rue
Traverse
Temple
Macé
Denver
R. A. Troude
Pont mobile de Recouvrance
Rue
Rue
Biblioth. Municipale
Palais de Justice
Salaun
Marie
Le
Bris
R. de Madagascar
Rue de l'Elorn
Nielly
Considère
Brossolette
Cours Dajot
Avenue
Jean
Rue
de
l'Ami
Arm.
Tour Tanguy
Bd. des Français Libres
Pl. du Gén.de Gaulle Rue
Rue
Av. Franklin Roosevelt
R. Monument Américain
Quai
Quai
Quai de la Douananqu.
Château
Préf. Maritime Mus. Naval
Comm.
Port de Commerce
Malbert

BREST
0   100   200 m

riod of great economic prosperity that the area enjoyed during the 16th and 17th centuries. For one thing, Léon became rich from sea trading: It was the time when buckwheat was discovered, and there were also opportunities to export rye and wheat. Secondly, the area was able to make an enormous amount of money from the flax industry, and the linen which was made from this flax was then exported widely to England, Spain and Portugal. The weavers, who of course were also farmers and peasants, became exceptionally well off and came to be known as *julots*.

This affluence soon began to be reflected in parish funds. Parishes were now able to embark on ambitious architectural projects. It was only by building the highest clocktower, or by carving the most elegant porch or church façade, that one parish established supremacy over its neighbor.

Above: The chapel at Saint-Thégonnec.
Right: A parish close at Guimiliau.

128

The typical parish close consists of an outer wall surrounding the cemetery and three buildings: the **church,** the ossuary and the calvary. The low stone wall has a doorway or monumental arch, and on either side of it there are narrower passages that are blocked by a slab that one has to step over in order to enter. The church is normally in the middle of the cemetery. The **ossuary**, on the other hand, comes in two forms: either a building standing on its own and possibly backing onto the low wall, or a reliquary or other small building adjoining the church.

There had previously been a problem caused by the fact that the amount of space in the small cemetery surrounding the church was severely restricted and could not be enlarged; the ossuary solved this problem. Every five years, the bones of the dead were exhumed and deposited in it, and every 20 or 25 years when the ossuary itself was full, the remains were transferred to a common ditch in an elaborate ceremony called "the great funeral."

The **calvary** can stand anywhere at all as long as it is inside the area of the close, although it is normally in the passageway which parishioners walk along on the way to Mass. It is an exclusively Breton monument, and customarily illustrates Christ's Passion using bas-reliefs and a large number of stone statues. It also sometimes happened that priests made use of these pictures to teach their parishioners about the New Testament.

Above all else, the close was the place where the living and dead meet, and there can be nothing more typical of Brittany than this preoccupation and familiarity with death. Death is symbolized by a supernatural person known throughout the region as the *Ankou*, and he is usually placed above the ossuary to make sure that the living do not forget what awaits them. The familiarity of Breton people with the Ankou is illustrated in a remark-

able way by the maxims and other brief sentences that are carved on the front of the closes. They include *I kill you all* and *Death, judgment, cold hell: when man thinks of them, he must tremble*.

The **Close of St Thégonnec** is dedicated to a companion of St Pol, a celebrated monk of the 6th century. It is a wonderfully balanced mixture of the Baroque, which had only just arrived from Italy, and Renaissance style. The close took over 200 years to complete, and is without question the finest building in Léon. Access to the close is through a triumphal arch (1587) consisting of four enormous blocks of granite surmounted by lantern turrets. The calvary (1610) comprises a simple plinth and three crosses: The cross in the middle bears a number of people, angels and knights and has two crosspieces. On the plinth, there is an even larger group of people witnessing Christ's Passion. The ossuary has a fine façade in the Renaissance style, including a broken pediment, an arched door and windows, and niches. Inside the

ossuary there is a fine Burial of Christ, dated 1706 with life-size figures painted on wood. It was the work of the Morlaix sculptor, Jacques Lespagnol.

Access to the church is by way of a Renaissance porch which recalls the designs made by Philibert Delorme (1515-70) for the Tuileries. The interior architecture is not remarkable, but there is plenty to admire in the furnishings. For instance, the pulpit (1683-1722) shows God and the four Evangelists handing the Tables of the Law back to Moses, and the pulpit's sounding-board is decorated with small angels and is surmounted by the Angel of Judgment. Also of interest are the decorations in the choir, the celebrant's magnificent 18th-century chair, the Holy Sacrament altarpiece in the south wing of the transept, and the Rosary altarpiece in the north wing of the transept.

The **Close of Lampaul-Guimiliau** dates from 1553 and is the oldest of all. The calvary is very simple, but the church is quite outstanding. It is dedicated to Our Lady and combines a wide

range of styles. The church's structure is Gothic and is decorated with Renaissance motifs, and by the western façade there is a belltower (1573) which was struck by lightning in 1809. The nave and the south aisle, with bays decorated with chimeras and fantastic animals, are in the Flamboyant Gothic style and date from the first half of the 16th century. The south porch (1533) has retained its statues of the twelve Apostles, unlike so many other Breton churches which have lost theirs.

The richness of the interior decoration is extraordinary. The rood beam, one of the most beautiful in Finistère, bears carvings of the Crucifixion and statues of the Virgin Mary and St John. The six 17th-century side altarpieces are also superb. One of the most beautiful is that of the altar of St John the Baptist on the right of the choir; it depicts the life of the saint and episodes from the life of Christ.

Above: Detail of the calvary at Saint-Thégonnec. Right: The upper part of the calvary at Plougastel-Daoulas.

The side bas-reliefs include a wonderful Fall of the Angels. The left part of the altarpiece of the Altar of the Passion consists of eight sections; the most beautiful are those which represent the Birth of the Virgin and St Miliau, a king of Cornouaille who was beheaded. The church also boasts one of the best Entombments in Brittany: It was executed in 1676 in Touraine stone by a sculptor from the dockyard in Brest and a native of the Auvergne. Lastly, in the right-hand aisle there is a baptismal font with a canopy (1651), and a very beautiful Pietà (1530) with all six figures carved out of the same piece of wood.

The **Close of Guimiliau** has the most extraordinary of all calvaries in Brittany. It was made between 1581 and 1588, and contains an amazing number of granite figures demonstrating the excitement and fervor of popular story-tellers. Over two hundred people tell the whole of the New Testament, albeit in a somewhat jumbled way. In particular, the Entombment, the Descent from the Cross and the Descent into Hell, all of them masterpieces from the workshops of Landerneau (North Finistère), are exceptionally lifelike and expressive. The ossuary is to the east and contains an external pulpit which was used for open-air sermons, particularly on All Souls' Day. Inside, there is an altar dating from 1644 and an altarpiece dedicated to St Anne.

The south porch (1606) of the church is heavily decorated. It is made of Kersanton stone and the execution is typical of the High Renaissance. The decoration consists of the birth of Eve among the animals of Paradise, a fight between satyrs, and a saint performing a miracle. Inside, there are interesting altarpieces telling the life of St Milliau and St Joseph, together with some 17th-century statues, a marvelous baptismal font with a canopy, and a famous tribune bearing representations of David with his lyre and Cecilia with her organ.

The **Close of La Martyre** is one of Brittany's more discrete closes, but also one of the richest. This is because the parish is located in what was once an important center for trading with the whole of Europe. It is curious that it is called *La Martyre* as the use of *La* would suggest a female martyr, whereas in fact the close is dedicated to St Salaün, the martyr king who dates back to the earliest days of Breton history. The triumphal door is very beautiful and effective: although it was put up in the 16th century, it is in the Flamboyant Gothic style, and its combination of exuberance and modesty makes a much more profound impression than the triumphal arch at Sizun. The ossuary was built in 1619 and is decorated with a curious female caryatid that is wreathed in bandages like a mummy. The church has undergone so many restorations and alterations that it is somewhat indeterminate from an architectural point of view. However, the south door has several sculptures showing scenes from the birth and life of the infant Jesus, and there are

also some 16th-century stained glass windows of considerable interest.

The parishes of Ploudiry, **La Roche-Maurice**, Trémaouezan, Landivisiau and **Bodilis** also have fine 16th-and 17th-century examples of this form of religious art, but they are less important.

PENINSULAS OF CORNOUAILLE

Compared with Léon, **Cornouaille** covers a very large area; it extends from the far side of the Brest roadstead to the south of the Arrée peaks. It was also here that immigrants from Britain who belonged to the tribe of the Cornovii settled in the 6th century. The French word Cornouaille (*Kerne* or *Kernew* in Breton) is related to the English Cornwall. Cornouaille is a land with many different faces and a huge diversity of dialects, costumes and characteristics. A useful distinction may be drawn between Upper Cornouaille with its mountains, and Lower Cornouaille which stretches out towards the south and is bathed by the warm waters of the Atlantic. The result is, on the one hand, an area of tall, austere cliffs backed by mountains and misty moorlands, and on the other a flat, sandy coastline opening out into green, undulating countryside.

Plougastel Peninsula

Until 1930 when the **Albert-Louppe Bridge** was built across the River Elorn, the **Plougastel peninsula** (which is now crossed by the N165) was relatively cut off from the rest of the region. This isolation greatly influenced the way the people lived their lives. For one thing, the inhabitants of Plougastel belong to one clan; they are all more or less cousins, and most of them are called Kervella or Le Gall. For another, they have a keen sense of their identity, as can be seen from the originality of their costumes. Men's clothes are elaborate and highly colored, and date from a time when they were worn daily; they never fail to surprise and delight visitors. Women's headdresses, now rarely worn except on special occasions, call for exceptional skill in folding, particularly as they consist of three headdresses on top of one another. The people of this peninsula also had a reputation for hard work and a keen business sense. Plougastel's affluence was based mainly on vegetables and fruit, and in the 18th century its prosperity reached proverbial heights. The countryside has an exceptionally mild climate and the soil has always been ideal for the famous strawberries which were introduced from Virginia at the end of the 18th century.

Plougastel-Daoulas, the peninsula's main town, is best known for its **calvary**; together with the calvaries at Guimiliau and Pleyben it is the most important in Brittany, and its composition is quite perfect. It was probably constructed to fulfil a vow made by parishioners after an epidemic of the plague swept Cornouaille in 1598. The cross in the middle is a "plague cross" whose main shaft is covered with the inflamed blisters which characterize the illness. There are at least 150 sculpted figures on the plinth and, with the three crosses which rise above them, they comprise a beautifully balanced work of art. Two km (1.25 mi) to the east of Plougastel is the 15th-16th-century Fontaine Blanche Chapel; fragments of a statue of the Virgin Mary and of a Gallo-Roman fertility god have been found here.

A tour of the peninsula is an opportunity to enjoy the many splendid sights, like the Anse de Caro (Caro Cove) and, above all, the Pointe de l'Armorique. From here, there are good views of the straits of Brest, and of the Crozon peninsula dominated by Menez-Hom. Also worth visiting are the 15th-century chapel of St Christine and the 16th-century chapel of **St Guénolé;** both of them contain interesting statues.

Where the peninsula joins the mainland , the village of Daoulas has a lovely Romanesque abbey founded in the 6th century by a lord of the nearby town of Le Faou in atonement for a double murder (*daou laz*) of two local abbots. The 7th-century abbey **cloister** is one of the most delightful pieces of Romanesque architecture in Brittany. It comprises 32 arches supported on small columns 1.5m (5 feet) high, alternately single and in pairs, and in the middle of the courtyard there is an octagonal basin, decorated with heads and geometrical motifs, at which the monks used to make their daily ablutions.

Nearby is the hamlet of **Kersanton** which has given its name to the famous stone used in making all the major works of art in Finistère including statues, calvaries and rood screens. This unexpectedly malleable stone lends itself remarkably well to carving, and it also grows harder with time.

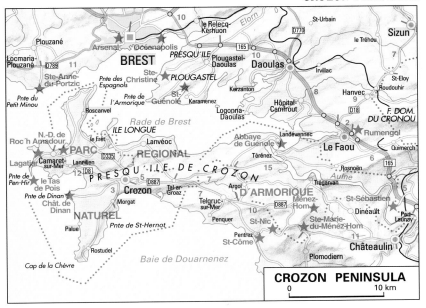

Crozon Peninsula

For those who love the wild beauty of coastal landscapes, the **Crozon peninsula** is quite unique in Brittany. Its cliffs, creeks and rocks make a magnificent backdrop for walking along signposted paths bordered with reeds, heather and sea-holly.

As a result of the constant erosion of the rocks, the peninsula has taken the form of a cross. Crozon seems to have lived for ever in deep, solitary meditation: Very few people live there, there is little agriculture to speak of, and no industry. Only the Defence Ministry has shown an interest by taking over the Île Longue to establish a top secret nuclear submarine base.

The town of Crozon is at the junction of three roads, the D335, D8 and D225. It boasts a number of old houses, and inside the **church** there is a fascinating altarpiece of painted wood. It contains several hundred figures and shows the martyrdom of the Theban Legion in which 10,000 soldiers who had been converted to christianity were crucified on Mount Ararat in Armenia.

Morgat, which is 3 km (1.8 mi) further on, is a fishing port and seaside resort well known for its lovely houses so characteristic of Breton architecture between the two World Wars. Its long sandy beach is one of the best sheltered on the coast and also enjoys a gentle climate. At either end of it are two rocky spurs, both full of **caves**. The spur to the south, called *Beg ar Gador* (Chair Headland), ends at an arch called La Porte. According to legend, it once opened suddenly to allow in a boat full of fishermen in distress who had prayed to St Marina. Some of the caves, known as *petites grottes* are accessible on foot at low tide; the *grandes grottes*, which are notable for their colored stones, may only be visited by boat.

Cap de la Chèvre makes for a splendid walk. There are lovely, old-fashioned villages, windswept moors and, from the top of some sheer cliffs, a magnificent view over Cap Sizun, Pointe de Pen-Hir

133

and – on a clear day – the island of Sein and even Ushant. The cape still has a large number of megalithic remains. Between Morgat and Saint-Hernot, there are stone alignments including a square wall consisting of a double row of vertical stones standing side by side. This wall, the only one of its kind, is called *Ty ar C'Huré* (The Priest's House). A Druid is thought to have lived here once, but it was probably the early Christians who substituted the word meaning priest (*curé*) for Druid. On the western coast, looking out to sea, are the long mudflats of La Palue, while at the northern extremity are the Pointes rocks and **Dinan Castle**.

Like so many other spots on this peninsula, **Camaret** was occupied by a colony of artists at the end of the 19th and beginning of the 20th century. They included the painter Eugène-Louis Boudin, the theater director André Antoine and

Above: Nightfall at Camaret-sur-mer. Right: Sunset over the bay of Dinan.

134

the poet Saint-Pol-Roux. The port is protected by a natural, curved bar of shingle called the *Sillon de Camaret* (Camaret Spit), and a polygonal tower, one of Vauban's defensive constructions, and the chapel of Notre-Dame-de-Rocamadour were also built here. The name of the chapel comes either from the Breton *roc'h am a dour* (rock in the middle of the sea) or from a famous place of pilgrimage in the Middle Ages. The port specializes in catching *langoustes* (sea crayfish) but it is currently suffering a severe recession and it is common to see dozens of wooden fishing smacks rotting on the beach.

On the moors just outside Camaret, there are 143 megalithic alignments at **Lagad-Yar** (the name means "chicken's eye"), somewhat fewer than the 700 or so which were there up to the 18th century. **Pen-Hir Point** nearby is an enormous rocky headland that looks down on the waves from a height of 70 m (230 ft), and extends into the sea along a line of huge reefs called the Tas-des-Pois (Heaps of

Peas). This culinary association may be due to a phonetic confusion between the Breton words *piz,* which means "peas" and *pezh* which means "piece of rock". From here the visitor may make a small detour along the Roscanvel peninsula to **Pointe des Espagnols** from where there is a panoramic view of the Brest Channel and the Plougastel peninsula.

It would be a shame to leave the Crozon peninsula without paying a visit to the town of Argol which has a fine parish close, including a monumental arch dating from 1659 and a charming 16th-century church. The **chapel of St Côme and St Damien** faces south towards the sea, and is only a short walk away. Lastly, a detour via **Trégarvan** with its beautiful 16th-17th-century church leads to the delightful Aulne Valley, and an opportunity to climb **Ménez-Hom** (330 m /1083 ft).

Landévennec Peninsula

The **Landévennec peninsula** contains a protected site of natural beauty. On a tall hill on the peninsula, at a spot where the Rivers Aulne and Faou meet, there is a Mediterranean climate which produces as many palm trees and subtropical flowers as Armorican chestnut and apple trees. **Landévennec Abbey** was founded here by St Gwennolé (Winwaloe) in the 5th century, but it was destroyed by the Normans in 913. On being rebuilt, it became one of the leading religious and intellectual centers in Brittany and exerted considerable influence over a very long period of time. The French Revolution put an end to that, but there was renewed interest in the abbey at the beginning of the 20th century, and in 1950 the Benedictines decided to rebuild the monastery only a few yards from the old abbey. Today, the ruins of the abbey may be visited, and there is a museum containing a number of objects dating from the 11th century. The capitals and the bases of the columns are of particular interest, since the designs carved on them – crosses, spirals and circles – date from early prehistoric times.

Douarnenez

The town of **Douarnenez** has given its name to one of the most beautiful and broadest bays in the world, and since it is one of France's leading fishing ports and an extremely charming seaside resort, Douarnenez should not be missed.

The most likely explanation of the word "Douarnenez" is that it is a corruption of *Tutuarn-Enez* (Island of St Tutuarn) after a hermit who lived during the 6th century on a rock that is now called Île Tristan. The port was in existence long before that, however – the Romans had already exploited the local industries of salt-curing and the production of *garum*, fermented fish oil much prized throughout their Empire for spicing dishes.

Early in the 6th century, the sea began to encroach on the land, submerging the town, or at least its more low-lying districts. Legend identifies Douarnenez as

Above: Apéritif time in Brittany. Right: Old woman on a Breton cemetery.

the celebrated sunken city of Ys, and the discovery of ancient Roman roads in the bay tends to support this hypothesis. Douarnenez's disappearance beneath the waves is regarded as an historical fact by some, but the way in which legend relates the story throws light on the conflict between Christianity, which was at the time establishing itself in the region, and ancient religions.

What legend tells us is that King Gradlon, who had been converted to Christianity by St Gwennolé, fell under the influence of his daughter, Dahud, who had remained faithful to the ancient beliefs. These beliefs can only have been those of the Druid religion since Douarnenez was consecrated to the Celtic horse-god, Marc'h. When the king's daughter and the inhabitants of the town opted for a life of debauchery, God decided to punish them. He did so by using Satan to seduce Dahud who in turn stole the keys to the lock gates, thus enabling Satan to submerge the town. Gradlon was warned of what was happening by St Gwennolé and

tried to flee on horseback with Dahud, but was only able to escape drowning by abandoning his daughter.

The little port of Douarnenez developed gradually over the centuries; it was not until 1851, when François Appert (d 1840), discovered that you could keep food by sterilizing it and sealing it hermetically in cans, that the first cannery could be opened. With that, the town's prosperity was established. Fishing has long been one of Douarnenez's main economic activities, but more recently the town has diversified into industries based on advanced technology. However, the true basis of the people's extraordinary dynamism lies in their exceptional success in publishing ventures covering Breton ethnography.

A number of organizations, together with magazines like *Le Chasse-Marée* and *Ar-Men* which are sold all over France and even abroad, have led to the development of a profound awareness of the town's cultural heritage, and a realization that it is something they must look after and make known to a wider circle of people. It was in this context that the **Boat Museum** was started, a most unusual place that has a number of ships on display but also recreates the atmosphere of life at sea. You can take a course on ancient navigation or a trip on a sailing ship.

The **port of Rosmeur** takes us back to a more traditional type of fishing village, with an auction first thing in the morning, the quays lined with cafés, the nets hung out to dry, and the ships – mainly sardine boats – hurrying to and fro. **Tréboul** to the west has been administratively part of Douarnenez since 1945, and is linked to it by a viaduct. There is something very captivating about Tréboul with its lovely sandy beach, its small marina and the Pointe de Leydé, which soars 50m (150 ft) above a wilderness of rocks. A walk along the **Sentier des Plomarc'h** just south of Rosmeur leads to the Plage du Ris and to the village of Ploaré with its beautiful 16th and 17th-century church topped by a fine tower 55 m (180 ft) high.

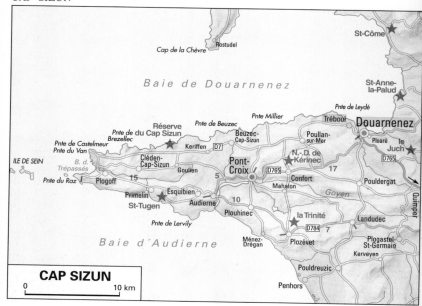

CAP SIZUN

0   10 km

Cap Sizun

Cap Sizun extends west from Douarnenez to the furthest extremity of **Pointe du Raz**, and is remarkable both for the architecture of the buildings and the violent beauty of the land as it goes to meet the ocean. It is an area of brutal, savage grandeur, and of sheer cliffs plunging straight down towards the waves which break onto them with a deafening roar.

It is a spectacle which led Flaubert to exclaim: *Man is not designed to live here; he cannot tolerate such a high dose of Nature.* Yet even here, people have learnt to adapt, and it is quite surprising to discover that there are 100 inhabitants to the square kilometer at the broadest part of the Cape, and as many as 200 at the Point itself.

Towards the far end of the peninsula, there are some almost vertical paths leading to magnificent headlands. The D7

Right: A small hotel on the Pointe du Raz.

runs along the north side of Cape Sizun and offers a succession of quite superb views from the tall cliffs. You should take a walk out to the end of **Pointe du Milier** and the see the majestic rocks at **Pointe de Beuzec.** The jagged rocks of Cap Sizun are also home to a **bird sanctuary** where whole colonies of sea-birds, some of them on the point of extinction, have found an ideal spot to breed. The best time to visit the sanctuary is between 1 May and 30 June, when there are large numbers of penguins, guillemots, puffins, cormorants and many types of gulls and terns. The view from **Pointe de Brézellec** might be followed by a strenuous climb to **Pointe de Castelmeur** where there are the remains of four earth ramparts from the Celtic era which defended the narrow neck of the isthmus. The **Pointe du Van,** at the furthest extremity of the north coast, is seldom visited by tourists but is unusually interesting. This rocky spur overlooks the sea from a height of 65 m (213 ft), and to one side of it is the **chapel of St They**, a very humble

church in an equally deserted spot. Lastly, there is the **Pointe du Raz** known to sailors the world over. The promontory descends by small ledges to sea level, but there are now complete tours of the 72 m (234 ft) high point organized by qualified guides. Of particular interest is the *Enfer de Plogoff* (Plogoff's Inferno), a deep chasm in which the waves swirl round and boil up before crashing noisily on to the rocks.

The moorland vegetation has been laid to waste by the trampling of countless tourists, and the character of the place has been spoilt by souvenir stalls and a shopping center. Accordingly, the visitor is advised to turn away and look out towards the horizon where, on a clear day, it is even possible to see the Île de Sein. The name *Raz* means "strong current" or "tide-race", and indeed the tide runs at a terrifying speed through the gap between the headland and the Île de Sein, making it a hazardous passage even in good weather. To the north of Raz Point lies the **Baie des Trépassés** (Bay of the Dead)

which has long been reputed to be the point of departure to the next world. According to tradition, the remains of dead Druids were taken from here to be buried on the Île de Sein .

The D784 passes through Plogoff, a village which achieved sudden fame when it successfully resisted the building of a nuclear power station, and then Primelin, before a short detour leads to the beautiful 16th-century **chapel of St Tugen.** It is best known for its centuries-old pilgrimage in honor of St Tugen, a saint with the power to cure rabies. Long ago, on the day of the *pardon,* pilgrims would acquire small keys made of lead which they would then keep; when approached by a rabid dog, they would throw one of the keys at it and the animal would leave them alone. The chapel is surrounded by an attractive close with a calvary, triumphal arch and cemetery.

The town of **Audierne** belongs to an altogether more tranquil part of Cornouaille. From a bridge over the River Goyen, there is a general view of this little port and a walk as far as Pointe de Lervily offers a range of pleasant views over the left bank of the ria (river mouth), the Plouhinec coast, Audierne's beach and the open sea. Like so many ports, Audierne has had to face up to competition from intensive fishing, and in response to this challenge the town has modernized its fleet, and built an *écloserie* (specially enclosed beds used as a nursery for lobsters) and the largest covered fish-breeding farm in France.

Pont-Croix (by the D765), the former capital of Cape Sizun, is notable for the beautiful church of **Notre-Dame-de-Roscudon,** a fine mixture of Romanesque, Gothic and Flamboyant styles. The late 16th-century south porch is surmounted by three tall, and highly original, gables that are either projecting or in a clover-leaf design. The 15th-century belltower is topped by a spire which reaches a height of 67 m (220 ft) and closely resembles that on the cathedral of St Corentin in Quimper. This tour of Cape Suzon then passes through the village of **Confort**, whose church has a carillon-wheel, and ends 2 km (1.25 mi) further on at the **Chapel of Notre-Dame-de-Kérinec** which has a calvary and is decorated with statues.

Île de Sein

Over the centuries, the **island of Sein** has been sanctified by myths. In Roman times, for instance, it was known as the *Insula Sena* and the nine priestesses who officiated there were endowed with exceptional powers; for the Druids, it was a burial ground called the Island of he Seven Slumbers. There is no doubt that the inaccessibility of this little bit of land, battered by the seas, has given rise to particularly potent legends.

Unlike Ushant, Sein is a flat island with an average height above sea level of a scarcely more than 1.5m (5 ft), and this explains why it has often been threatened

with being submerged. In 1830, 1868 and 1897, things got so bad, in fact, that the inhabitants were obliged to take refuge on the roofs of their houses. In 1820, the island measured 3 km (1.8 mi) long by 900 m (830 yards) wide; today it is only 2 km (1.25 mi) long and 800 (720 yards) wide. When Sein was first inhabited, those living there had a very unsavory reputation, being known as the "devils of the sea" because of their their habit of pillaging shipwrecks. After they were converted to Christianity, their behavior mellowed somewhat and they subsequently became famous for their heroic and daring deeds. Many are the stories of the inhabitants of Sein linking arms to form a human chain in the rough seas to rescue people from ships that had foundered on the rocks. Today, the 500 souls who inhabit the island scrape a living from fishing. Older women still wear the *jobelinen*, a mourning headdress that was introduced after the cholera epidemic which swept the island in 1886.

From the Sein lighthouse, there is a view over the Chaussée de Sein, a line of reefs extending 10 km (6 mi) into the open sea. At the far end of these rocks is the **Phare d'Ar-Men** (Ar-men Lighthouse), one of the most remote anywhere on this coast; it took fifteen years to build, and there are two keepers who take it in turns to work there.

FROM THE MONTS D'ARRÉE TO THE BLACK MOUNTAINS

Mountains form the boundaries of Finistère's peaceful countryside. The Monts d'Arrée and the Montagnes Noires(Black Mountains) are to be found on either side of the Aulne Valley.

Monts d'Arrée

The **Arrée Mountains** are unquestionably the wildest region in all of Brittany and four mountains, **Tuchenn Gador**

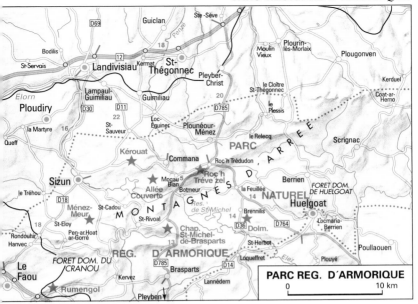

(the highest point in Brittany at 384m), **Roc'h Trévézel, Saint Michel** near the village of Brasparts, and Roc'h Trédudon form a natural basin where the River Elez has its source. The desert-like appearance of the landscape has given the area a special significance. The famous peat moor of Yeun Elez with its damp climate and thick, choking mists, was for many years a place where witchcraft was practiced. When the soul of a dead man or woman refused to leave its home and tormented the family with bizarre manifestations, a priest was called in to carry out an exorcism. after a long and distressing ritual the priest would drive the soul from the dead person into the body of a black dog which was then hastily drowned in the bog of Yeun Elez.

The Elez basin is encircled by green wooded areas, like the **Forests of Le Cranou and Huelgoat,** and the **Parc Naturel Régional d'Armorique** extends to the very heart of this region. It was set up in 1969 and covers an area of 110,000 hectares (425 square miles). It is divided into two parts: the larger of the two, containing the massif of the Arrée Mountains, and a coastal and island section including the islands of Ushant, Molène and Sein, the Crozon peninsula and the Aulne Estuary. The park's administrative center is on the **Ménez-Meur Estate.**

The park may fail to come up to some people's expectations because of a shortage of money, but it does try to fulfil its dual role of protecting nature and welcoming tourists, be means of numerous special events linked to rural traditions. In addition, there are museums which present certain traditional aspects of peasant life: these include the **mills at Kérouat**, the Maison Cornec which is a typical example of Breton architecture, the Maison de la Rivière et de la Pêche, the Maison des Minéraux, the Maison de l'Ecole Rurale Bretonne (an agricultural school), the Maison des Pilhaoueriens (rag-and-bone men who, at one time, used to go around collecting pieces of material, rabbit skins and bits of metal) and the Maison des Artisans.

141

The town of **Le Faou** to the west used to be a prosperous port where timber was loaded for shipment to the naval dockyards . Today, its main street is lined with granite corbelled houses whose façades are attractively covered in slate. The D18 going north passes through the small town of Hanvec and then **Sizun** (*seizun* means "seven slumbers"). This village has a **parish close** crowned by a magnificent and unique triumphal door (1588-90) with three semi-circular arches; the platform, which has a balustrade and skylights, is supported by Corinthian capitals, and the whole is surmounted by an altar and a calvary.

To the east, and not far from Roc'h Trévézel, lies **Commana.** This village stands on a bare hillside and can be recognized from a long distance by the height of its clocktower (57 m or 187 ft, which is so dark and massive that it al-

Above: Breton craft work – painted meerschaum pipes. Right: A fisherman in the port of Audierne.

most looks like one of the Arrée mountain peaks.). There is also a **parish close** complete with triumphal arch, cemetery, ossuary and 18th-century church, but it is the church that contains the most important pieces: two large painted altarpieces, both outstanding examples of 17th-century peasant Baroque art. The **St Anne altarpiece** depicts the saint with Mary and Jesus, and the Five Wounds altarpiece has Jesus showing his wounds and being crowned by the angels. It always comes as something of a surprise to discover such superb decorations in the modest parishes of the Arrée; however, the parishes of the Elorn Valley, rather like those in Léon, owe their considerable prosperity to the linen industry which dominated all economic activity in the region from the 16th to the 18th centuries. Two km (1.25 mi) from Commana lies the **covered avenue of Mougau-Bian** which dates from 2000 B.C. This truly magnificent monument comprises five horizontal slabs 14 m (46 ft) long in all, supported by 28 pillars, and there are axes and daggers carved on the walls.

North of here along the D785 are Plounéour-Ménez and Relecq, the latter interesting for the ruins of its 12th-century abbey and the St Thégonnec Cloister, formerly the priory of Relecq's abbey. From here, there is a very wild path that winds in and out of the Caragou rocks and the St Barnabé rock to Huelgoat.

Huelgoat (the name means "high wood") is situated to the south-east, on the D764. It is a place that is more mythical than real, another vestige of the ancient Forest of Brocéliande. A place where the forest is scattered with huge piles of rocks, with tumbling streams and legends reaching back into the mists of time. Local imagination has peopled this area with ghosts, devils, giants and other supernatural beings. That is the reason why, in order to explain the forest's unusual geography, the local story goes that the giant Gargantua was so furious at being given only one meal in Huelgoat that he hurled down rocks where they can still be seen in the forest. These granite rocks have for centuries been used in building the churches and other monuments of Finistère. Walking through the woods you will come across many unusually shaped rocks with picturesque names.

The path by the right bank of the Argent leads to the *Grotte du Diable* (Devil's Grotto), said to be the gates of Hell, and a deep crevasse takes an utterly enchanting route along the banks of the river. Meanwhile, the left bank boasts a very strange geological phenomenon, the **Roche Tremblante** (Logan Stone or Rocking Stone), a stone weighing over 100 tonnes which sways slightly if pressed very gently in the right spot. Further on is another strange rocky outcrop, the **Ménage de la Vierge:** in popular imagination, the Virgin Mary had her first home here with a bed, cooking pot, cupboard and cradle for the baby Jesus. A walk in a different direction will take in the *Grotte d'Artus* (Artus' Cave – i.e. King Arthur's Cave) and the *Mare aux Sangliers* (Wild Boars' Pool), a pond with wonderfully clear water sheltered by huge trees. Not far from that is the Camp d'Artus, probably all that remains of a Celtic double ditch and rampart with an entrance flanked by exceptionally large blocks of stone and defended by a bastion. Nearby, there is a parish close at Berrien (5 km or 3 mi from Huelgoat), and 6 km (3.7 mi) to the south there is the church at Plouyé which has many chapels with springs said to have miraculous powers.

The tour of the Arrée Mountains continues to the west along the D14 through **Saint-Herbot,** the patron saint of horned beasts. In former times, in order to gain the protection of this animal-loving saint, the peasants would come to the *pardon* and place on a stone table tufts of hair taken from their animals' tails.

The **chapel,** which was built between the 14th and 16th centuries in the Gothic Flamboyant style, is one of the architectural jewels of Finistère. The huge tower 30 m (98 ft) high is inspired by the tower on the cathedral at Quimper; then there is the magnificent main door with two smaller doors on either side, and the south porch is adorned with painted statues of the Apostles.

The church's splendidly decorated interior includes a chancel in carved wood, carved stalls and, in the apse, a fine 16th-century stained glass window showing the Passion.

The end of this journey is reached through Loqueffret with its 16th-century church, Lannédern, a village under the protection of the 8th-century St Elern, a hermit who is traditionally always represented riding a stag, the village of Brasparts, and the **mountain of St Michel** from whose summit there is a wonderful view over the whole region. The farm of St Michel in Brasparts produces a wide range of fine craftwork including carved

wood, leather, ceramics, weaving and jewelery (tel 98 81 41 13).

Aulne Valley

The **Aulne Valley** lies between the Monts d'Arrée and the Montagnes Noires , and much of it is followed by the N164. The town of **Châteaulin** stands on a bend of the river and was once a prosperous city. Its finest monument is the **Notre-Dame Chapel** which stands in a particularly charming spot beneath a cliff on the left bank of the river. Its triumphal arch and 15th-century calvary are very fine, and inside the church there are statues from the same period. Not far downstream from here is the tiny village of **Port-Launay,** a lovely place for walks, with its low houses hugging the curve of the river, against a backdrop of green hills. To the north west is the important and richly decorated **chapel of St Se-**

Above: Taking a walk over the magnificent rocks at Huelgoat.

bastian and St Ségal. Like so many country chapels, this one was built in the hope of the keeping the plague at bay. The 16th-century monumental door and calvary are both made of Kersanton stone and are very beautiful, and inside the church there are magnificent painted altarpieces decorating the choir. In front of the nave stands a marvellous 17th-century rood beam surmounted by a crucifix and representations of the Virgin Mary and St John.

The town of Pleyben is famous for its superb parish close. The imposing **Church of St Germain** (St Germanus), which was built in 1564 and restored in the 19th century, has two belltowers. One of them has a spire designed with typical Gothic delicacy and finesse, and is connected to a corner turret which is surmounted by a pinnacle turret. The other one, known as the St Germain Tower, is less tall and more robust; it was started in 1588 but, because of the Wars of the League, was not completed until 1642. It is an adaptation of the classic, large

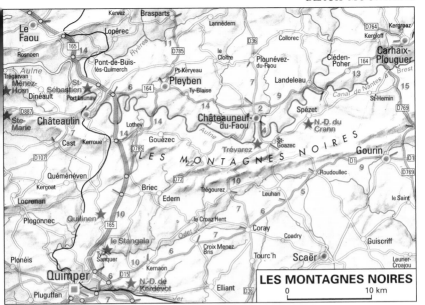

Anglo-Norman tower in the Renaissance style, and is surmounted by a dome with lantern turrets. The decoration in the interior of the church is magnificent. This includes the high altar made in 1667, the Rosary altarpiece, a large number of hanging keystones adorning ribbing in the nave, decorated rood beams, and painted carved stringers. The latter contain highly imaginative scenes from daily life, the Bible and even pagan mythology including the ever-present *Ankou.* The ceiling is in the form of an inverted ship's hull, and there is also a splendid 16th-century stained glass window depicting the Passion. In the apse, there is a sacristy dating from 1719 and built in the style of Bramante, and this is dominated by a half dome and a cupola with lanterns. The ossuary (1550) is one of the oldest in Brittany; it is also beautifully designed with wonderful pointed segmental arches decorating the bays of the façade.

The most remarkable monument in Pleyben is unquestionably the **calvary**. For a long time, it was thought to date from the 17th century because of the date carved on it. The date of 1650 is probably when restoration was carried out, however, and the carved figures wearing 16th-century clothes suggest that it dates back to as early as 1550. The 28 episodes of the life of Christ which are depicted on this calvary are notable for the attention to detail and realism of the carving.

Montagnes Noires

The **Montagnes Noires**, or Black Mountains, called the *Menzioù-Du* in Breton, run parallel to the Arrée Mountains and are separated from them by the Châteaulin basin. They contain a series of relatively gentle landscapes extending for 60 km (37 mi) from Ménez-Hom to the woods of Conveau in the Department of Morbihan. These mountains must have been well wooded at one time, and they reserve their charms for nature-lovers who seek out , on foot or by bicycle, the sunken roads, the woodland paths, and low houses built of dark coloured schist.

To the west of Châteaulin stands **Ménez-Hom** (330 m or 1083 ft), the last peak of the Noires range, and offering a stunning view from its summit. On a clear day, it is even possible to see the Brest roadstead, the Pointe du Van, Cape Chèvre and the inland valleys. Once upon a time, this peak, together with the summit of Méné-Bré and the peak of Saint-Michel-de-Brasparts, was amongst the most important places of worship for the Celts.

According to some legends, King Marc'h is buried not far from here by the road to Trégarvan. However, the legend continues, because of his many sins he will not be allowed to enter Paradise until he can, from the saddle of his horse, see the belfry of the Chapel of **Sainte-Marie-du-Ménez-Hom.** This chapel seems like an oasis of civilisation in a landscape of bare heathland and lonely pines. Here, beyond the arched doorway built in 1739, is a close with a calvary (1544). Most of the chapel, a mixture of Gothic and Renaissance styles, was constructed during the period 1570-91, and the interior is mainly memorable for the three altarpieces dating from the early years of the 18th century.

From **Châteauneuf-du-Faou,** a peaceful little town overlooking the Aulne Valley with a splendid view of the mountains, the road leads to the **Domaine de Trévarez** (Trévarez Forest Park), a delightful area for walks which contains a castle and a flower garden. The village of Saint-Goazec is followed by the hamlet of Spézet, whose **chapel of Notre-Dame-du-Crann** contains some remarkable stained glass windows from the 16th century; they were influenced by either German or Italian designs, and depict scenes from the Passion, the childhood of Jesus, and the legends of St James, and St Eloi, the patron saint of blacksmiths.

Right: The square at Locronan with its granite houses.

The town of **Carhaix-Plouguer** (by the N164) in the center of the **Poher** region was an important strategic and commercial crossroads as early as the Gallo-Roman period. However, its prosperity declined over the centuries, to such a point that during the reign of Louis XIV some 30,000 peasants from Carhaix and the vicinity mounted a rebellion against a tax which they considered unfair.

In the town center, there are some very beautiful corbelled Renaissance houses, and the Place du Champ-de-Bataille has a statue of Théophile-Malo Corret de la Tour-d'Auvergne, a great hero of the imperial armies. The church of St Trémeur was rebuilt in the 19th century, although its 16th-century combined porch and belltower survives. The church of St Peter has parts of an 11th C. sanctuary. The most important monuments nearby include the **Kerbreudeur Calvary,** which dates from the second half of the 15th century and is thought to be the oldest calvary in Brittany, equal with the calvary at Tronoën. Not far away is the village of Saint-Hernin which boasts a lovely 16th-17th-century parish close; the calvary shows the two thieves crucified on either side of Christ, being rent asunder on their crosses and punished in a particularly cruel manner.

Locronan

Locronan is in the south west of the Aulne Valley and is thought by many to be one of the most beautiful villages in France. One reason for this is that it has retained a remarkable degree of architectural homogeneity with its granite houses decorated with pedimented dormer windows, and narrow paved streets which seem to echo still with the sound of horses' hooves.

The origin of the town lies in the cult of St Ronan, an Irishman who came to these parts to find the solitude necessary for his contemplative vocation. He is now re-

membered by a *pardon* known here as a *troménie*, a word derived from the Breton *tro minihy* which means "the monk's walk".

Every year there is a short procession of 6 km (3.7 mi), and every six years there is a *grande troménie* of 14 km (8.7 mi) which takes in the roads which the saint himself used to walk. The ceremony starts on a Sunday morning in July with a blessing of the banners, and the procession moves off in the afternoon to the sound of drums; stops are made at 44 resting places along the route. The procession then climbs the mountain to the chapel of St Ronan and goes all the way round a granite rock called the Kador Saint-Ronan (St Ronan's chair).

Locronan's more temporal riches were based mainly on the manufacture of sail-cloth, and on the 300 looms which supplied the port of Brest during the 17th century. The end of the great sailing ships and the onset of the industrial revolution in the 19th century signaled the end of this kind of work; today, the town makes a very good living out of tourism because it has been wise enough to cherish its architectural treasures. One of the greattest of these is the **church of St Ronan** which was built in 1420 with the help of the Dukes of Brittany, and is one of the most beautiful examples of Flamboyant style. It has had no additions made to it nor undergone any alterations at any time since it was built.

Adjoining the church is the Chapelle du Pénity, built in 1504 on the orders of the Duchess Anne; the two buildings are joined through an inner doorway. The church is in the Anglo-Norman style, and the steeple recalls the spire of the cathedral at Quimper; the top part of the steeple was destroyed by lightning in 1808. There are also two other belfries, one in the center of the church and another belonging to the chapel. The interior of the church is notable for the extremely beautiful and rare stone vaulting supported by elegantly carved pillars; the nave was constructed on a slope and offers an unusual perspective.

The pulpit in carved wood contains a remarkable series of images, consisting of ten medallions recounting the most important details of St Ronan's life. There is also a superb 17th-century Rosary altarpiece and 15th-century stained glass windows recounting Christ's Passion in 18 panels. The chapel contains a splendid Deposition from the Cross in multicolored stone dating from 1413, and the tomb of St Ronan carved in Kersanton stone. In the square in front of the church there is a well, and lining the square itself are several unusual houses made of ashlars and dating from the 16th and 17th centuries. Another building in this square is the *Pâtisserie Guillou* which sells *houing-aman,* a Cornouaille specialty. Close by is **Locronan Mountain**, the destination of the *troménies*. A walk to the top is extremely pleasant, and from the peak there is a lovely view over Douarnenez Bay and the surrounding countryside.

Above: Cottage industry, a flax-weaving workshop in an old house at Locronan.

QUIMPER AND THE BIGOUDEN COUNTRY

Quimper, a lively town of considerable charm, is queen of the Cornouaille region. It makes a good starting point for exploring the Bigouden country with its wealth of monuments and traditions.

Quimper

The name of the town of **Quimper** (in Breton: *Kemper*) corresponds to the French word *condé,* meaning confluence, being situated at the head of an estuary, where the waters of the Steir and Odet once mingled. Only the Odet now remains, a river whose character is determined by the rise and fall of the tides, and whose banks are ideal for walking.

Historical and economic capital of the Cornouaille, Quimper is also the chief town of the *préfecture* of Finistère, despite an interminable power struggle with its rival, Brest. The site has been occupied since prehistoric times, and at Kergaradec the outlines of a vast Celtic settlement are still visible.

The town grew rapidly during the Middle Ages, when work was begun on the cathedral, but over the centuries Quimper was racked by political and religious strife and frequently besieged and looted. Since the last century, there has been considerable commercial and industrial development, and in recent times a number of advanced food-processing and electronics firms have been attracted to the area.

The **cathedral of Saint Corentin** was begun in the 13th century, during the reign of Saint Louis, and building work continued off and on until 1854-6, when the spires were finally added. So well do they blend in with the whole that they might be taken for 15th-century work, contemporary with the facade. Above the facade stands a statue of King Gradlon, an 1858 copy of the original, which was

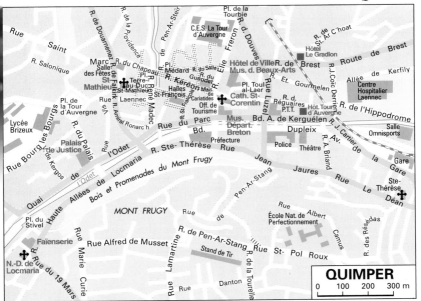

destroyed during the Revolution. Perfectly preserved is the magnificent south door, dedicated to Saint Catherine.

Amazingly, the choir (13th century) is not in line with the nave (15th century), deviating by 15 degrees to the left. Some have interpreted this as a reference to the angle of Christ's head on the cross, but a more down-to-earth explanation is that the architects did not take into account the location of the existing bishop's palace and were then reluctant to destroy the building. Ten or so fine stained glass windows are preserved in the upper part of the nave, where they escaped the attentions of the Revolutionaries.

The **Musée Départemental Breton** is housed in the former bishop's residence beside the cathedral, featuring costumes, furniture and folk art of the region, while the **Musée des Beaux-Arts** has a fine collection of Flemish (Van Dyck, Rubens Breughel), French (Fragonard, Corot), Spanish, German and Italian paintings, fine pictures by the Pont-Aven school and works by contemporary Breton artists.

Though lacking conspicuous monuments, the old town is rich in atmosphere, and the visitor should explore beyond the **rue Kéréon** (street of the cobblers) opposite the cathedral. In the rue de Guéodet stands the most picturesque of Quimper's buildings, the **Maison des Cariatides,** erected by an inn-keeper in the days of the League, during the Wars of Religion. Its stone pillars bear striking sculptures of townspeople who distinguished themselves during the seige of 1595. Another town house of comparable dignity is the Minuellou, in the rue du Sallé. The Pont Médard, once a drawbridge, which commands a fine view of the remains of former ramparts, the rue Saint-Mathieu, the place Terre-au-Duc, the rue René-Madec with its 18th-century façades, together with the Venelle Saint-Nicolas and other alleys, form an old-world architectural setting of great charm. At the foot of the 70 m (230 ft) Mont Frugy, which overlooks the town, narrow streets lead to the suburb of Locmaria, home of Quimper's ceramics (*faïence*) industry. A potter from

149

the South of France settled there in 1690, founding a factory whose fame was to spread beyond the borders of France. There is a **Musée de la Faïence** (route de Bénodet), and it is possible to visit the Kéraluc potteries (rue de la Troménie). Items can be purchased at the l'Art de la Cornouaille (place Saint-Corentin) or at thes hop of the pottery firm, *Faïencerie H.B. Henriot* (allée Locmaria).

Around Quimper

Overlooking the Odet, on the right bank of the river, is one of Brittany's oldest religious buildings, the **church of Notre-Dame de Locmaria,** an 11th-century Benedictine abbey consecrated to the Virgin Mary.

The countryside around Quimper is rich in châteaux, chapels and calvaries. On the way to Plogonnec, beguilingly

Above: The gothic cathedral of Saint-Corentin at Quimper. Right: A plate in Quimper pottery.

hidden among the greenery, the chapel of Ti-Mamm-Doué (house of the mother of God), built in 1541, merits a visit. Other picturesque chapels in the district include Notre-Dame de Kerdévot, and **Notre-Dame de Quilinen,** with its remarkable calvary in reddish stone, which dates from the 16th century. A sight not to be missed are the **Gorges du Stangala,** a magnificent vantage point, from which one can trace the valley of the Odet 70 m (230 ft) below. Much of the route can be covered by car, on one bank or the other, but the gorge itself can only be reached on foot, along dirt tracks.

A boat trip on the Odet is a must, following the wooded banks of the river downstream from Quimper or upstream from Bénodet. Into view come the châteaux of Lanniron, Kéraval, Kebernez and **Pérennou,** some of which are open to the public, and there are some magnificent vantage points, such as the **Site des Vire-Court**, where the river snakes between high wooded cliffs. The name is explained by the fact that the river forms a hairpin bend at this point, and sailing ships were forced to tack (*virer*) frequently to negotiate the bend.

Bigouden Country

The **Bigouden country** lies between Plozévet to the west and Sainte-Marine to the south of Quimper. The term *bigouden* is a reference to the costumes worn by the inhabitants of the region. The origins of these people have long been shrouded in mystery. They were even said to have had an Asiatic or Eskimo provenance! There has in fact been a good deal of racial mixing, as a result of foreign vessels being shipwrecked on this coast.

The area is one of contrasting landscapes. The west coast, where the D2 runs parallel with the shores of the Baie d'Audierne, is somewhat desolate, with low cliffs and sand dunes running as far as the prominent **Rocher de la Torche.**

The south coast, on the other hand, starting at the **Pointe de Penmarc'h,** is far more picturesque, with busy little fishing harbors such as Saint-Guénolé, Kérity, Le Guilvinec, Lesconil and Loctudy. The land is low-lying, and the sparse coastal vegetation is swept by strong south-westerly winds. Only some way inland does one find more sheltered valleys and parkland with wild flowers.

This country is the setting for an enchanting short story, *Le Cheval d'Orgueil* (The Horse of Pride), in which Per Jakez Hélias recalls his poor peasant upbringing. The landscape is flat, the earth grudging; a sense of melancholy pervades these barren wastes, yet they inspire one to flights of imagination. **Plozévet** boasts the church of Saint Démet, built over a spring which wells up on either side of the south porch. Its 15th-century doorway, with ogival vault, is decorated with empty niches and slender columns, creating a honeycomb effect. In the old cemetery stands a simple but moving memorial. It depicts a man of

humble origins beside a menhir: an inhabitant of Plozévet who lost his four sons and two sons-in-law in the Great War of 1914-18. The **chapel of Notre-Dame de Penhors**, with its central bell-tower, is another local curiosity.

In the village of Plovan, where the attractive calvary forms a roundabout for traffic, the figure of the Virgin Mary seems to be wearing a Breton head covering. One km (0.6 mi) away are the ruins of the charming **Chapelle de Languidou,** dating from the 13th century. The magnificent rose window in the Flamboyant Gothic style still survives. Some believe that this was the birth place of the Pont-Croix school of sculpture, of Anglo-Norman inspiration, which in the 13th century influenced the whole of the lower Cornouaille.

From an austere landscape of dunes, hedges and fallow fields now emerges one of the oldest and most impressive of Breton calvaries, that of the **chapel of Notre-Dame de Tronoën,** built between 1450 and 1470. The chapel is one of the

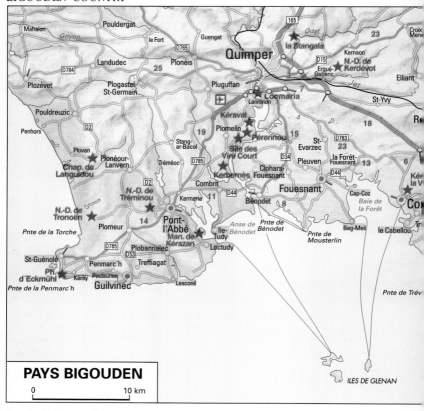

PAYS BIGOUDEN

0 ——————— 10 km

ILES DE GLENAN

few in Brittany with stone vaulting. The Breton writer, Yves Le Gallo, has described the calvary in poetic terms: *Powerful emotions emanate from this tall mass of raw stone, firmly anchored in the flat grassland of the heath, so unexpectedly does it fill the surrounding solitude with its silent throng. Crowded together more closely than in the windows of a cathedral: the Virgin, the Wise Men, Mary Magdalene and Pilate, St John and Christ himself. Frozen in ritual gesture, they mime different episodes of the long liturgical drama, with no one for an audience but the Spirit of God, hovering over the waters... At dusk, with its three decks facing toward the ocean, this remarkable calvary resembles Noah's Ark left high and dry by the retreating waters.*

Southwards along the D57, there is a fine view to be enjoyed from the headland of la Torche, before coming to the port of **Saint-Guénolé** with its **Musée de la Préhistoire.** A little further on stands the powerful **lighthouse of Eckmühl,** 65 m (213 ft) in height. It is named after a village in Bavaria, in gratitude for a bequest made by the daughter of Marshal Davout, Prince of Eckmühl. For those prepared to climb the 307 steps to the top, there is a magnificent view of the Penmarc'h peninsula, the Glénan archipelago and Île de Sein. **Penmarc'h** (via the D53) is a translation of the old designation Cap Caval or "horse's head," recal-

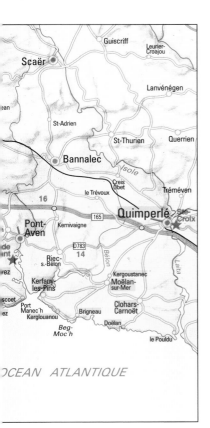

ling the sacred horse of the Celts. In medieval times, the name Penmarc'h was applied to the whole coast, but has gradually become limited to its south-west extremity and the village itself.

Until the 17th century, Penmarc'h was a busy, prosperous town, thriving on cod and hake fishing and on trade with Spain, Bordeaux and England. Decline set in when the coastal cod fisheries failed, violent storms decimated the fishing fleet and, during the Wars of Religion in 1596, La Fontenelle sacked and ravaged the area.

Little remains of the town's former glories, except the **Eglise Saint-Nonna,** a fine church in the Flamboyant Gothic style, built with contributions from the rich ship-owners of the parish. In honour of these benefactors, fish, fishing craft and larger vessels were sculpted on the towers.

Near the bustling little port of **Guilvinec** are a number of megalithic sites, including a covered way at Poulguen and a menhir at Kerscaven. **Loctudy** boasts the best-preserved Romanesque church in Brittany (12th century), despite the fact that its facade and bell tower were re-modeled in 1760. The east end consists of a choir with domed vault, ambulatory and apsidal chapels, while the capitals and bases of columns are heavily ornamented with animals and human figures carved in the granite.

From the harbor, there is a splendid view of the Pont-l'Abbé estuary and over to the Île Tudy, a narrow tongue of land with a cluster of old fisherman's cottages. Leaving the harbor and taking the D2 towards Pont l'Abbé, one passes a strange cross of Celtic type close to the chapel of Croaziou. A little further on is the 18th-century **Château de Kérazan,** which houses a fine collection of 19th-century paintings.

Pont l'Abbé is the chief town of the Bigouden country. It takes its name from a bridge said to have been built by the abbots of Loctudy. The **château** houses the local administrative offices and also the **Musée Bigouden,** which illustrates the history of the area, its peasant and seafaring traditions, and the way people dressed. For those interested in buying fabrics, lace or a real fisherman's cabin, *Le Minor,* at 3 quai Saint-Laurent, is able to satisfy all requirements.

Another place of interest is the **church of Notre-Dame-des-Carmes** (14th-15th centuries), which has beautiful rose windows. On the way out of the town stands the **chapel of Notre-Dame-de-Tréminou,** which witnessed the revolt of the *bonnets rouges.* Here, in 1675, peasants from fourteen parishes who had risen up against royal authority proclaimed the

fourteen articles of the *code paysan*, demanding an easing of taxes and the abrogation of aristocratic privileges. The insurrection was brutally repressed and, by order of Louis XIV, the bell towers of the rebel parishes were razed to the ground.

THE COUNTRY AROUND FOUESNANT AND PONT-AVEN

The south coast of Finistère, with its mild – almost Mediterranean – climate, superb beaches and sailing harbors, is deservedly popular with holiday makers.

Fouesnant Area

Lying between the River Odet, the Bay of Bénodet and the Baie de la Forêt, the **Fouesnant area** is a haven of peace and prosperity. The country abounds in apple

Above: The Bigouden headdress, a stylish folk tradition. Right: The easy-going nature of the Fouesnantais, a touch of the Mediterranean.

orchards, which produce an excellent cider, woods and green pastures. Its coast consists of fine sandy beaches to attract the summer visitor. There could be no greater contrast with the Cape Sizun area or the Pagan country, where man seems constantly pitted against a harsh natural environment. Not surprisingly, the character of the Fouesnantais is more jovial and relaxed, more in tune with the pleasures of life. Flaubert, when visiting the area, remarked on the beauty of the local women. They have long been known for their coquettish headdresses, decorated with ribbons and delicate lace, and their fetching costumes, set off with red and gold. The men, for their part, have never shown much inclination for the religious life. From 1803 to 1964, only five men from this locality were ordained as priests; a poor showing when compared with Pont-Croix, which gave 233 of its sons to the Church.

Tourism has played an important role in the economic life of the area since the 19th century. The town of **Fouesnant** has

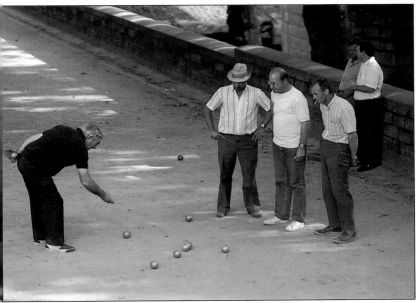

also developed major food-processing industries and is famous for its cider, which can be tasted and purchased at the *Caveau de M. Blin,* 15 rue Parc-Lann.

The pride of Fouesnant is the **church of Saint-Pierre.** Though remodeled in the 18th century, it remains a jewel of Romanesque architecture. Features worthy of note are its characteristic double-angled roof flanked by lower roofs on either side, a double-decker calvary, the hull-shaped roof of the sacristy and, inside, a magnificent five-arched nave with wooden panelling.

From the D44, a number of minor roads lined with oaks and chestnut trees lead to manor houses and chapels, fishing harbors and yachting resorts. To enjoy the full flavor of the area, it is worth walking the coastal path which runs from Cape Coz to the Roche-Percée. There are fine views over the Baie de la Forêt to Concarneau and the headland of Trévignon.

Beg-Meil, so named for a windmill which once stood on the site of the pre-sent signal-station, is a well-known seaside resort. Such famous personalities as the writer Marcel Proust and the actress Sarah Bernhardt spent holidays here. There are pleasant walks to the headland of Mousterlin, with a fine view of the Glénan archipelago, and the 17th-century chapel of Notre-Dame-des-Neiges.

Between the Mousterlin and Bénodet headlands is an interesting geological curiosity, the *Mer Blanche* or White Sea: a huge lagoon separated from the open sea by a 4 km (2.5 mi) bar of sand.

Bénodet is a prestigious holiday resort, the Breton name indicating its position at the mouth of the river Odet. The poet Guillaume Apollinaire spoke warmly of its charm: *Benodet makes one think of the Côte d'Azur; for here you have the same climate, the fig-trees, the clear skies.* Take time to stroll along the corniche overlooking the estuary, before exploring the port and the many rocky inlets on its right bank. Several buildings in the surrounding area are worth a detour. The chapel of Drennac stands not far from

155

one of the finest sacred springs in Brittany, where there is a granite *Pietà* dominated by a cross. Also in the vicinity are the church of Clohars-Fouesnant, the Château of Cheffontaines, and the chapel of Saint-Thomas, built in 1674 in memory of the martyred Thomas à Beckett, archbishop of Canterbury.

The **Glénan archipelago,** known mainly for its nautical center and sailing school, consists of a dozen or so islands. The islands consist mainly of low-lying sand-dunes, and beaches dotted with the abandoned hulks of fishing boats. From the high point of the Île Saint-Nicolas, there is a good view of the enclosed area of sea – known as the Chambre – and of the coast, from Penmarc'h to le Pouldu.

Concarneau

Concarneau, reached by the D783, occupies a sheltered position in its own

Above: A yacht at Bénodet. Right: The ramparts of old Concarneau.

156

bay. The Breton *Konk-Kerné,* or "inlet of Cornouaille", is derived from the Latin concha, meaning seashell and, by extension, inlet or bay. Concarneau is France's third fishing port, and lands the largest catches of tuna, with 1600 m (nearly one mile) of docks and a market area of 14,000 square metres (three-and-a-half acres). Fishing and related activities (boat-building, fish wholesaling, canning, etc.) provide the livelihood and prosperity of the town. These modern activities co-exist harmoniously with the old town, or **Ville Close,** with its circle of **ramparts** and network of narrow streets, which bear witness to the town's eventful history. It stands on an island, where, in the days when Christianity was being introduced into Brittany, the abbots of Landévennec founded a priory. Fortifications were erected in the 13th and 14th centuries, rebuilt in the years 1451 to 1477, and finally repaired and completed by Vauban in the 17th. The port was long considered an important strongpoint in the defense of the realm, and withstood many sieges. In recognition of this, its coat-of-arms, three axes on a background of ermine, symbolises a barrier preventing enemies from entering Britanny.

On entering the harbor, one comes face to face with the 380 m (416 yd) of ramparts defending the island. Nowadays the only sentry is the slate-roofed belfry with its sundial. The Ville Close lies within an inner circle of walls, and is distinctly medieval in character. Its main artery, the **rue Vauban,** is of considerable interest. The **Musée de la Pêche** houses models of boats and maps showing the areas of the world where different types of fish are caught. The former chapel of the Hôpital de la Trinité has a remarkable façade, and there is a fine fountain in the place Saint-Guénolé. Finally, a walk on the ramparts gives good views of the inner and outer harbors, the village of Lanriec and its charming 16th-century church, and the beach at Cabellou, a very pleasant sea-

side resort. To sense the real atmosphere of the place, visit the nightly fish auction, the market, and – in August – the *Fête des Filets Bleus,* one of the most popular festivals in Brittany (the blue nets are used for sardine fishing). Locally-made fish preserves, obtainable at the *Etablissements Courtin,* 3 rue du Moros (by the harbor), make a tasty souvenir.

In the vicinity, it is possible to visit the unusual **Château de Kériolet –** a 19th-century Neo-gothic fantasy built by a Russian princess on the ruins of an old manor house. It was inspired by Breton buildings such as the Château de Rustéphan at Nizon. One former inhabitant was the Russian Prince Yusupov, who assinated Rasputin.

Pont-Aven

Sited on the banks of the River Aven, **Pont-Aven** (reached by the D783) is the sort of place one falls in love with at first sight. It is hardly surprising that, with its mild climate and ideal light conditions, it became a favorite haunt of painters, notably Gauguin. An earlier visitor, writing around 1794, gave this enthusiatic description of the scene. Quite likely, this was the same landscape the artists discovered a century later: *This little port is the most capricious place you can imagine, if I may use an Italian expression. It is built over water, on rocks, at the foot of two high cliffs, whose flanks are strewn with enormous rounded blocks of granite – which seem about to break away at any moment ... Mills located on the banks use these huge stones to support the axles of their water wheels.* So rustic a setting was bound to attract Gauguin, who wanted to get away from city life and settle in an unspoilt natural environment. Painter colleagues and friends such as Paul Sérusier, Emile Bernard and Maurice Denis were also drawn to this spot. To quote Gauguin: *When my clogs strike the granite underfoot, I hear the earthy, unpolished, robust sound I am seeking to capture in my painting.* Local scenes and social life also provided a fertile source

of inspiration for Gauguin. At Pont-Aven, he broke free of the prevailing trend in contemporary painting – Impressionism – and discovered a new form of expression, which became known as symbolism.

The **Pont-Aven museum** stages temporary exhibitions relating to Gauguin and his friends, and tells the story of the Pont-Aven school of painting. Strolling through the streets, one passes the small hotel run by Marie-Jeanne Gloanec, where the painter lodged, then, following the river bank one comes across several mills – still standing – as if to illustrate the old saying: *Pont-Aven needs no telling; fourteen mills and fifteen dwellings.*

A walk to the Bois d'Amour and the heights above the town, brings one to the chapel of Trémalo. Inside, a 17th-century figure of Christ carved in wood is supposed to have provided the model for Gauguin's *Christ Jaune.* The celebrated

galettes de Pont-Aven (a kind of biscuit) can be bought at the *Biscuiterie Traou Mad.*

Two and a half km (1.5 mi) out of town, the small 15th-century church at Nizon has some superb primitive statues. The calvary was used by Gauguin as a model for his *Christ Vert* or *Calvaire breton* of 1889.

South of Nizon stand the romantic ruins of the Château de Rustéphan.

Aven Area

There are some delightful excursions to be made in the vicinity of Pont-Aven. To the north-west, the village of **Melgven** boasts no less than four chapels. The most remarkable is the Chapelle de la Trinité, whose granite doorway is carved with garlands of thistle and vine leaves. To the south-west is **Névez,** which also has its chapel. From here, there is a fine view of the Château de Hénan, a fortress built in the 15th and 16th centuries against raiding parties. A little further on

Above: Bridge over the river at Pont-Aven.

s **Kérascoët**, a hamlet of restored Breton cottages with thatched roofs. A magnificent coast road runs from Raguénès-Plage to the headland at Trévignon.

On the opposite bank of the Bélon estuary one will find the holiday resort of **Kerfany-les-Pins,** still in mourning for its parasol pines, which were blown down in the 1987 storm. The Bélon estuary and its chief town, **Riec-sur-Bélon**, are famous for their numerous oyster beds. The local oysters have been highly prized since classical times. The shore can be reached from Lanriot or via the right bank, on which lies the charming little port of Bélon. From here, a 9 km (5.5 mi) coastal path leads back to Pont-Aven. Five km (3 mi) to the west of Riec-sur-Bélon, from the harbor at Rosbras, there are fine views of the wooded banks of the river.

The coastline between the Aven and Laïta estuaries is a constant delight. Following the twisting roads, one comes upon tiny harbors, with fleets of fishing boats or pleasure craft.These little waterside villages, tucked away in sheltered creeks and estuaries, enjoy a blissful tranquillity. A good example is **Brigneau**, whose fine stone houses have traditional thatched roofs. From here, there are various excursions to be made on foot. One can follow the right bank of the estuary, via Beg Moc'h, to Kerglouanou, or walk east and follow the Port-Merrien inlet inland. Be sure to visit this charming little port, which is concealed in a bend in the river, surrounded by 60 hectares (150 acres) of woodland and heath.

At **Moëlan-sur-Mer**, it is worth visiting the graceful Renaissance chapel of Saints Roch and Philibert, dating from the 16th century, with its calvary and fountain. Near the village are many megalithic remains, including an 18 m (59 ft) covered way and a line of menhirs at the hamlet of Kergoustanec.

After visiting the fishing-village of Doëlan and crossing the Clohars-Car-noët, home territory of the great painter Tal-Coat (1905-1985), one arrives at the village **Le Pouldu**, at the mouth of the Laïta estuary. An attractive seaside resort, Le Pouldu was a meeting-place for the painters of the Pont-Aven school. It is possible to visit the Marie-Henry boarding house, where the artists stayed: they painted its walls and ceilings, and even its windows.

The old town of **Quimperlé** stands at the confluence of the rivers Isole and Ellé, which together form the Laïta estuary. When the novelist Flaubert discovered it, he wrote that it was one of the greatest strokes of fortune on his trip, adding: *It seems that Quimperlé only exists to be painted in watercolours."*

The town is indeed a place of poetry and character, with old streets of quaint houses, set in a gently undulating landscape.

Built on the steep sides of the valley, Quimperlé consists of an upper town dominated by the church of Notre-Dame (13th to 15th centuries) and a lower town arranged around the ancient abbey. There are some fine old timber-framed houses, especially in the rue Brémond d'Ars, which also includes the double balustraded staircase of the Présidial, while the rue Dom-Morice is the setting for the **Maison des Arche**rs, housing a museum of Breton traditions.

The glory of Quimperlé is nevertheless **the church of Saint-Croi**x, on which work was begun as far back as 1083. In those days, Western Europe still had its eyes set on Jerusalem, and many undertook the pilgrimage to the Holy Land. It was common to build copies of the Church of the Holy Sepulchre, with its characteristic circular plan. Such was the inspiration for Saint-Croix, the only Romanesque church of its type in Brittany, apart from Lanleff (Côtes d'Armor). The capitals of the columns in the crypt, like those of Landévennec, are carved with typically Celtic motifs.

Tourist Information
Information about the region: **Comité départemental du Tourisme du Finistère**, 11, rue Théodore-le-Hars, BP 125, 29104 Quimper cedex, Tel: 98-530900.

AUDIERNE
Tourist Information
Office de Tourisme, place de la Liberté, Tel: 98-701220.

PARC REG. D'ARMORIQUE
Tourist Information
Informations and access to the nature reserve, Maison du Parc, Ménez-Meur Hanvec, 29224 Daoulas, Tel: 98-219069.

ÎLE DE BATZ
Ferry Connections
Ferries to the island, Tel: 98-617698 or 98-617775.

BENODET
Tourist Information
Office de Tourisme, 51, avenue de la Plage, Tel: 98-570014.

BREST
Accommodation
MODERATE: **Les Ajoncs d'Or**, 1, rue Amiral-Nicol, Tel: 98-451242. *BUDGET:* **Le Régent**, 22, rue Algésiras, Tel: 98-442977.
Museums / Sightseeing
Musée des Beaux-Arts, 22, rue Traverse, Tel: 98-446627. **Château**, Tel: 98-221239. **Tour de la Motte-Tanguy** and **Musée du Vieux Brest**, Tel: 98-450531. **Océanopolis**, port de plaisance du Moulin Blanc, Tel: 98-344040.
Tourist Information
Office de Tourisme, 8, avenue Clémenceau, Tel: 98-442496.

CARHAIX-PLOUGER
Tourist Information / Religious Festival
Office de Tourisme, Tel: 98-930442.
Fête folklorique du Pardon de Sainte-Anne, religious festival on July 26, Tel: 98-931335.

CHÂTEAULIN
Tourist Information
Office de Tourisme, quai Cosmo, Tel: 98-860211 in summer, otherwise Tel: 98-860111.

CHÂTEAUNEUF-DU-FAOU
Festival
Festival des Danses et Traditions populaires, August 10-15, Tel: 98-818010.

COMMANA
Museum / Sightseeing
Moulin de Kérouat, windmill with **Écomusée des monts d'Arrée**, Tel: 98-688776.

CONCARNEAU
Accommodation
LUXURY: **Relais Belle Étoile**, Le Cabellou

Plage, Tel: 98-970573. *MODERATE:* **Océan**, Plage des Sables Blancs, Tel: 98-505350.
BUDGET: **Les Sables Blancs**, plage des Sables Blancs, Tel: 98-970139.
Museum / Castle
Musée de la Pêche, fishing, Tel: 98-971020.
Château de Kériolet, open June–September.
Tourist Information / Festival
Office de Tourisme, quai d'Aiguillon, Tel: 98-970144. *Festival international de Folklore*, July 31–August 5, Tel: 98-503885. *Fête des Filets bleus*, August 15–18.

CROZON-MORGAT
Accommodation
BUDGET: **Hostellerie de la Mer**, le Fret, Tel: 98-276165.
Tourist Information
Office de Tourisme, Toul an Trez, boulevard de la plage, Tel: 98-270792.

DAOULAS
Sightseeing
Abbey and **Centre culturel**, Tel: 98-258439.

DOUARNENEZ
Accommodation
MODERATE: **Clos de la Vallombreuse**, 7, rue d'Estienne-d'Orves, Tel: 98-926364.
BUDGET: **Bretagne**, 23, rue Duguay-Trouin, Tel: 98-923044.
Tourist Information / Museum / Festival
Office de Tourisme, 2, rue du Dr.-Mével, Tel: 98-921335. **Musée du Bateau**, Tel: 98-926520.
Festival des Minorités, end of August.

LE FOLGOËT
Religious Festival
Grand Pardon de Notre-Dame, in September.

FOUESNANT
Accommodation
LUXURY: **Manoir du Stang**, La Forêt-Fouesnant, Tel: 98-569737.
BUDGET: **Armorique**, 33, rue de Cornouaille, Tel: 98-560019.
Tourist Information / Religious Festival
Office de Tourisme, 5, rue d'Armor, Tel: 98-560093. *Pardon de Sainte-Anne*, Sunday following July 26.

GLENAN ARCHIPELAGO
Ferry Connections
From Concarneau, Tel: 98-970144, from Quimper, Bénodet and Loctudy, Tel: 98-949794.

HUELGOAT
Tourist Information
Office de Tourisme, rue des Cendres, Tel: 98-997232 in summer, otherwise Tel: 98-997155.

CHÂTEAU DE KERJEAN
Tourist Information
Informations in the castle, Tel: 98-699369.

LANDERNEAU
Accommodation
MODERATE: **Le Clos du Pontic**, rue du Pontic, Tel: 98-215091.
Festival
Festival celtique Kann al Loar, July 10–14, Tel: 98-216150.

LESNEVEN
Tourist Information / Museum
Office de Tourisme and **Musée du Léon**, 14, place du Général-Le-Flô, Tel: 98-830147.

LOCRONAN
Tourist Information / Festival
Office de Tourisme, place de la Mairie, Tel: 98-917014 in summer, otherwise Tel: 98-917005.
Petite Troménie, July 14.

MONTAGNES NOIRES
Sightseeing
Château and **Parc du Domaine de Trévarez**, 29520 Saint-Goazec, Tel: 98-268279.

MORLAIX
Tourist Information / Museum
Office de Tourisme, place des Otages, Tel: 98-621494. **Musée de Morlaix**, Tel: 98-886888.

ÎLE D'OUESSANT
Ferry Connections
From Brest, Tel: 98-802468 or 98-488013.

CHÂTEAU DE PERENNOU
Tourist Information
Information in the castle, Tel: 98-942272.

PLEYBEN
Tourist Information
Office de Tourisme, Tel: 98-266811.

PLOUGASTEL-DAOULAS
Tourist Information
Office de Tourisme, place du Calvaire, Tel: 98-042629.

PLOZEVET
Festival
Festival de Folklore, in July, Tel: 98-914433.

PONT-AVEN
Tourist Information / Festival
Office de Tourisme, 5, place de l'Hôtel-de-Ville, Tel: 98-060470. *Fête des Fleurs d'Ajoncs*, folklore festival with costumes and dancing.

PONT-CROIX
Tourist Information
Office de Tourisme, Tel: 98-704038 in summer, otherwise Tel: 98-704066.

PONT-L'ABBE
Accommodation
BUDGET: **Tour d'Auvergne**, 22, place Gambetta, Tel: 98-870047.
Tourist Information / Museum
Office de Tourisme and **Musée du Pays Bigouden**, in the castle, Tel: 98-872444.

LE POULDU
Accommodation
MODERATE: **Armen**, route du Port, Tel: 98-399044.

QUIMPER
Accommodation
MODERATE: **Le Gradlon**, 30, rue de Brest, Tel: 98-950439. *BUDGET:* **Tour d'Auvergne**, rue des Reguaires, Tel: 98-950870.
Tourist Information / Festival
Office de Tourisme, rue de la Déesse, Tel: 98-950469. *Festival de Cornouaille*, 4th week in July, Tel: 98-555353.
Museums
Musée départemental breton, rue du Roi-Gradlon, Tel: 98-952160. **Musée des Beaux-Arts**, 40, place Saint-Corentin, Tel: 98-954520.

QUIMPERLÉ
Accommodation
MODERATE: **Ermitage**, Manoir de Kerroch, route du Pouldu, Tel: 98-960466.
Tourist Information / Museum
Office de Tourisme, Pont du Bourgneuf, Tel: 98-960432. **Maison des Archers**, 5, rue Dom-Morice, Tel: 98-960432.

ROSCOFF
Accommodation
MODERATE: **Brittany**, boulevard Sainte-Barbe, Tel: 98-697078.
Tourist Information
Office de Tourisme, chapelle Sainte-Anne, rue Gambetta, Tel: 98-697070.

SAINT-GUENOLE-PENMARC'H
Accommodation
BUDGET: **Les Ondines**, Plage de la Joie, Tel: 98-587495.
Museum / Sightseeing
Musée Préhistorique, Tel: 98-586117. **Phare d'Eckmuhl**, lighthouse, Tel: 98-586117.

ÎLE DE SEIN
Tourist Information / Ferry Connections
Office de Tourisme de Sein, town hall, Tel: 98-709035. **Ferry connections** from Audierne, Tel: 98-700237 or 98-700237.

CAP SIZUN
Nature Reserve / Religious Festival
Réserve ornithologique du Cap Sizun, bird reserve, Maison de la réserve, Kerizit Vihan, 29770 Goulien, Tel: 98-701353. *Pardon de Loïc Ildut*, religious festival end of July, in Sizun.

CHÂTEAU DU TAUREAU
Tourist Information / Castle
Informations in the castle, Tel: 98-670030.

CHÂTEAU DE TREMAZAN
Tourist Information
In the town hall of **Landunvez**, Tel: 98-899102.

MORBIHAN

CORNOUAILLE AND POURLET
PONTIVY
FROM LORIENT TO QUIBERON
OFF-SHORE ISLANDS
CARNAC AND THE LAND OF
MEGALITHS

The estuary south of Vannes must have had something special about it to have given its name to a whole *département.* And the Morbihan has plenty to commend it, not least its coast-line, wide open to the Atlantic: the *Mor Braz* or great sea, with its endless sandy beaches fringed with low dunes. A friendly climate, smiling sea and hospitable shores, which, from Le Pouldu to the Vilaine, are are practically free from dangerous cliffs and rocks – all these have made it one of Brittany's tourist playgrounds, attractive to sailor and sunbather alike. Then, in the background, there is the aura of mystery surrounding its amazing menhirs, dolmens, cromlechs and cairns. There is also much of interest in its ports – Lorient, Auray and Vannes – and a string of sleepy islands: Groix, Hoëdic, Houat and Belle-Île, which though close to the coast, still have something exotic about them. Such is the spell of this coast that one easily forgets the Argoat country further inland. Le Faouët, Kernascléden and Josselin are on the tourist map. But who is familiar with the heath country of Lanvaux, the Rohan plateau, the Blavet valley, the Porhoët region, and the Montagnes Noires?

Preceding pages: The Atlantic on a calm day. Left: The manor of Beg-er-Lan.

CORNOUAILLE AND THE POURLET COUNTRY

Forests to the north, forests to the south, and in between them a countryside of small fields and copses. There is no cause for boredom: a shifting pattern of valleys, trout streams and small villages lends variety to the north-west quarter of the *département.* And there is a staggering concentration of historic monuments. The humblest parish boasts its church, calvary, chapels and reputedly miraculous covered fountain. These take the form of vaulted niches capped with a pointed roof, touched with gold and silver by the lichens and overrun with weeds. The working of the granite and richness of the decoration reflect the generosity of the faithful, and some are of monumental proportions. The chapel or church will not be far away. Most were built between the 15th and 17th centuries. Standing in open country or dominating the village square, each has some special feature to commend it: skilled timberwork, a colonnaded porch, a highly wrought bell-tower, a fine reredos or rood-loft, at the very least some Romanesque capitals or an exquisitely sculpted holy-water stoup.

The Breton enthusiasm for sculpture is given full rein in the furniture and the

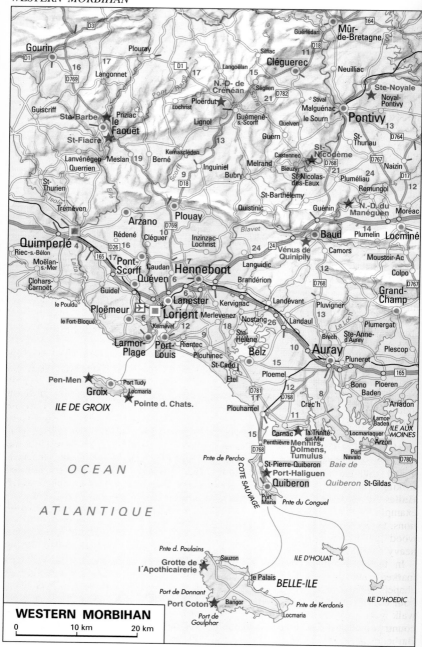

WESTERN MORBIHAN

0   10 km   20 km

painted statues of wood or stone, whose colours have now, alas, faded.; in the tracery and the friezes of dragons, ghouls and other fantastic creatures.

The more remote of these chapels, easy prey to thieves, stand locked and empty, slowly decaying. Moved by their plight, some have tried to come to their rescue. For instance, the *Breiz santel* association exists to revive old traditions, festivals and *pardons*, and to protect unlisted items of national heritage, from rural chapel to abandoned bread oven. It is a labor of Sisyphus: the life is draining out of the region, with countless houses for sale in the local villages – well-built granite dwellings, and some with their thatched roofs still intact.

Echoes of Cornouaille

The north-west corner of Morbihan is a little piece of the **Cornouaille** country, stolen from neighboring Finistère. This small area of the Black Mountains, barely 60 km (37 mi) long and 4 km (2.5 m) wide, has a reputation for extreme poverty, comparable with rural Ireland. So overwhelming has been the rural exodus that at Gourin, once a center of the slate industry, there is talk of founding a museum on the theme of emigration.

The D790 follows the river Ellé southwards to **Le Faouët**, a pearl of a town, set amid woods and valleys. Old houses decorated with carvings surround a most striking monument, the 16th-century **Halles**, or covered market, a perfect example its kind. Of gigantic proportions, the structure rests on long rows of wood and stone pillars, supporting a heavy slate roof.

In the surrounding country, a way-marked route takes in two picturesque chapels, **Saint-Fiacre** and **Sainte-Barbe**, both built in the late 16th century. The walk gives a true appreciation of the countryside. The first stop is Sainte-Barbe, its massive shape squatting on the wooded slopes of a ravine, 100m (300ft) above the river Ellé. The spot is reputed to attract lightening. This is understandable, since St Barbe is not only the patron saint of fireman, but also the mistress of fire from heaven. A spectacular stairway in the classical style leads to the church. Naveless, for lack of space, it is nevertheless surrounded by secondary buildings: the oratory of Saint-Michel, reached via a fine stone arch, and a pavilion in which hangs a bell. It is rung by pilgrims as a protection against storms. Saint-Fiacre, exquisitely decorated, is in a quite different style, of rare elegance despite its asymmetrical layout. Inside, the focal point is the rood screen, skilfully carved and colored with the brilliance of an illuminated manuscript. But the real masterpiece is the gabled bell-tower, elaborately sculpted, with a tall spire, its two arches holding the pinnacled turrets carrying the staircase.

Pourlet Area

Far more pretentious is the bell-tower of the **Chapelle de Kernascléden,** 15 km (9 mi) east along the D782. Too big, too fine, too triumphant for this insignificant village, the chapel has an almost arrogant air. The corbelled tower positively bristles with sculpted balustrades. Porches gabled and plain, a rose window and a host of pinnacles jostle with it in calculated disorder. The chapel is renowned for its 15th-century wall-paintings, which include a *danse macabre* worthy of Hiëronymous Bosch. The area also has some more modest chapels in store (reached via the D18 and the D3): The naive chapel of Saint-Yves in **Lignol**, whose disproportionate bell-tower balcony gives it the appearance of a pointed mushroom; **Notre-Dame de Crénénan,** with its rich furnishings and tree of Jesse in blue and gold; Saint-Barnabé in **Langoëla**n, topped by an openwork tower; and the squat Chapelle de Lochrist, hid-

den in woodland, with a lean-to farm building propped against its wall.

For fishing or sailing enthusiasts, there are some well-equipped stretches of water in the vicinity: the lac de Bel-Air at Priziac (via the D109) and the Étang du Dordu, between Langoëlan and Gué-méné. It is also possible to go canoeing on the River Scorff. Gastronomes will head for **Guéméné-sur-Scorff,** which, according to the signs outside pork-butchers' shops, has been producing *andouille* for generations past. These are some of the best chitterlings to be found, tightly rolled, smoked for three months, cooked for three hours If you want to taste this local delicacy, here are three addresses to remember:

L. Quidu, 12 place Loth
P. Saille, 26, rue Emile-Mazé
M.Guillemot, 2, rue Joseph-Pérès.

Above: The chapel of Sainte-Barbe, near Faouët. Right: Breton bagpiper, at Gourin.

PONTIVY AND THE BLAVET COUNTRY

Lower-lying but still rugged and deep-ly carved by streams and rivers such as the winding Blavet, the region around Pontivy is known as the plateau de Rohan. This is something of a misnomer, since the area is hardly a plateau, and Rohan, a pleasant center for boating, lies on its eastern fringe, beside the Nantes-Brest canal. But these former heathlands, now almost entirely brought under culti-vation, were once the estates of the Dukes of Rohan.

Pontivy and its Surrounding Area

Like Rennes, though for quite different reasons, **Pontivy** is a town with a double identity: The picturesque area around the château and church, the rue du Fil and the **place du Martray,** where the Tuesday market is held, are distinctly medieval in character; but as one descends the rue Nationale, the style becomes brutally ge-

ometrical, in the imperial style. The fact that you can see here a rectangular parade-gound, a hospital, barracks and a high school, the *Lycee Impérial,* is evidence that Napoleon wanted to install a garrison here, at the junction of the Nantes-Brest canal and the Blavet, in the heart of the traditionally rebel *Chouan* country. Pontivy was a convenient location for his purposes. The massive **Château des Rohan** still stands, built of reddish schist (the foliated clay stone typical of the region). It has a self-confident air, with its empty moats and thick walls, large towers and reassuringly sober square courtyard. Since the 1970s, it has been open to the public and is used to stage a variety of exhibitions.

North and south of Pontivy lies the **Blavet country**, which merges into the Baud region just short of the Lanvaux heathlands. Made navigable by Bonaparte, the Blavet descends to Lorient through a system of 28 locks; but northeastwards its course is blocked by the Guerlédan dam. South of the artificial lake thus created lies the **forest of Quénécan**, the mecca of environment-friendly tourism in the Côtes-d'Armor region. The alternating heath and woodland is a paradise for roe deer, mushroom gatherers and admirers of out-of-the-way chapels. And do not miss the magical cave of Argondia, haunt of dragons and horned devils, as depicted by the Czech painter Réon, who hangs his fantastic paintings on its walls.

West of Pontivy again, in the region of **Cléguerec, Seglien** and Silfiac, there is an abundance of chapels in the Flamboyant Gothic style, lost among the bracken, together with crosses, fountains, manor houses and aristocratic farms, surrounded by woodland and running waters. Megaliths are to be seen, for instance the covered ways of Saint-Nizon and Bot-er-Mohed, while Stival is renowned for the fountain of **Saint-Mériade**c.

At **Quelven**, the **tower of Notre-Dame** seems to have grown to the improbable height of 70 m (230 ft). Inside, there is a curious statue of the Virgin,

which opens out like a wardrobe to show scenes of the passion. The local religious festival is quite spectacular: the model of an angel (formerly a real child) is lowered from the tower, torch in hand, to light the bonfire.

A similar rite is practiced at the **chapel of Sainte-Noyale** (6 km or 4 mi northeast of Pontivy), which is famous for its fine Flamboyant Gothic architecture: its square, three-roofed tower, adorned with slender pinnacles, has a charming feel of *chinoiserie* about it. Hard by the chapel are an oratory, a sculpted cross and a fountain. On the opposite side of the village of Noyal-Pontivy, a pathway leads to the **Trois-Fontaines**, an elaborate complex of three fountains: Legend has it that, at this spot, Saint Noyale was decapitated by a petty tyrant whose advances she had scorned, and water sprang from the ground where three drops of her blood fell. At Noyal-Pontivy itself, the

church presents an enigma for scholars: do the *bas-reliefs* it contains refer to secret practices known only to alchemists? A final stop at **Notre-Dame-de-la-Houssaye** (2 km or 1.25 mi south of Pontivy), renowned for its white stone reredos crowded with a hundred or so figures, brings us back to the banks of the Blavet as it descends towards Baud, home of cabinet and clog-makers.

Blavet Valley

Despite their graceful fountains, Bieuzy and **Saint-Nicolas-des-Eaux** are counting on the waters of the Blavet to ensure their futures as centers of tourism: Here it is possible to enjoy water sports, take a trip in a launch, or visit the waterways museum or the leisure park. The amazing **chapel of Saint-Nicodème** is also worth going out of one's way to see. Set in open country, its steeple rises 46 m (151 ft) into the sky. Nearby are two fountains, one sculpted, with three apertures, for human drinking requirements;

Above: A vessel in dry dock at the naval shipyard, Lorient.

the other more simple, for the use of cattle. To the west is **Melrand** (by the D2), whose unusual calvary features the truncated heads of the twelve apostles. Nearby, on the archaeological site of a medieval village, life in the year 1000AD has been recreated, with a farm, peasant dwellings, vegetable garden and livestock. On the other side of the Blavet (via the D142) rise the slopes of **Mané-Guen** (the white mountain), where the fine church of **Notre-Dame-du-Mané-Guen** stands amid a pile of rocks, one of which – known as the sacrificial stone – bears the imprint of a human body.

Returning to the Blavet again, one comes to the site of **Castennac,** enclosed by a meander of the river, which was once a Gaulish settlement. From here, there is a good view of the **hermitage of Saint-Gildas**, overshadowed by an enormous mass of rock. Compared with the more uplifting sights in the vicinity, it has the austere, silent air of a deserted barn. At Castennac, centuries ago, was discovered a granite idol more than 2 m (6 ft) in height. The **Vénus de Quinpily** was finally set up on a grassy site near Baud, but the well-rounded buttocks of the fertility goddess gave rise to less-than-Christian practices, and the statue was first buried, then sunk in the depths of the Blavet. The Venus was finally rescued, in the 17th century, by the local squire, who out of modesty had the offending backside reduced in size. The origin of this Venus, which – according to Flaubert – was far too ugly to be of Roman workmanship, remains a mystery. Some scholars believe the affair to have been a 17th-century hoax.

FROM LORIENT TO QUIBERON

This stretch of the coast is distinguished by long beaches of white sand which are broken by deep and ever-changing estuaries, a gentle interpenetration of land and ocean.

Lorient and its Surrounding Area

Lorient has little in the way of architectural heritage. Its oldest buildings date from the 1930s, and the church of Saint-Louis, four-square and built of concrete, will come as a relief to those who have had an overdose of Gothic. The reason is that Lorient was entirely destroyed in 1944, and rebuilt in a hurry. Maybe its destiny is to be a town without a past. Certainly this was the case when, on Colbert's orders, it was first laid out on the flat coastal plain facing the estuary. On the opposite bank, Port-Blavet – renamed **Port-Louis** in honor of Louis XIII – had been trading with Africa and Madagascar for years past. The minister would have set up his famous Compagnie des Indes there, but the port was run by a veritable mafia, with low taverns, brothels, and shady business. So Colbert established his shipyard opposite.

The first vessel to be built there was named the *Soleil d'Orient*. Workmen were taken on for *L'Orient*, and the new town, initially a collection of work-site huts, was soon known by the same name. Sixty years later, it had grown to be a town of 14,000 inhabitants, and Port-Louis went back to tuna and sardine fishing. The only consolation is that today its fine 17th-century **citadel,** with **rampart**s overlooking the narrow entrance to the estuary, houses the **Compagnie des Indes museum**, as well as a maritime museum which will appeal to admirers of scale models.

Lorient has three roadsteads and four harbours (not counting the landing-stage for Groix and Port-Louis). After World War One, a huge modern fishing port was built in the Keroman estuary, where trawlers dock at dead of night and the fish is loaded on to trucks. Auctions take place at dawn, but unfortunately spectators are not admitted. The haunt of the fishermen is the bar *Chez Finette* (64 avenue de la Perrière), though you may prefer the musical atmosphere of a genuine Irish pub, the *Galway Inn* (18 rue de Belgique).

The second harbour is the Arsenal (naval dockyard) with its gigantic submarine base, while the third, Kergroise, is reserved for commercial traffic. Kernevel is a lively sailing marina, though unfortunately surrounded by ugly council housing. It includes a Maison de la Mer, designed by the architect J. Rougerie, its roof shaped like a sail, which is used for exhibitions on the life of the ports and fishing.

Upstream, the suburb of Lanester is so populous that it counts as Morbihan's third urban area. There is an air of nostalgia about it: Low tide reveals an old timber store on the Scorff where masts were once seasoned in the mud, while on the Blavet, located upstream of the Bonhomme bridge, the hulks of old two-masters are haunted by seagulls.

At the head of the estuary lies **Hennebont**, which stll has its its **ville close.** The few old houses which survived the war-time air raids (Grande-Rue, rue des Lombards and rue de la Paix) are protected by ramparts and the heavy pepper-pot towers of the Broërec gate. In the old town rises the miraculous and monumental porch and bell-tower of Notre-Dame-de-Paradis, 65 m (213 ft) high, soaring above a host of lesser pinnacles. The great park of the former monastery is now home to the national stud, which is open to visitors and offers riding facilities (tel. 97 65 16 34). Out of the town, the former ironworks at **Inzinzac-Lochrist,** which closed in 1966 after a hundred years, now house a **museum,** devoted partly to the history of iron working, partly to the River Blavet. Further north, towards Quistinic on the D159, stands **Poul Fétan,** a hamlet of traditional thatched cottages, which serve to illustrate a former way of life. It is un-doubtedly a touristic venture, but its promoters have avoided the excesses of an American-style development. It includes self-catering accommodation, crêperie and craft-shop.

From the beaches and naval base of Larmor-Plage as far as Guidel and the Laïta estuary, the coast road west of Lorient (the D152) winds its way through a succession of holiday resorts and fishing villages, passing sandy creeks and tiny harbors before reaching the 5 km (3 mi) long beach of **Fort-Bloqué.** At migration time, bird watchers will find plenty to observe at the **étang de Lannélec**. Binoculars are equally useful on 24 June, when a procession of boats comes out from Larmor to bless the Coureaux channel north of Groix.

East of Lorient, as far as Etel and then down to Quiberon, there is an almost un-interrupted succession of sandy beaches. The starting point is the Gâvres headland, at the end of a spit of land in places scarcely wider than the road (D158). It encloses the **Mer de Gâvres,** an inland sea at high-tide, mud-flats when the tide is out. Rich in shell-fish, it provides a winter sanctuary for ducks and Canada geese. Gâvres itself, standing on its cramped headland, has a magnificent seventeen-stepped fountain and, almost on the beach, a tumulus with decorated burial chamber. The dunes between Gâvres and Plouharnel are used by the army as a firing range. Parking of cars is not allowed and bathing permitted only on weekends. The *Conservatoire du Littoral* – a voluntary association which plays a vital role in preserving the coastline – is trying to buy the land in order to safeguard its threatened eco-system.

From Etel to Quiberon

Half way to Quiberon is the mouth of the **River Etel**. The estuary is a world apart, more isolated, wilder and more thrilling than others of its kind. There are

Right: Cleaning oysters is part of their job.

no charts of the river. They would serve no purpose. In this world of deceptive calm, it is impossible to tell exactly where mud bank ends and water meadow begins, and wildly swirling currents change the position of the channels with each tide. The perils of entering the estuary are notorious: the **bar** at the mouth of the river is responsible for many a shipwreck, despite the warning signals. From the hill of Saint-Symphorien to the north, there is a view over the whole estuary, and the road leading to Sainte-Hélène (D158) offers many fine points of vantage. But this little world is best appreciated from close quarters, from roads flooded at high tide, or from the estuary's tiny harbors: Three or four blue and white thatched cottages and a rough stone jetty, with a moored rowing boat dancing on the waves. Secret paths lead to oyster beds, past mud banks where gulls dabble and reeds where long-legged wader and heron wait in ambush.

Etel is a melancholy village not far from the narrow mouth of the estuary,

downstream from the suspension bridge. The fish market is closed, the port empty; the last trawlers have defected to Lorient; Yachtsmen find the tides too dangerous. Of the 150 proud tuna boats of pre-war days, the last hulks lie rotting in the surrounding coves. The villages have their fair share of chapels, including some very fine examples, cheek by jowl with Gaulish *stelae*, dolmens and menhirs. Undoubtedly, the jewel of the Etel river is **Saint-Cado**, attached to its own islet by a granite causeway. It has a Romanesque chapel haunted by the grumbling of the waves, and oysters and clams are on sale at the little harbor.

From Etel to Penthièvre, the coast is again an endless strip of sand edged by a narrow band of sand dunes and pine trees. It culminates in the **Quiberon peninsula,** virtually an island, connected to the mainland only by a fragile bridge of sand, so narrow in places that road and railway run shoulder to shoulder. The windward side of the peninsula is wild and lacerated by the fury of the elements,

while its lee is an oasis of calm, overlooking a magnificent sheltered stretch of water, which has ensured its success as a family holiday resort.

From Saint-Pierre-Quiberon to Port-Maria, on the leeward side of the peninsula, the beaches are packed. Inland, hedged fields struggle to survive against the encroachment of holiday homes. If Quiberon still has charm, albeit imperfect, it can still be found in the bright sunlight, the ebb and flow of the tides, the harsh cries of the gulls, and out in the bay the cheerful confusion of sails, of all colors and sizes.

Nothing can destroy the charm of the wild windward coast, with its broken, foam-flecked cliffs, ridges of sand set with black rocks worn smooth by the undertow, and dangerous, unpredictable swell, which sweeps all before it as it drives in from the off-shore plateau des Birvideaux. Out to sea, the location of this island-size reef, which lies some 10 m (33 ft) beneath the surface, is marked by a lighthouse. Legend has it that there was once a village on the spot, but the land on which it stood was swallowed up by the sea; every year on 23 November, the inhabitants return to the land of the living, dressed in red capes! At opposite ends of this wild coast, the headland of **Percho** and the **Beg er Goalennec** offer awesome views over the coast and offshore islands.

From Port-Maria on the western side of the peninsula, boats leave for Belle-Île, Houat and Hoëdic, from a quay that is encrusted with lichen, moss and sea-weed.

Facing the bay, Port-Haliguen was once just a small tidal harbor. Today, it accommodates more than a thousand yachts, and is turning custom away!

Between the two, the **Pointe du Conguel** juts out into the sea, famous for its views and many beaches, and also for the perennially popular sea water therapy founded by Louison Bobet.

Above: The shore at Port-Blanc, on the east coast of Belle-Île. Right: Quiberon harbor.

Other places of interest include the **national sailing school at Beg-Rohu;** the famous blow-hole in the cliff above Port-Maria, where the sea rushes in with a hellish din; and, near Plouharnel at the foot of the peninsula, a rather phoney replica of a galleon housing a collection of models made of shells (tel: 97523956).

OFF-SHORE ISLANDS

Millions of years ago, the Île de Groix, together with Quiberon, Hoëdic and Houat, was part of a long ridge of land running parallel with the mountains of Brittany. These are sister islands, while Belle-Île is a cousin, sole survivor of a land causeway which extended as far as the bay of Bourgneuf.

Île de Groix

The **Île de Groix**, island of witches, lies like a ship at anchor 3 nautical miles (5.5 km) off Lorient. The crossing takes almost an hour, whether one takes the ferry from Kerneval or Port-Louis. At Port-Tudy, the arrival of the *Jean-Pierre Calloch* is always something of an event. In the season, the ferry may make the trip up to eight times a day.

Port-Tudy is the symbol of the island's heyday, a prosperous period lasting from the mid 19th century until the last war. In those days, the biggest tuna-fishing fleet on the whole Breton coast was based here: tall, wide-beamed two-masters, bristling with poles and other tackle.

In the 1930s, there were more than 300 of them. The harbor had been created especially, in what was no more than a "miserable little bay". The Breton novelist, Henri Queffelec, wrote: *There were three docks, quays, breakwaters and slipways... The boats were crammed in, gunwale to gunwale... Oh, the wonderful confusion of mooring ropes, which crossed over each other, got tangled up in tillers and grappling-hooks, and plunged beneath the keels!* (From: *The Six Sailors of Groix*).

175

The tuna boats have disappeared, but in summer there is still a glorious chaos of pleasure boats in the little marina and in the anchorage of the outer harbor below the lifeboat station. A few trawlers still dock at the old port, and sometimes you can see the *Kenavo*, a small local cutter restored in traditional style, which takes enthusiasts for trips in the Courreaux channel. On the road leading up to the town is the **Groix eco-museum**, installed in the premises of a former cannery. It is worth visiting for in-depth information on Groix and the tuna fish. The port also boasts two cafés, a high-class restaurant, and tourist accommodation with a chip shop and terrace. A little further on is the picturesque *Ti Beudeff* inn (tel. 97 86 80 73), where Celtic atmosphere is guaranteed. For other needs, visitors have to climb the steep road to the town, between old two-story houses and newly built homes for fishermen.

Above: Gulls are seen everywhere on the coasts of Britanny.

The town is laid out in a star shape around its shady square, at the center of which, surrounded by a low wall, stands Saint-Tudy. Instead of a cockerel, the weather vane of the church is in the form of a tuna fish. At number 19, hidden away in a normal dwelling house, is the tiny but friendly crêperie of *Ti Ar Krampouz.*

It is possible to take cars over to Groix (having made an advance booking), or even hire one, but there is little point. The island – a plateau of schist 30 metres above sea level, with only slight undulations – is just 8 km long by 2 km wide. (Roughly 5 miles by one-and-a-quarter). And far more interesting than the few roads are its steep cliff-top paths, cutting through bramble and fern. For exploring the island, the best form of equipment is a bicycle, preferably a mountain bike. The interior is a patchwork of meadows and fields, broken up by heathland. The traditional strip cultivation has disappeared, unsuited to mechanical cultivation. There are no hedges and only a few copses. The hamlets consist of unpretentious houses with gray roofs and white gables. Apart from these, there is the odd fountain, a menhir at Clavezic, two dolmens at Kerard, and a lighthouse at either end of the island. In the west, Pen Men, austerely black and white dominates a bird sanctuary. In the east is the red and white Pointe les Chats, and an area of mineralogical interest. Groix is unique from a geological point of view, possessing such uncommon rocks as blue glauconite, green epidote and garnet.

Not far away, Grands Sables beach wraps its circumflex of sand around the La Croix headland. **Locmaria,** the second settlement of the island, can hardly be called a port, despite its jetty. A few dozen one-or two-story houses, rendered in white, pink or yellow-ocher, huddle together on a flat expanse of heathland. Often, in the hottest part of summer, only a few children are to be seen on the beach, and a couple of fishermen passing the time in the single café. Further round, the southern coast is rocky, its cliffs broken by miniature valleys carpeted with greenery. In the deepest of these inlets, Port-Saint-Nicolas, the occasional yacht may be seen riding out the tide in the intense green water. To the north, the inlet of Port-Melin has been transformed into a reservoir to supply the islanders with water. Port-Lay, a Tom Thumb harbor identifiable by the bright orange buoys of an anti-pollution boom (which presumably has to be kept somewhere), is home to a sailing school.

Houat and Hoëdic

South of Quiberon, beyond the rocks of the Teignouse and the Béniguet – much feared by sailors when a mist descends or the sea begins to get choppy – ie the **islands of Houat and Hoëdic**, wallowing in the Atlantic swell like a duck and its duckling. Splendid in their isolation, they have the charm of simplicity: stiff dry tracts of grass, dunes clothed in spiky quitch, thistles and marram grass, jumbled rocks interspersed with white sands. Houat, slightly the larger of the two, is almost 300 hectares (740 acres) in area (you can walk round it in a matter of hours). Hoëdic is lower (a mere 25 m or 82 ft at its highest point, as opposed to 30 m or 98 ft for Houat), and has only a quarter of its rival's population: 120 inhabitants in winter time. Each year, its school is threatened with closure.

For many years, the islands have lived under a strange regime, governed by a rector, who, as well as father confessor, acted as mayor, judge, gendarme, midwife for Hoëdic, café owner on Houat (*La Cantine*), and person responsible for lighthouses and buoys (he still fulfils this role on Hoëdic, and remains town clerk on Houat). The islands were accorded the status of *commune* a century ago, but Houat has remained quite archaic in its social organization. On the other hand, as the only island still seeking to live by fishing alone, it has had to adopt the very latest technology. Twenty years ago, to replenish its stocks of lobsters, the island set up a hatchery and research center, and is now turning its attention to the breeding of shellfish and phytoplankton. Its fleet, consisting of forty or so trawlers and lobster boats, has doubled in the last forty years, and has just taken delivery of a state-of-the-art catamaran, able to manage over a thousand shrimp and crab pots. Long ago, to supplement its single well, Houat installed a desalination plant, which makes it possible to tolerate, without too many complaints, the thousand or so visitors who camp around the magnificent **beach of Treacher-Goured** each summer. With 1.5 km (nearly a mile) of sands, this can hardly be described as overcrowding, but the *mairie* has sent the promoters packing, not wanting their new houses and yachting marina. The island wants to preserve its identity. Already, Saint-Gildas is saturated in summer, as is the diminutive

Port-Argol on Hoëdic. There is often friction between the fishermen, who are fiercely insular and suspicious, and owners of pleasure craft, who often behave as if the island belonged to them.

Houat boasts a grocer's, a baker's, a bar and, during the summer, two hotels, a restaurant and a crêperie; a handful of cars that are never seen; some houses rendered and freshly whitewashed, others empty, their walls bare and covered in moss; dry-stone walls, a few vegetable gardens, a church, an old port destroyed by storms, five menhirs, three dolmens, a tumulus, and an old fort built by Vauban in the center of the island, with a commanding view of the surrounding islets and reefs. All of these are accessible, as one explores the network of pathways – preferably in spring, when carnations and tamarisks are in flower and the heathland is carpeted with golden gorse and sweet-scented helichrysum.

Above: A delicious harvest of clams. Right: Every man to his boat.

Hoëdic is sandier, and the heathland is flatter. The village is less friendly-looking, more orderly, its houses all facing south, in rows of three or four. The camp site above the harbor is small but well organized; the old fort is used for sailing courses; and several houses are available as self-catering accommodation. There is an old-fashioned grocery and general store. which for many years was run by two old sisters, known to generations of yachtsmen. Again, a relaxed stroll is the order of the day, after trying the seafood at the *Hôtel des Cardinaux* or *Chez Jean-Paul,* or before having an aperitif at *La Trinquette,* opposite the church. The old port of la Croix, behind the lagoon, is well worth a visit. At low tide, it faces out over a vaste expanse of rock, covered in sea-weed and alive with winkles and barnacles. Sailing boats brave the tortuous channel to come and beach on the sand. At evening, the shores of the eastern end of the island are a good place to watch for the Grands Cardinaux lighthouse to begin beaming forth its warning.

Belle-Île

To the west of its diminutive cousins, Belle-Île is a continent by comparison: Hoëdic would fit forty times into the area between the headlands of **les Poulains** and Kerdonis, Le Palais and **Port-Goulphar!**

The island has passed through many hands. Its masters have included monks; pirates; and from time to time the English; it was once owned by Gondi, the banker of Charles IX, who loved the place; and by Fouquet, who wanted to make it the nerve center of his trading empire but fell into disgrace, partly because of the unauthorized defense works he was erecting; Louis XIV had Vauban remove the offending fortifications; and the Compagnie des Indes leased it as an entrepôt. But in its long history it has only grown in beauty.

Today, Belle-Île, so named for the fertility of its schist soils rather than for any picturesque qualities, is practically the only island south of Penmarc'h which still lives by agriculture. Even so, there remain no more than 200 farms, mostly engaged in breeding livestock. The potato, which Belle-Île prides itself on having discovered before Parmentier (thanks to its settlers in the New World), is now rarely cultivated. Inland, where few tourists venture (except perhaps to see the menhirs on Kerlédan heath or the village of Bangor), pasture land is reverting to wasteland.

Le Palais is more port than town. It is a thrilling experience to slip slowly past the walls of the **citadel** in a small boat, pass the jetties, then inch one's way through the needle's eye of a lock and tie up at the quay in the narrow confines of the inner harbor. Such pleasures are reserved strictly for winter sailors. In summer, there is all the chaos and disorder typical of crowded harbor approaches, periodically disturbed by the wash of the ferry arriving from Quiberon. In the main, the crowds disgorged by the ship confine their investigations to the town itself (which does not take long), the port

with its chicane-like gates, and the star-shaped ramparts of the fort. Those with good appetites find their way to the *Boulangerie du Port*, to feast on Breton pastries.

A more select company will push on to **Port-Coton** or the **grotte de l'Apothicairerie.** The first, its needles of black rock standing amid the foaming sea, shrouded by a curtain of spray as soon as a wind gets up, is said to have inspired 38 canvases by Monet. More recently, it must have accounted for thousands of miles of photographic film! The grotto, whose Breton name is *Groc'hen-Ver,* gets its nickname from the bird's nests which, in former times, clung in serried ranks beneath the vault, like jars at the chemist's. In those days, the cavern could be reached only by boat, and the birds' eggs were easy pickings. There is now a treacherous stairway for those wanting to get closer to the deafening roar of the surf.

Above: Fishermen repairing their nets at Audierne harbor.

These are the highlights of the southwest coast, its wild cliffs cut to shreds like the frayed edge of a wind-torn flag, though one should not forget the Pointe des Poulains, haunted by the ghost of Sarah Bernhardt. Here, the actress created a fantastic holiday kingdom around an abandoned fort. The complex was destroyed (fortunately, some would say) during the last war. The sunny beach of Port-Kérel; the wooded inlet of Port-Goulphar, whose little hotel, the *Castel Clara*, overlooked by the tall silhouette of the Grand Phare (lighthouse), has a reputation for good food; the beautiful but dangerous beach of **Port-Donnant;** the twin inlets of Ster-Wraz and Ster-Wen, though not deserted, are known only to those who actually holiday or camp on the island.

And there are plenty of places where you can get away from it all: the crumbling cliffs crowned with heather or thorny scrub, steep valleys concealing patches of woodland and, down by the sea, reed-beds, deep inlets, anarchic reefs, and no end of places called "Port Such-and-Such," but where no ship could make a landfall, since the Breton *porz* means cove and not harbor. All in all, the coastal path is more than 80 km (50 mi) in length, giving access to a bewildering variety of scenery.

Even in the height of summer, motor traffic is light. The island's roads, numerous enough to enable you to avoid the main thoroughfares, are ideal for cycling. On Belle-Île, the only really big beach is the **plage des Sables Blancs**, on the gentle, friendly north-east coast. But the most delightful spot on the whole island, a place that immediately wins one's heart, is **Sauzon,** *a charming little port backed by a wooded fiord.* The miracle is that Sauzon is still quite unspoilt. The inlet has something English about it, with its demure, pastel-colored houses, rather like the river ports of the Cornish coast. From the terrace of the *Hôtel du Phare,* which faces the breakwater in splendid isolation, one looks out onto neat white turrets capped with green and red roofs. Coasters and sailing boats are dotted around, the bigger craft anchored in the outer harbor, the small fry pulled up on the sands of the estuary. A shop selling nautical souvenirs displays engravings, water-colors, ships-in-a-bottle, and some superb models by J. Guillaume.

On the quay, amid mooring rings, ropes, nets, piles of lobster-pots and up-turned dinghies, there are almost always two or three stalls selling freshly-caught lobsters – furiously waving their claws – as well as sole and mackerel. But you will not find the famous *pouce-pied* (a sort of edible barnacle), surely a queen among crustaceans, generally unknown to the French because it lives only here on the *côte sauvage* and the catch is immediately exported to tickle the palate of Spanish gastronomes. In any case, they may only be harvested two months a year, in winter. And winter in the islands is something quite different.

CARNAC, LAND OF MEGALITHS

Between the Etel and Auray rivers, especially around Carnac, la Trinité and Locmariaquer, the map is literally black with menhirs, dolmens, tumuli and burial chambers. The islands of the Golfe du Morbihan also have their fair share. The gulf itself is an immense labyrinth of land and water, a complex pattern of islands, islets, peninsulas and mud banks, channels, creeks, coves, rivers, beaches, grasses swaying in the wind, marshland and the marker poles of oyster beds: the very soul of the Morbihan.

One stone laid on others is called a dolmen, whether horizontal or vertical. A number of standing stones roofed with a series of slabs is a fairy grotto. When the stones are arranged in an oval with no hat to cover them, you say: There's a cromlec'h. A peulvan, also called a menhir, is a marker stone of larger or smaller dimensions, standing alone in the middle of the countryside. What better guide to the land of megaliths than the writer Flaubert? Since he visited the area, little has changed, except perhaps that the ground around these ancient monuments has been much trodden down and the menhirs now have to be banked up. He describes the "alignements" at Carnac as: *Eleven rows of black stones, set at regular intervals, the stones diminishing in size the further they are from the sea.*

As to who erected them, when, how and – most difficult of all – why, all is conjecture. We can at least say that they were not the work of Druids or Celts. They would appear to date from the neolithic period, between 3500 and 1800 years before Christ, with some monuments built over even older ones. As for the means, we can but wonder. To drag on rollers the **Grand Menhir** which today lies fallen and broken at Locmariaquer would have taken, it is reckoned, the strength of 12,000 men and 125 yoke of oxen. It must be added that this menhir

is exceptional, standing 81 m (266 ft) high and weighing 350 tonnes. Why did they do it? There is no lack of theories: It was a military cemetery, a zodiac table, an astronomical observatory, and so on. Legend speaks of sinners turned to stone, armies stopped dead in their tracks, wanton girls or lewd monks punished for their misdemeanors. A more down-to-earth explanation is that the stones served as landmarks for sailors far out at sea.

The name **Carnac** means "piles of stones." And there are almost 3000 of them, without taking into account the **tumulus of Saint-Michel** and the **alignements du Ménec.** Locmariaquer, for its part, boasts the great *galgal* (tumulus) of **Mané-Lud,** the **Table des Marchands** (Merchants' Table), the dolmen of Mané-Rutual and **a covered way of flat stones.** The list of other megaliths is almost endless, including the **alignements de Kerzerho, the dolmen of Crucuno,** the

Champ des Pierres Bleues (Field of Blue Stones), la Quenouille et le Fuseau de Brigitte (Brigitte's Distaff and Spindle) at Locoal-Mendon, their strange forms standing amid the glassworts on the banks of the Etel, the dolmen of Penhap on the Île-aux-Moines, and its counterpart, the Gréavo dolmen, on the Île d'Arz. Visiting them each in turn is tiring work, despite the magnificent setting of pines and heath, and after one's archaeological investigations, the animation of the **Grand'plage de Carnac** or the beach of Kerpenhir at Locmariaquer comes as a welcome relief. Some may prefer the atmosphere of **La Trinité-sur-Mer,** once the port of Carnac, on the Crach estuary. Nowadays, it is full of ocean-going yachtsmen, the favorite harbour of the great catamarans and trimarans, which are not easy to accommodate elsewhere.

Gulf of Morbihan

Locmariaquer is the gateway to the **Gulf of Morbihan.** It is a tranquil place

Above: One of the famous lines of menhirs, in the vicinity of Carnac.

and the climate is almost Mediterranean. The vegetation includes pines, mimosas, camellias, tamarisks, eucalyptus, and even palms brought home from distant places. The **Île-aux-Moines** is proud of its figs and three olive trees. Violent storms are few and far between.

The water, though, has only an appearance of calm. Below the surface run turbulent tidal currents, tearing at the sandbanks, crossing, clashing, or devouring one another in swirling fury. To fill these 10,000 hectares (24,700 acres) of drowned valley – the result of fluvial erosion and subsidence – the ocean has to pass through an opening so narrow (less than a kilometer between Port-Navalo and the headland of Kerpenhir) that the gulf can fairly be described as "a sea in a bottle." The rising waters take a full two hours to reach Vannes, only 25 km (15.5 mi) away. In these circumstances, calculating the tides is no mean feat.

Twice a day, the metamorphosis takes place: Where, at high tide, the water licked at grass and houses, at low tide the islands are left high and dry on the slick gray-green of the mud-flats, and oyster catcher, sandpiper, redshank and silent heron feed amid flocks of gulls. At migration time, thousands of mallard, brent geese and shelduck invade the salt marshes. Several areas have been designated as **bird sanctuaries**. Dignified cormorants stretch out their wings to dry on the half-submerged stones of the cromlec'h of **Er Lanic**, proof that the water level has risen since prehistoric times.

Of the forty or so islands, half are marked on maps, some fifteen are inhabited, and all but two are privately owned: the communes of **Arz** and the **Île-aux-Moines**, respectively 3 and 6 km (1.8 and 3.7 mi) long. The Île d'Arz is harsher, but both are quite delightful. Like all the holiday resorts in the area, their populations multiply tenfold in summer. Even then, they are not really crowded, except perhaps on 15 August,

when the Île-aux-Moines regatta is held. **Gavrinis**, too, is served by a regular boat service, bringing visitors to see the finest of all dolmens, a barrow almost 10 m (33 ft) tall concealed beneath a great heap of pebbles, which constitutes the highest point of the gulf! There are few clues to the meaning of the serpentine reliefs which adorn the walls of its 14 m (46 ft) underground chamber, and the other carvings and inscriptions discovered in the environs are equally mysterious. A visit to the **museums of prehistory at Carnac and Vannes** simply underlines the extent of our ignorance.

One is allowed to land on the other islands in one's own boat, but not to go beyond the high-water mark. Avoiding the more popular beaches of Conleau, Arradon, Larmor-Baden or Noyalo, small (flat-bottomed!) craft are ideal for discovering, at leisure, the tiny deserted cove of one's dreams. However, it is wise to steer clear of strong currents, the routes taken by tourist launches, and especially oyster beds.

The reputation of **Auray** (reached by the D101 from Vannes), lying at the head of its narrow estuary, needs no reinforcing. Though its port is no longer very active, it maintains the atmosphere of a trim, sea-faring town. A quay is named for Benjamin Franklin, who in 1776 landed here on his way to negotiate a treaty with the French against the English during the American War of Independence. In the **Saint-Goustan quarter** across the ancient stone bridge are the fine old houses of the ship-owners and masters of bygone days.

It still has its charterhouse, the specter of Cadoudal (the royalist counter-revolutionary who plotted against Napoleon), and, nearby (via the D17), the church of **Sainte-Anne-d'Auray**, which has become the main place of pilgrimage of the peninsula, the Breton *pardon* par excellence. It all goes back to 1624, when the insistent apparition of a "white lady" in-

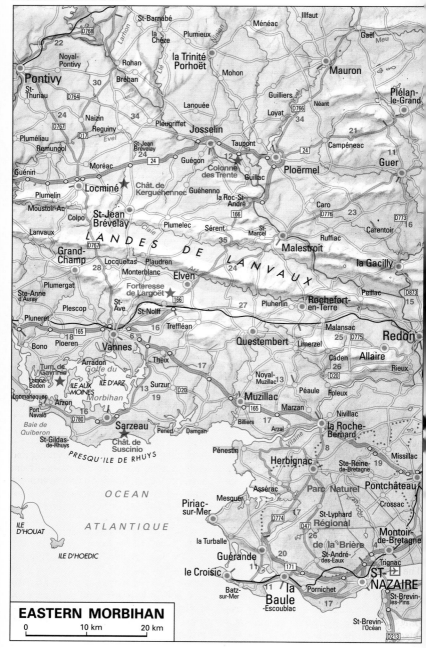

EASTERN MORBIHAN

0   10 km   20 km

structed a ploughman named Nicolazic (a house purporting to be his is open to the public) to build a chapel. On the designated spot, Nicolazic unearthed an ancient wooden statue. The clergy dated it – with great precision as it turned out – to the year 701, had it recarved in accordance with Christian criteria, then, in response to a wave of popular fervor, methodically organized pilgrimages of the strictest orthodoxy. The present **basilica** and *Scala Sancta* – which is to be climbed on one's knees – date from the 19th century and are not the most attractive monuments of their kind. The varied and moving collection of offerings, on the other hand, is worth a look.

Nine km (6 mi) to the north-west stands the **farm and inn of Réserdoué,** so renowned for its pancakes that it is wise to reserve a table (Tel: 97 24 45 19). Up the Auray river, there is an **ecological museum at Saint-Degan-en-Brech** (can be reached via the D19), a hamlet of perfectly restored thatched cottages, while downstream (via the D101) lies the charming port of **Le Bono**, where the fishermen have abandoned their old sailing boats and gone in for salmon-trout farming.

From the head of its estuary, **Vannes** lords it over the gulf. Historically, it was never the capital of the Veneti tribe, but came to prominence in the 9th or 10th century, when its chieftain, Nominoé became the first king of Britanny. It is a handsome town, justifiably proud of its corbelled and half-timbered houses, classical façades and churches. It takes particular pride in its **Cohue:** an ancient covered market and seat of the Parlement, which has been converted into a center for exhibitions and cultural events. The complex includes the **Musée des Beaux-Arts, du Golfe et de la Mer.** Vannes also likes to show off its charming wash-houses at the foot of the **ramparts**, its **towers** and gates: the machicolated Prison Gate, and the Poterne and Saint-Vincent Gates overlooking the harbor. Other glories include the dignified **Château de l'Hermine**, a striking 19th-century prefecture, gardens in the French style, and the shady, moss-covered quays of the Rabine, where nowadays only pleasure boats moor. Despite its sense of superiority, the town is open, lively and welcoming to visitors (though parking facilities are poor!).

The **Rhuys peninsula,** fringed with fine beaches on the Atlantic side, forms the southern shore of the gulf. **Sarzeau** (reached by the D780) draws large numbers of tourists, as does **Arzon**, a little further on. Here different ages meet: Near the village is an ancient covered way, but all is overshadowed by the ultra-modern marina and tourist development of Crouesty (via the D198), whose construction is nearing completion.

At **Saint-Gildas-de-Rhuys,** the church is all that remains of an ancient monastery, which, in its heyday, acquired an evil reputation. Peter Abelard was sent to restore order, but was unable to deal with the unruly monks – in fact, he was almost poisoned before beating a hasty retreat. As for the **Château de Suscinio,** hunting lodge of the Dukes of Brittany, the fact that the best of its dressed stones were auctioned off after the Revolution has merely reinforced its massive medieval austerity.

Finally, if you have a free evening and enjoy a good story, drive north-east from Vannes (via the D135) to the **fortress of Largoët**: In summer, its imposing medieval ruins provide the setting for a *son et lumière* entertainment on some legendary themes.

Porhoët and the Basse Vilaine

The Argoat country defies easy definition. The only guidelines are its rivers – the Blavet, Oust and Vilaine – and, to the south, the hilly barrier of Lanvaux heath (les Landes de Lanvaux).

Lanvaux Heath

Between Vannes and its hinterland and the Porhoët region, **Lanvaux heath** (flanked by the D1 and the D10) forms something of a frontier, a wall of hard schist which even the rivers have not been able to penetrate. But it could hardly be called a mountain range: it extends 60 km (37 mi), from Baud to Rochefort-en-Terre, is a mere 5 km (3 mi) wide, and the average altitude is only just over 100 m (328 ft). At 175 m (574 ft), its highest point is little greater than the plateau around Vannes. Nevertheless, those who live "on the other side" are still regarded as somewhat foreign.

At one time a real wasteland of gorse and scrubby bushes, the heath was colonized during the last century, cleared, reafforested, and cultivated as far as was possible. There are still more broom

Above: Ancient wash-houses and Tour des Connétables, Vannes.

thickets, menhirs and woods than villages. The forest of Lanvaux and the woods of Colpo, Treulan, Saint-Bily and Molac form an almost continuous belt, to delight the rambler in search of majestic trees and solitude (GR38 footpath). Provided they have no fear of thick undergrowth, lovers of megaliths can explore to their hearts' content, for there are standing stones in profusion concealed in the dense woodland. At least, there are no crowds around the dolmens of Coh-Coët or Roh-Koh-Koëd (near Saint-Jean Brévelay), under the "roof" of the Loge aux Loups (the Wolves' Lair), or at the feet of Babouin and Babouine (the Baboon and his Wife), two column-like stones.

Colpo is associated with Elisa Bocciochi, a cousin of Napoleon III, cold-shouldered by the Court, who retired to these estates and spent her time improving and organizing them. At **Larcuste**, two cairns of flat stones recently discovered and restored are of exceptional interest. From **Moustoir-Ac**, a waymarked itinerary akes in a dozen or so dolmens, menhirs and sacrificial stones. **Locminé** is notable for its unashamedly modern church. The 20th century has also broken in on the 18th-century **Château de Kerguéhennec,** where exhibitions of contemporary art are shown.

The **oak of Le Pouldu,** standing beside the road to Guéhenno, is thought to be nearly two thousand years old! The story of the **Guéhenno calvary,** the most elaborate to be found in the Morbihan, is one to warm the heart. It was torn down during the Revolution but, 60 years later, the parishioners gathered together the fragments and, although there were no sculptors among them, restored it with their own hands, replacing missing pieces as necessary. With the passage of time, the different parts have blended together.

Situated on the banks of the Nantes-Brest canal, where canoeists plough up and down, **Malestroit** is known as "the pearl of the west." Around its church and along the riverbanks is a profusion of old half-timbered houses, some of them decorated with satirical carvings: a pig threading a distaff, a rabbit playing the bagpipes, Malestroit himself beating his wife. Similar motifs can be found at Questembert, Josselin, Vannes, and even on the church at Ploërmel, and some commentators like to think they have a deeper meaning. The "new" **church of Saint-Gilles** (16th century) has absorbed an older edifice (12th century), resulting in a structure with a split personality. On one of the buttresses of the side door, a splendid carving of an ox – which may symbolize Saint Hervé, Saint Luke or Saint Cornély (patron saint of cattle and of the original church) – is said at certain times of day to take on the profile of Voltaire. The village of Saint-Marcel specializes in more recent history. Its **museum of the Breton Resistance movement** includes models, tanks, film-shows and reconstructions of key events, all thoroughly modern and educational.

But first prize for picturesque charm must go to **Rochefort-en-Terre,** reached by the D764 along the river Oust. A tiny jewel, set in a changing landscape of narrow valleys, heath, wooded slopes and pretty villages, the town clings to the flank of the Grée, a somber spur of schist jutting into the deep gorge of the Gueuzon. Its fine old houses are bedecked with geraniums, ensuring that, for the last twenty years, Rochefort has never failed to win the best-kept-village competition. The **château,** which an American painter restored in eccentric style in the early years of the century, now houses a municipal museum of popular art, featuring tools, implements and regional headdresses. To encourage tourism, self-catering accommodation has been made available, and the nearby lake of Pluherlin (2 km or 1.25 mi away) has been equipped for bathing and sailing.

Porhoët Area

In the north-west corner of the *département* lies the **Porhoët** area, a name meaning "beyond the forests", though the forests in question have shrunk to a shadow of their former selves. But the memory remains, and on the borders of the Ille-et-Vilaine one enters a region of magnificent heathland. Néant-sur-Yvel (on the D766), site of a *nemeton* or sacred clearing used by the Druids, is the starting point.

At the **camp des Rouets** near Mauron are preserved the remains of a wooden fortress, thought to have been used from the 7th to the 9th centuries. A visit can be combined with a walk in the **forest of Lanouée.** Here, and in the twin forest of Paimpont, there was once an important iron industry.

Formerly a town of substance and the favourite hunting center of the Dukes of Brittany, **Ploërmel** still has a flourishing economy and is a proud bastion of the *Gallèse* language, the French-based dia-

lect of eastern Brittany. Its **church of Saint-Armel,** in the Flamboyant Gothic style, has a splendid stained-glass window, which survived war-time air raids, and a richly sculpted doorway. Its farcical scenes include one of the clog-maker sewing up his wife's mouth ! Beside the road to Josselin (the N24) stands the *Colonne des Trente,* a kind of obelisk commemorating a battle between 30 Breton knights of the English party and 30 who took the French side.

Of all the places to visit in the Porhoët area, **Josselin** is the most rewarding. Its **château,** rising beside the Oust canal is undoubtedly one of the finest sights in the whole of Brittany. Viewed from the river, its high ramparts of brown schist, extending from the bare cliff, must have discouraged the boldest attacker. The fortifications consist of three regularly spaced towers, linked by a curtain wall, with the slate roof of the living quarters visible be-

hind. From the garden side, the château is elegance personified: a long, low residence graced with mullioned windows and, to avoid monotony, a crenellation of beautifully carved pinnacles. The slope of the ground hides all trace of fortifications, apart from the pepper-pot tops of the towers. Though it was built, rebuilt, strengthened and embellished many times over, the town of Josselin has kept the name it was originally given in 1008 by its founder, in honor of his son. The choice of site is explained by the not unusual story of a statue of the Virgin, which refused to be removed from the bramble bush in which it was discovered. Hence, the **church** is dedicated to **Notre-Dame-du-Roncier.** Her festival, held on 8 September, used to be known as the "shouters' *pardon*", because epileptics, yelling and gesticulating, were constrained to attend.

The **doll museum,** housed in the castle mews, is maybe not everybody's cup of tea, but the church and the narrow streets of old houses which surround it are an inviting place for a stroll.

Lower Vilaine

The D764, which follows the course of the **Oust,** leads to the Redon area. Those with a nose for smells will make a detour to La Gacilly, headquarters of Yves Rocher, son and benefactor of the town, who pioneered "biological" perfumes. His factory employs 1200 people, and there is also a plant at Ploërmel. The town has a perfume museum (where you can really savor the scents, not just gaze at bottles) and a botanical garden, and there are plenty of art and craft shops. Between La Gacilly and Redon, where the Nantes-Brest canal temporarily parts company with the river, there are small islands and reed beds, a haven for moorhens, ducks and eels. The Île-aux-Pies, where there is a sharp bend in the river, is a center for canoeing and rock-climbing.

Above: Monastery at Paimpont. Right: Café terrace and old houses, at Josselin.

From Redon to the sea, the only way to explore **the river Vilaine** and its watery marshlands is by boat. No road runs close to the river, and even the villages keep a safe distance. It is true that the flow is now regulated by the Arzal dam downstream, but better safe than sorry! From the road which runs like a balcony along the wooded right-hand side of the valley, there are occasional glimpses of the river. First comes Rieux, an ancient fording place, and the remains of its citadel, then the little harbor of Foleux, then Marzan, which was once an imposing fortress.

From here, the modern suspension bridge on the N165 is one's introduction to **La Roche-Bernard,** a staging post on the old salt route, which has become a center for sailing and water sports. From the bridge, suspended 50 m (164 ft) above the wooded banks, there is a superb view of the harbor and old town, which clings to the slope of the Ruicard promontory. This is pretty country, devoted largely to tourism, and there are some good walks in the area for those

who like more strenuous exercise. The Vilaine and its seagoing history are brought to life by a **museum** housed in the **Château des Basses-Fosses**.

Further downstream is Arzal, with its dam and lively sailing harbor. In winter, at dead of night, you may come across men catching baby eels with hoop-nets. They hate being watched, even if they are not poaching outside the prescribed times of year. Elver fishing is big business.

On the north bank of the estuary stands Muzillac and, beside the long **lake of Penmur,** a mill where it is possible to buy rag paper produced in the old style. The surrounding area is generally deserted, except for two months in the summer, when camp sites are filled to capacity. Places of interest include Billiers, at the head of its inlet; the beaches of Damgan; and the small harbor and estuary of Penerf (12 km or 7.5 mi long, but with a shore-line of 50 km or 31 mi), where at low tide only trickles of water lick around the oyster beds. It is deserted except in the two summer months.

Tourist Information
Information about the region: **Comité départemental du Tourisme du Morbihan**, Hôtel du Département, BP 400, 56009 Vannes cedex, Tel: 97-400680.

AURAY
Accommodation
MODERATE: **La Diligence**, 160, av. du Général- de-Gaulle, Tel: 97-240018. *BUDGET:* **Le Loch**, La Petite Forêt, Tel: 97-564833.
Tourist Information / Festivals
Office de Tourisme, place de la République, Tel: 97- 240975. *Festival international* and *Fête folklorique*, both middle of July, Tel: 97-240975.

BELLE-ÎLE
Accommodation
MODERATE: **Le Manoir du Goulphar**, Port-Goulphar, Tel: 97-318010. *BUDGET:* **Bretagne**, quai Macé, Le Palais, Tel: 97-318014.
Restaurants
Castel Clara, Port-Goulphar, Tel: 97-315169, moderate prices. **Le Contre-Quai**, rue Saint-Nicolas, Sauzon, Tel: 97-316060, inexpensive.
Museum / Sightseeing
Citadel with **Museum**, Tel: 97-318417. **Le Grand Phare**, lighthouse, Bangor, Tel: 97-318208.
Tourist Information / Ferry Connections
Office de Tourisme, quai Bonelle, 56360 Le Palais, Tel: 97-318001 and 97-500690. **Ferry connections** from Quiberon, Tel: 97-318001 and 97-500690.

CARNAC
Accommodation
LUXURY: **Le Diana**, 21, bd. de la Plage, Tel: 97-520538. *MODERATE:* **Plancton**, 12, bd. de la Plage, Tel: 97-521365. *BUDGET:* **La Marine**, 4, place de la Chapelle, Tel: 97-520733.
Restaurant
Lann-Roz, 36, avenue de la Poste, Tel: 97-521048, moderate prices.
Tourist Information / Museum
Office de Tourisme, avenue des Druides, Tel: 97-521352. **Musée de la Préhistoire**, Miln-le-Rouzic, Tel: 97-522204.

CLEGUEREC
Festival
Festival de Musique traditionnelle en Arwen, 2nd week in May, Tel: 97-380165.

ELVEN
Sightseeing / Special Events
Forteresse de Largoët, fort, Tel: 97-535279. *Son et Lumière*, in June, Tel: 97-535279.

LE FAOUËT
Accommodation
BUDGET: **La Croix d'Or**, 9, place Bellanger, Tel: 97-230733, with inexpensive restaurant.

Tourist Information / Religious Festivals
Office de Tourisme, 1, rue de Quimper, Tel: 97-232323. *Pardon de Sainte-Barbe*, end of June. *Pardon de Saint-Fiacre*, end of August.

GOURIN
Religious Festival
Pardon des Sonneurs, at the end of September.

ÎLE DE GROIX
Tourist Information / Ferry Connections
Office de Tourisme, 4, rue du Général-de-Gaulle, 56590 Groix, Tel: 97-055308. **Ferries** from Lorient, Tel: 97-868037 and 97-210397.
Museum
Écomusée de Groix, ancienne conserverie, Port-Tudy, Tel: 97-868460.

HENNEBONT
Tourist Information
Office de Tourisme, place du Maréchal-Foch, Tel: 97-362452.

ÎLE D'HOËDIC
Ferry Connections
Ferry services from Quiberon, Tel: 97-500690.

JOSSELIN
Accommodation / Restaurant
BUDGET: **Le Château**, 1, rue du Général-de-Gaulle, Tel: 97-222011. **Restaurant Blot**, 9, rue Glatinier, Tel: 97-222208, inexpensive.
Museum / Castle / Religious Festival
Château, Tel: 97-223645. **Musée des Poupées**, museum of dolls, Tel: 97-222250. *Pardon de Notre-Dame du Roncier*, September 8.

CHÂTEAU DE KERGUEHENNEC
Tourist Information / Castle
Exhibitions of modern art in the castle, information Tel: 97-602119 and 97-605778.

LOCMARIAQUER
Accommodation
BUDGET: **Relais de Kerpenhir**, Tel: 97-573120.
Tourist Information
Office de Tourisme, place de la Mairie, Tel: 97-573305.

LORIENT
Accommodation
MODERATE: **Mercure Lorient**, 31, place Jules-Ferry, Tel: 97-213573.
BUDGET: **Le Victor-Hugo**, 36, rue Lazare-Carnot, Tel: 97-211624.
Restaurant
Le Bistrot du Yachtman, 14, rue Poissonnière, Tel: 97-213191.
Festivals / Special Events
Festival interceltique, August 2–12, Tel: 97-212429. *Les Océanes*, 2nd week in July, Tel: 97-656301. *Kan ar Bobl*, Breton songs, at Easter, Tel: 97-212051.

Tourist Information
Office de Tourisme, place Jules-Ferry, Tel: 97-210784.

GULF OF MORBIHAN
Nature Reserve / Tourist Information
Réserve naturelle de Falquérec, information: l'Apothicairerie, SEPNB de Vannes, Tel: 97-409295, or in the Vannes tourist office, Tel: 97-472434.

Accommodation
BUDGET: **Le Gavrinis**, "Toul-Broch", Baden, Tel: 97-570082.

PLOËRMEL
Accommodation
MODERATE: **Le Cobh**, 10, rue des Forges, Tel: 97-740049. *BUDGET:* **St. Marc**, 1, place Saint-Marc, Tel: 97-740001.

Tourist Information
Office de Tourisme, place Lamennais, Tel: 97-740270.

PONTIVY
Accommodation / Restaurant
BUDGET: **Friedland**, 12, rue Friedland, Tel: 97-252711. **Le Gambetta**, place de la Gare, Tel: 97-255370, restaurant, moderate prices, good food.

Tourist Information / Castle
Office de tourisme, rue du Général-de-Gaulle, Tel: 97-250410.
Château des Rohan, Tel: 97-251293.

PORT-LOUIS
Accommodation / Restaurant
BUDGET: **Le Commerce**, 1, place du Marché, Tel: 97-824605. **Avel Vor**, 25, rue de Locmalo, Tel: 97-824759, restaurant, moderate prices.

Museum / Sightseeing
Citadel and **Musée de la Compagnie des Indes**, Tel: 97-211401.

QUIBERON
Accommodation / Restaurant
LUXURY: **Sofitel-Thalassa**, Pointe de Goulvars, Tel: 97-502000. *MODERATE:* **Ker Royal**, Chemin des Dunes, Tel: 97-500841. *BUDGET:* **Druides**, 6, rue de Port Maria, Tel: 97-501474. **La Chaumine**, 36, place du Manémeur, Tel: 97-501767, inexpensive restaurant, good food.

Tourist Information
Office de Tourisme, 7, rue de Verdun, Tel: 97-500784.

RHUYS PENINSULA
Tourist Information / Castle
Office de Tourisme de Sarzeau, Tel: 97-418237. **Château de Suscinio**, Tel: 97-419191.

LA ROCHE-BERNARD
Tourist Information
Office de Tourisme, place du Pilori, Tel: 99-906798.

Museum / Castle
Château des Basses-Fosses and **Musée maritime**, Tel: 99-908347.

ROCHEFORT-EN-TERRE
Restaurant
Lion d'Or, rue du Pélican, Tel: 97-433280, good food at moderate prices.

Castle / Museum / Religious Festival
Château, with the **Musée d'Art populaire**, Tel: 97-433505. Religious festival *Pardon de Notre-Dame de la Tronchaye*, 3rd Sunday in August.

Tourist Information
Office de Tourisme, Tel: 97-433357.

SAINT-PIERRE-QUIBERON
Accommodation
MODERATE: **Hôtel de la Plage**, 25, quai d'Orange, Tel: 97-309210. *BUDGET:* **La Godaille**, Penthièvre, Tel: 97-523128.

Sports
École nationale de Voile, sailing, Beg Rohu, Tel: 97-502702.

SAINTE-ANNE-D'AURAY
Accommodation / Restaurant
BUDGET: **La Croix Blanche**, 25, rue de Vannes, Tel: 97-576444.
Les Rahed Koët, Plougonmelen, Tel: 97-563496, inexpensive restaurant.

Religious Festival
Pardon de Sainte-Anne, at the end of July.

TRINITE-SUR-MER
Accommodation / Restaurant
BUDGET: **Le Rouzic**, 17, cours des Quais, Tel: 97-557206. **L'Azimut**, 1, rue du Men-Dû, Tel: 97-557188, restaurant, moderate prices.

Tourist Information
Office de Tourisme, cours des Quais, Tel: 97-557221.

VANNES
Accommodation / Restaurants
MODERATE: **La Marébaudière**, 4, rue Aristide-Briand, Tel: 97-473429. **Manche Océan**, 31, rue du Lt-Colonel-Maury, Tel: 97-472646. *BUDGET:* **Hôtel des Remparts**, 4, rue des Vierges, Tel: 97-541190.
La Marée Bleue, 8, place Bir-Hakeim, Tel: 97-472429. **La Varende**, 22, rue de la Fontaine, Tel: 97-475752, both inexpensive restaurants.

Festivals
Fêtes historiques, 2nd week in July, Tel: 97-472434. *Fêtes folkloriques d'Arvor*, August 10–15, Tel: 97-472434.

Museum
Musée des Beaux-Arts du Golfe et de la Mer, La Cohue, place St-Pierre, Tel: 97-473586.

Tourist Information
Office de Tourisme, rue Thiers, Tel: 97-472434.

NANTES AND ITS HINTERLAND

NANTES
CÔTE D'AMOUR
BRIÈRE REGIONAL
NATURE RESERVE

Is Nantes and its hinterland part of Brittany? Ask this question in a crowded bar and passions are bound to run high. Administrative convenience has dictated that the historic seat of the Dukes of Brittany be detached to become capital of the Loire country, while the surrounding region has been renamed Loire-Atlantique. From an historical point of view, the issue is not in doubt. So long as Brittany was an independent state, Nantes was an inseparable part of it. Language is not really a consideration, since there are also other parts of Brittany where Breton is not spoken. The geographical aspect of the question is, however, more controversial. The Nantes region borders on Anjou and the Vendée, and not surprisingly its landscapes are softer, its rivers more easy-going, its fields and woodlands more open and sunny. Slate roofs give way to red tiles. Its coastline, significantly named the Côte d'Amour, is more voluptuous. The traveler leaving the purple-hued heathlands of the north and suddenly awaking on the tranquil banks of the Loire has entered another world. The traditional image of Brittany has been replaced by sun-kissed vineyards,

Preceding pages: Grid pattern of salt pans at Guérande. Left: Angling from the jetty at Le Croisic.

stylish châteaux, the canals of the Brière country, the salt pans of Guérande, and smart, fashionable holiday resorts. While not venturing south of the river, in this chapter we will look at the areas most characteristic of the Loire-Atlantique: Nantes itself, historic capital of the Dukes of Brittany; the Brière regional nature reserve; and the Côte d'Amour.

NANTES

Nantes is a river port, situated at the confluence of the Erdre and the Loire on the final stage of their journey to the sea. The town is steeped in history, which greets the visitor at every turn, in the form of commemorative plaques, museums, different styles of architecture, and buildings from every period. Medieval town houses grace the rue du Château, place du Pilori, rue de la Juiverie, place du Bouffay and the former quays of the Loire, their façades decorated with bas reliefs, their jutting upper stories drawing the eye skyward. The unashamedly 19th-century frontage of the brasserie *La Cigale*, in the **place Graslin**, comes as a sudden surprise, standing shoulder to shoulder with the typically 18th-century Crucy Theater. The eastern and western districts of the city, divided up by 1920s boulevards, are charac-

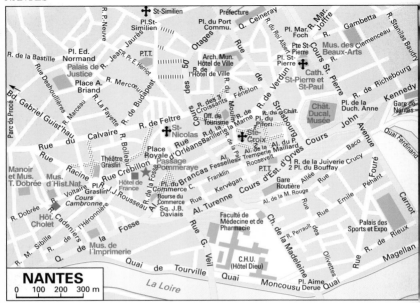

terized by groups of late 19th-century apartment buildings; the **parc de Procé,** designed by Noisette and frequented by poet André Breton; or the **Château du Grand-Blottereau,** a reminder of the great wealth enjoyed by merchants trading with the colonies. Nantes is a true metropolis, complete with factories, crowded student cafés, and a **botanical garden** (the Jardin des Plantes).

The old town begins at the place Maréchal Foch, site of the fortifications defending the porte Saint-Pierre. In the center of the square stands a statue of Louis XVI, dispensing his royal greeting to all comers.

The way ahead is blocked by the **cathedral of Saint-Pierre,** a masterpiece on which the Nantais were engaged over several hundred years. Begun in the 6th century, destroyed in the 9th and 10th, rebuilt in the 11th, finished in the 12th,

completely remodeled in the 15th in accordance with the wishes of Duke John V, restored in the 18th as a consequence of the Revolution, it assumed its present form as late as 1802! The harmonious effect of the whole is a matter of wonder, and one could linger for days over the details. Of the original Roman building, there remains only a crypt under the choir. The façade and towers were erected in the early 16th century. The effect on crossing the porch and entering the nave is breathtaking: The choir is aflame with colored light from 500 sq.m (5500 sq. ft) of stained-glass window. In the south transept stands the Renaissance tomb of Duke Francis II and his wife, Marguerite de Foix, its four corners guarded by statues personifying prudence, strength, temperance and justice. In the niches are figures of the twelve apostles, together with Saints Francis of Assisi, Margaret, Louis and Samson.

The venerable **Château des Ducs de Bretagne** is reached by the **place de la Psalette**, where *boules* players polish

Right: Gateway to the Château des Ducs de Bretagne, Nantes.

196

their skills in the shadow of Renaissance town houses. Its walls formerly lapped by the waters of the Loire, the handsome, tower-girt fortress has witnessed episodes of immense historical importance. Gilles de Retz was imprisoned and sentenced within its walls; it saw the birth of the Duchess Anne, and her marriage to Louis XII; an inscription in the courtyard quotes Francis I's speech formalizing the perpetual union of the lands and duchy of Brittany with the kingdom of France; here, Henry IV signed the Edict of Nantes granting rights to Protestants. Finally, excavations undertaken in the early years of the century brought to light remains of the town's Gallo-Roman ramparts.

Between the place Royale and the place Graslin lies the 19th-century quarter. Designed by local architect Mathurin Crucy, the **place Royale** was so badly damaged by air raids during the last war that it had to be rebuilt from the ground up. The modern copy is entirely faithful to the late-18th-century original. A blue-granite fountain comprises statues sym-

bolizing the Loire and its tributaries, surmounted by the city of Nantes in white marble.

The **basilica of Saint-Nicolas** is in the Neo-gothic style, its monumental spire, which soars to 85 m (279 ft), covered with stone shingles. Inside, the fine nave has five tripartite bays, and there are paintings by Elie Delauney. The place du Commerce is the bustling heart of the city. Here, the Nantais come to meet their friends in the surrounding cafés, and to visit the **media center** (*médiathèque*) and cinemas. In the 18th century, a stock exchange for the city's merchants was built in this square, site of the old wine dock. The exchange was damaged during the war and now only the façade remains, decorated with statues of famous seafarers. The apartment buildings, houses and palaces, and the nearby Quai de la Fosse are eloquent of a time when ship owners, engaged in the slave trade, brought prosperity to the town. The fine buildings on the **Île Feydeau** (which ceased to be an island at least 60 years

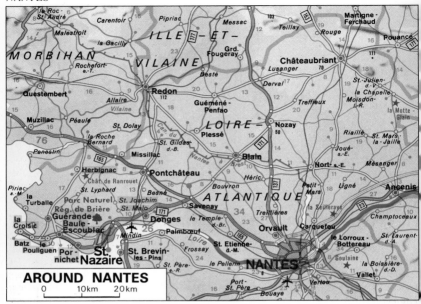

AROUND NANTES

0   10km   20km

ago) were then used as warehouses and offices. Some façades still preserve their wrought-iron balconies, and windows are decorated with sculpted pediments and grotesque masks, often of pirates.

Museums

The castle has become a municipal museum and houses three distinct collections. The Musée des Arts Décoratifs specializes in contemporary wall-hangings, particularly from the 1970s, which are displayed on the second floor. The ground and first floors are regularly used for temporary exhibitions.

The **Musée d'Art Populaire** has seven rooms devoted to the history of Brittany and its people. A whole floor is given over to costume, head-wear, housing and furniture. The Pays Blanc of the Guérande peninsula is specially featured, with a display of the furniture, clothing and tools used by the salt workers. An exhibition on the second floor traces the development of wrought and cast-iron

work in the Nantes area, and there are collections of pottery and ceramics.

The **Musée des Salorges** is concerned with the commercial, colonial and industrial history of the city since the 17th century. It includes many models of boats, nautical instruments, a model of the port at the turn of the century, and documents and paintings of historical interest. There is also an auditorium, where films are screened to illustrate current exhibitions.

The **Musée des Beaux-Arts** possesses an exceptional collection of paintings and sculpture, from the 13th century to the present day. Some of the masterpieces on show – by Delatour, Ingres, Courbet or Monet – have been exhibited worldwide.

The **Musée de l'Imprimerie,** housed in a room at the media center is devoted to printing. There is a display of old artefacts, combined with a workshop where professionals explain the techniques of composition, printing, typography and binding. You can even make up your own newspaper.

Located in the **Saint-Anne district** on a hill overlooking the river, the **Musée Jules Verne** (19th century) draws on models, games and personal items to bring to life the fantasy world of a writer who has fascinated readers everywhere. At the **Planetarium,** with its 8 m (26 ft) dome, you can undertake a journey from the Earth to the Moon and beyond.

The **Natural History Museum** is housed in the former mint (Hôtel de la Monnaie) and features a particularly varied range of exhibits. There is a gallery devoted to the evolution of fish, rooms concerned with pre-history, palaeontology, mineralogy and general zoology, a vivarium, and 20th-century natural history.

The **Musée Thomas Dobrée** and the **Musée Archéologique** are spread over several buildings: the Manoir de la Touche (15th century), the Manoir Thomas Dobrée (19th century), built in the English Neo-romanesque style, and a modern edifice. The collections of Thomas Dobrée, son of a rich dynasty of ship owners, include precious illuminated manuscripts and a celebrated example of the goldsmith's craft: a reliquary designed to hold the heart of Anne de Bretagne. The archaeological museum gives a chronological account of the people who lived in the area from the stone age to the Norman invasion. It includes some fine collections of Celtic art, and Gallo-Roman and Merovingian artefacts.

CÔTE D'AMOUR

Nestling in a semi-circle of sand dunes amid resinous pine woods, **La Baule** has grown up along its magnificent beach. The pulse of the resort is felt in the comings and goings of holiday-makers, the mass occupation and abandonment of holiday homes, bathers returning from the beach, sailing boats putting out to sea. With **Pornichet** and **Le Pouliguen,** Brit-

tany's premier holiday resort forms a Riviera worthy of comparison with the Côte d'Azur. Palatial hotels, casinos, residential complexes, golfers, polo players, horse riders and yachtsmen combine to give the place social status and a slightly old-fashioned charm. Its story is nevertheless one of rags to riches. Because the area was subject to subsidence and moving sands, a major public works project was put in hand, and extensive belts of pine trees planted to stabilize the terrain. Quite by chance, an agreeable micro-climate was created. The result was that the south-facing stretch of fine sand from La Baule to **Pornichet** quickly became a fashionable holiday resort, with attractive parks and gardens, and comfortable residences in elegant *fin-de-siècle* style. But for all the seductions of the sea front, with its luxury shops and procession of sports cars, the attractions of the esplanade in the quiet residential Benoit district, or the appeal of the woodlands at La-Baule-les-Pins, the resort leaves something to be desired. Amid all the *dolce vita*, one looks for old-world charm. The place is too young; one must turn elsewhere for a sense of the past.

It can be found at **Le Pouliguen.** The oldest of the three holiday resorts has maintained a thriving port for a good 400 years, and the fishermen still live in their ancient dwellings, arrayed along the channel which feeds the salt marshes of Guérande. The past also comes to life at the **Château de Carei**l, whose exterior Gothic façades conceal a Renaissance inner courtyard. Pouliguen's neighbor, **Le Croisic,** has also conserved its fine 16th-and 17th-century houses – for instance the **Hôtel de Aiguillon** – grouped around the little harbor, where traditional fishing boats and modern pleasure craft maintain a peaceful coexistence. From **Batz-sur-Mer,** the road to Guérande crosses the salt marshes atop a narrow causeway. The first stop is **Kervalet,** a pretty marshland village, then Saillé,

whose **Maison des Paludiers** gives an historical account of the highly specialized activity of making salt.

BRIÈRE REGIONAL NATURE RESERVE

Guérande, sheltering behind its granite ramparts, is a living fossil, guardian of the region's past. The old town is entered by the porte Saint-Michel, which leads into the street of the same name, lined with fine granite or rendered houses. There is a regional museum, showing local furniture, costume and pottery.

A few kilometers to the east begins a region of mud banks and reeds, the **Brière regional nature reserve**, whose marshy carpet covers an area of 40,000 hectares (100,000 acres) north of the Loire estuary. Little has changed since Alphonse Chateaubriand waxed eloquent on the remoteness of this great peat bog

Above: Le Croisic harbor, on the Guérande peninsula.

drained by the Brivet river. Silence still hangs over the reed beds, broken by croaking, a brush of wings, the lapping of the gray water. The marshes seem devoid of human presence.

Near Herbignac, one comes upon the ruins of a fortress, the **Château de Ranrouët**, now being restored. The inhabitants must be sought around the periphery of the marsh or on the islands. Owners of the central area of the marsh (7000 hectares or 17,300 acres) since 1461, the Brièrons are spread over 21 communes, mostly sited on the peaty islands of the Grande Brière. They lived by hunting and fishing, exploiting the peat, which they used to sell in Nantes, and the reed beds, and keeping a few herds of cattle. In so doing, they developed a unique way of life.

The **Maison de l'Eclusier,** or the lockkeeper's house, at Saint-Malo-de-Guersac, gives an historical account of life in the Brière marshes. The most remarkable living example is the **Île de Fédrun**, an island fringed with reed beds, its squat cottages pressed down by a weight of thatch. Entirely dependent on the water, each house has its own dock giving onto the *curée,* or peripheral canal. Here the family barge is moored, without which travel in the marshes is impossible. The **Chaumière Brièronne** (Brière cottage), at Saint-Joachim, is a reconstruction of traditional living conditions: a single room with a low ceiling, a fire-place, a few items of furniture, and stairs leading up to a hayloft. Another precious key to this ancient way of life is the **museum village of Kerhinet** (no cars allowed), whose houses have been restored with great care. To encourage observation of the marsh's abundant wildlife, the authorities have set an area aside as a **bird sanctuary.** From the path, binoculars to hand, it is possible to watch harriers, bitterns, purple herons, coots and teal going about their business undisturbed in the willow plantations.

Tourist Information

Information about the region: **Comité départemental du Tourisme de Loire-Atlantique**, place du Commerce, 44000 Nantes, Tel: 40-895077.

LA BAULE
Accommodation

LUXURY: **Royal**, Esplanade François-André, Tel: 40-603306. *MODERATE:* **Bellevue-Plage**, 27, bd. de l'Océan, La Baule, Tel: 40-602855. *BUDGET:* **Hostellerie du Bois**, 65, avenue Lajarrige, Tel: 40-602478.

Festivals / Special Events

Rencontres internationales de la Danse, 2nd week in July, Tel: 40-242424. *Festival du Film européen*, October 3–11, Tel: 40-243444.

Tourist Information

Office de Tourisme, 8, place de la Victoire, Tel: 40-243444.

BRIERE NATURE RESERVE
Tourist Information

Information about the nature reserve and the bird sanctuary *réserve ornithologique* from the **Maison du Parc**, 180, Île de Fedrun, 44720 St-Joachim, Tel: 40-884272.

CHÂTEAU DE CAREIL
Tourist Information

Informations in the castle, Tel: 40-602299.

LE CROISIC
Accommodation

MODERATE: **Grand Hôtel de l'Océan**, Port Lin, Tel: 40-629003. *BUDGET:* **Hôtel des Nids**, 83, bd. Général-Leclerc, Tel: 40-230063.

Museum / Sightseeing

Hôtel d'Aiguillon and **Musée naval**, Tel: 40-231536 and 40-629117.

Tourist Information

Office de Tourisme, place du 18 juin, Tel: 40-230070.

GUERANDE
Accommodation / Restaurant

BUDGET: **Roc Maria**, 1, rue des Halles, Tel: 40-249051. **Au Dé d'Argent**, 3, rue du Pavé de Beaulieu, Tel: 40-249017, budget restaurant.

Museum / Sightseeing

Porte St-Michel and **Musée régional**, Tel: 40-429652 and 40-249037.

Tourist Information / Festivals

Office de Tourisme, 5, place du Marché, Tel: 40-249671.
Festival d'Art sacré, in June, Tel: 40-247373. *La Voix des Orgues*, organ concerts, Friday evenings in July and August, Tel: 40-249671.

HERBIGNAC
Castle

Château de Ranrouët, Tel: 40-889011.

NANTES
Accommodation

LUXURY: **Sofitel**, 15, bd. Alexandre-Millerand, Tel: 40-476103. *MODERATE:* **Hôtel de France**, 24, rue Crébillon, Tel: 40-735791. *BUDGET:* **Cholet**, 10, rue Gresset, Tel: 40-733104.

Restaurants

Le Gavroche, 139, rue des Hauts-Pavés, Tel: 40-762249, moderate prices. **La Cigale**, 4, place Graslin, Tel: 40-697641, inexpensive.

Festivals

Festival atlantique d'Art lyrique, July 10–25. *Festival international d'Été*, July 5–10, Tel: 40-697414 and 40-470451.

Museums / Sightseeing

Château des Ducs de Bretagne, Tel: 40-415656. **Musée des Salorges**, Tel: 40-415656. **Musée d'Art populaire régional**, Tel: 40-471815. **Château du Grand Blottereau**, Tel: 40-419860. **Manoir et Musée Thomas Dobrée**, place Jean-V, Tel: 40-697608.
Musée des Beaux-Arts, 10, rue Georges-Clémenceau, Tel: 40-739923. **Musée Jules-Verne**, 3, rue de l'Hermitage, Tel: 40-697252.
Planétarium, 8, rue des Acadiens.

Tourist Information

Office de Tourisme, place du Commerce, Tel: 40-470451.

PORNICHET
Accommodation

MODERATE: **Sud-Bretagne**, 42, boulevard de la République, Tel: 40-610268. *BUDGET:* **Les Charmettes**, 7, av. Flornoy, Tel: 40-610430.

Tourist Information

Office de Tourisme, place Aristide-Briand, Tel: 40-610388.

LE POULIGUEN
Accommodation

BUDGET: **Beau Rivage**, 11, rue Jules-Benoît, Tel: 40-423161.

Tourist Information

Office de Tourisme, port Sterwitz, Tel: 40-423105.

SAILLE-EN-GUERANDE
Sightseeing

Maison des Paludiers, Tel: 40-622196.

SAINT-JOACHIM
Sightseeing

Chaumière Brièronne, 160, Île de Fédrun, Tel: 40-884272.

SAINT-LYPHARD
Museum

Musée de Kerhinet, Kerhinet, Tel: 40-619406.

SAINT-MALO-DE-GUERSAC
Sightseeing

Maison de l'Éclusier, Rozé, Tel: 40-911780.

FESTIVALS, FEAST DAYS AND FOLKLORE

It is easy to make the mistake of thinking that festivals are the sole prerogative of the South of France. Brittany, fiercely proud of its culture, is also home to many cultural events, some of which are of international importance. Each summer, Brittany reverberates to the sounds of bagpipes, gavottes, Celtic harps, Celtic rock groups, and opera singers.

The **Festival de Cornouaille** at **Quimper** – a kaleidoscope of color, music and song – is today one of the foremost European spectacles devoted to popular arts and traditions. During the third week in July, hundreds of musicians, dancers, actors, puppeteers, chefs, and instrument makers bring life to the old streets in the town center, while exhibitions of photography and painting form a backdrop to all the story-telling, concerts and dancing. A grand procession, held on the fourth Sunday in July, brings together folk groups of Celtic origin from Wales, Scotland and Ireland, as well as Brittany itself, and the festival ends with a gargantuan *festnoz.*

An **Inter-Celtic Festival** takes place at **Lorient** during the first fortnight of August, with ten days of continuous celebrations. Each year, some 200,000 spectators attend events staged at twelve different venues by thousands of artists from Scotland, Wales, Cornwall, Galicia, Ireland, the Isle of Man and, of course, Brittany itself – a glorious vindication of the seven Celtic nations. Concerts continue day and night; the various groups parade through the town; choirs sing themselves hoarse; competitions draw the crowds. Pipe bands, dances and harps accompany a wide variety of street entertainments.

Preceding pages: A heavy Atlantic swell smashing against the rocks. Hydrangea bush. Left: Girl in traditional costume, Pont-Aven.

The **Oceans Festival,** first staged at **Lorient** in 1988, is a mixture of concerts, exhibitions, displays of dancing, dramatic readings, and story-telling during cruises on the River Etel or the open sea. The festival takes place in mid-July and begins with a spectacular show.

Auray's International Festival is also held in mid-July, mainly at the municipal theater, which plays host to exhibitions of painting and decorative art, and concerts of folk music and dancing with an international flavor.

The **Historical Festival at Vannes** aims to take the visitor on a journey back in time. During the second week in July, the town is transformed in accordance with the chosen historical theme. The period settings thus created are used to stage contemporary dance entertainments, concerts and plays, and on the final evenings, the streets are thronged with wandering minstrels, acrobats and actors in period costume.

The **Festival de Suscinio** is staged by the commune of **Sarzeau** in the week leading up to 15 August. The setting is the magnificent courtyard of the Château de Suscinio, one-time summer residence of the Dukes of Brittany, which since 1981 has been the venue for concerts of classical music, lectures, folk dancing and poetry readings.

The towers of the ancient fortress of **Largoët** form the backdrop for a *son et lumière* entertainment organized by the inhabitants of Elven. From late June to late August, famous legends are given a new lease of life.

In 1980, wishing to stage a festival calling attention to the city's cultural heritage, the tourist authority in **Rennes** began to stage a series of evening events (**Tombées de la Nuit**), distinguished by an owl emblem. Organized with amazing panache, the festival, which embraces architecture, the sciences, town planning and the arts, now attracts over 60,000 visitors. During the first week in July,

Rennes is transformed into a giant theater. The hundred or so cultural offerings include poetry, song, plays, dance, mime, classical and ancient music, café-théâtre, films, even comic strips.

An **Art Rock Festival** gets the autumn off to a noisy start in **Saint-Brieuc**. Organized by the Wild Rose association, since 1983 the event has attracted a host of musicians from around the world, together with artists of all kinds. The aim is to build bridges between the different arts and rock culture. The concept may seem daring, but it has won the acceptance of a growing following, who invade the town during the last week in October. Dance, drama and concerts are all transmitted to public buildings by closed-circuit television. This ultra-modern festival is accompanied by another original event: an **International Festival Devoted to Music-videos and Films.**

Above: 18th-century hurdy-gurdy. Right: Young women in traditional head-gear, at Pont-Aven.

Since 1986, **Nantes** has organized les **Musicolores,** a festival featuring music and musicians from around the world. During the first week in July, the town plays host to a thousand or so artists from 30 different countries, who come to take part in the biggest event of its kind in France. Concerts and shows are staged at the Château des Ducs de Bretagne, while more spontaneous events take place in the streets of the town.

Paimpol had to be the venue for a **Festival Devoted to Sea Shanties and Old Ships.** Since 1990, during the second week in August, the town and regional development board have organized some events featuring restored sailing vessels – particularly Icelandic fishing schooners – and the songs of their sailors. The aim is to renew interest in the town's maritime past and the epic courage of its fishing fleet.

An **International Festival of Popular Dance and Traditions** takes place each year at **Châteauneuf-du-Faou.** From 8 to 15 August, a dozen or so groups gather

from all parts of the world to celebrate the diversity of their folk traditions. For a week, this small town in Finistère can take pride in being a meeting place of cultures, a place to appreciate the originality of each country's contribution, without fear of invidious comparisons.

Each year at the end of August, the **Festival des Minorités Nationales** is held at **Douarnenez** to encourage filmmaking by people of minority cultures. As well as producers from Celtic countries, representatives of other cultures are invited to present their works. More than 30 films are screened, and there are supporting exhibitions, concerts and discussion groups.

The **Fête des Fleurs d'Ajoncs** (Gorse Flower Festival), held at **Pont-Aven** on the last Sunday in July, was instituted in accordance with the wishes of the chansonnier Théodore Botrel, to celebrate the customs and costumes of the Aven country.

At **Lannion,** the **Fête de sa Majesté Mallarge** (Festival of His Majesty Mallarge) corresponds to the Lenten carnival in other parts of the world. Faithful to tradition, the Lannionais let their hair down to celebrate *Mallarge* (Breton for Shrove Tuesday) with robust humor. The festivities begin on the Saturday preceding Ash Wednesday, when His Majesty arrives on a cart. A procession takes place on the Sunday morning, with carts, musicians and people in disguise taking over the town. The inhabitants give free reign to their imagination in inventing pranks and sketches, while His Majesty Mallarge benignly observes the horse-play. On the Wednesday evening, straw effigies of the saints are set on fire and cast down from the Sainte-Anne bridge to a great chorus of lamentation from the observers.

The **Fête de la Saint-Loup** is traditionally held at the Château des Salles de **Guingamp** on the Sunday following 15 August. The performance of folk dancing culminates in a *dérobée* – an old dance from the Trégor region – in which all participate with gusto.

BRITTANY BY BOAT

To say that Brittany is a land of boats is to state the obvious. Images of old salts and deep-sea fishermen immediately spring to mind, but rarely does one think of inland waterways. And yet, with 650 km (over 400 miles) of navigable rivers and canals, France's greatest seagoing province also offers holidaymakers some delightful fresh-water sailing. Its varied and often wild landscape is scored by a number of canals and rivers, from which one has leisure to enjoy the sight of a castle on the bank, the purple of the heather, or sunsets reflected in the still waters. The slow pace of inland navigation and the many locks to be negotiated concentrate the mind on the surrounding countryside. House-boats and traditional narrow-boats are available. Spacious, comfortable and safe, they are easy to manoeuvre and can be hired for a week or

Above: Traditional boats on one of Brittany's many canals.

a weekend. Côtes d'Armor, Ille-et-Vilaine, Morbihan, Finistère and Loire-Atlantique all offer many possibilities for water-based exploration.

The lower reaches of the Rance are more like the sea than a river. It is difficult to negotiate its magnificent estuary without a suitable boat (yacht or powerful motor vessel) and unless one is fully acquainted with the techniques of marine navigation. However, once it joins the **Ille-et-Rance canal** at the Châtelier lock near Dinan, the joys of river-boating begin. From Dinan to Rennes, where it connects with the Vilaine, the canal snakes through a landscape of small fields, woods and meadows, punctuated by the flowerbeds of the lock-keepers' cottages. Châteaux and water mills come into view, and one is tempted to moor in front of the church at Evran or Treverien, or stop off at a miniscule inn. **Tinténiac** is not to be passed by. As well as the village and its church, there are two museums to be visited: an international natural history museum, and a museum of tools and trades, right beside the canal. This region has a wealth of historic castles, in particular at Montmuran and Combourg. The canal reaches **Hédé** in spectacular fashion: having climbed a stairway of eleven locks and risen 27 m (89 ft) in the process, it emerges into picturesque woodland. The village, which stands on a hill some distance away, is well worth a visit, if only for its fine Romanesque church and the incomparable view to be enjoyed from the top. As it continues towards Rennes and the Vilaine, the canal then descends into the valley of the Ille, whose banks support a profusion of honeysuckle, hazel and dog rose.

The **Vilaine** is a long river, navigable over almost half its course, offering an ideal way to explore the Gallo country. Its banks have witnessed the building of innumerable fortresses, ports, salt warehouses and churches, and are intimately linked with the history of the Dukes of Brittany. From Rennes, the river flows through soft rural landscapes towards Redon. Stretches of canal have been dug at certain points to give some semblance of order to the excentricities of its course. The most attractive part of the itinerary begins with the high purple cliffs in the vicinity of the Boël nature reserve, where rocky islets rise from the river bed. An imposing manor house announces the approach to Port-de-Roche and, a little further on, the 28 menhirs des Demoiselles. Now, the sandstone becomes redder in color, reeds begin to appear in the marshes, and sleepy châteaux and watermills bask lazily in the sun. Downstream from Beslé, fishing villages come into view, and it is interesting to study the old fish ponds, said to have been created by medieval monks. At Redon, the Nantes-Brest canal cuts across the Vilaine at right angles. To complete one's exploration of the area, it is worth first heading downstream towards the Arzal dam. This stretch, where the river opens out towards the sea, is not tidal, and it is possible to sail down among the coasters as far as the suspension bridge at La Roche-Bernard.

The **Nantes-Brest canal** forms an inland link between the three Atlantic regions, running from the mouth of the Loire, via Lorient, to the extremities of Finistère. Completed in 1840, it was used for commercial traffic until 1950. West of the Guerlédan reservoir, which was created in 1928, only a few stretches are navigable, but the 200 km (124 mi) of canal from Nantes to Pontivy gives access to a range of interesting historic sites. Starting from Sucé on the River Erdre, one joins the canal below Nortsur-Erdre and turns west into the Blinois country. Around Blain, the gentle valleys and well-wooded landscapes provide a verdant setting for châteaux, churches and the remains of Gallo-Roman towns. After Rieux, the canal turns north towards Redon – frontier town between Brittany and the Loire country and a crossroads of inland waterways. Westwards, the river **Oust** forms a 90 km (56 mi) link between Redon and Pontivy. By branching off north onto the **Vilaine** or taking a trip up the river **Aff**, it is possible to explore reed beds, the heathland of the Forêt Noire, and the flower-decked fields around La Gacilly. This region fairly bristles with dolmens, churches, châteaux and menhirs. Returning to the Oust, the ancient fortified island of Malestroit and the medieval town of Josselin are further invitations to stop and stare. Planted firmly on a cliff above the river, the castle of the Rohan family is the dominant landmark on this stretch of the canal. While in Rohan country, the town of Rohan itself is worth visiting for its architectural treasures. The canal now traverses twenty or so locks and a not particularly distinguished landscape before reaching Pontivy, a pleasant terminus and point of junction with the Blavet valley.

The **canal du Blavet** is really no more than a navigable river dubbed a canal for

no very obvious reason. Conceived by Napoleon but not opened until 1825, it was used for the transport of pit props to Britain. From Pontivy, it runs through undulating wooded country, before the valley gives way to cultivated fields. Villages and farms are few and far between. At the prehistoric site of Castennec, a stone statue stands out on the horizon. An aura of myth and legend pervades the region, extending its mysterious influence as far south as Hennebont.

In Finistère, between Port-Carhaix and Châteaulin, boats can navigate the canalized sections of the **Aulne** and **Hyères** rivers, which form part of the western end of the Nantes-Brest canal. The 76 km (47 mi) journey through the forests of the Hyères valley and down the meandering course of the Aulne is a real delight. Calvaries, chapels, historic sites and monuments are thick on the ground for those who wish to stop and explore. The Black

Mountains stand out above Saint-Goazec, the countryside is more arid, and villages infrequent. At Pont-Coblant, the ground opens up to reveal gigantic slate quarries. It is worth disembarking here and taking the road to Pleyben, which has the finest complex of ecclesiatical buildings in all Finistère – a monumental church and 16th-century calvary. Châteaulin and Port-Launay are the final stops, before the river mingles majestically with the sea at Landévennec.

For further information, the Comité Régional de Tourisme (in Rennes) or the Maison de la Bretagne (in Paris) will be pleased to help.

Exploring the Estuaries by Motor Launch

As well as hiring out narrow boats, Breton tourist offices organize boat tours of various **river estuaries.** Lasting a few hours, these excursions are an ideal way to get an overall impression of the often spectacular coastline, complementing

Above: Traditional costume, still worn with pride. Right: Trawler.

land-based exploration. The boats stop off at various islands, and there is time to visit the most interesting historic sites before moving on.

Blessed by Saint Anne, the small town of Auray stretches along the delightful banks of the Loc stream. South of the town, the valley widens out to form the tidal **Auray river,** an estuary 5 km (3 mi) in length. From the landing stage at Saint-Goustain, launches leave on trips round the **Gulf of Morbihan.** Châteaux and fine private houses may be glimpsed amid dense woodland, before the boats enter the gulf proper. The tour includes stops on the Locmariaquer peninsula to explore the menhir country, then at Port-Navalo and the Île-aux-Moines, the most attractive island of this inland sea. Further information can be obtained from the tourist office at Auray (tel. 97 24 09 75).

Formerly of major economic importance, nowadays the **River Odet** sees only the odd tramp steamer or dredger. *All bends and inlets, mudbanks and stretches of shining water,* as Jean-Edern Hallier

described it, the waterway can be negotiated without any anxiety. To admire the châteaux which adorn its banks and the profusion of wild flowers, it is possible to take a launch from Quimper or Benodet. The tour of the estuary takes a little over an hour. Information is obtainable from Corniguel harbor at Quimper (tel. 98 57 00 58) or at Benodet (tel. 98 57 00 58).

The best way to get one's first sight of **Cap Fréhel**, one of the most spectacular headlands in Brittany, is undoubtedly to approach it from the sea. Boats leave from Saint-Malo and Dinard, skirting the whole Côte d'Emeraude and revealing its inlets, deep bays and sheer cliffs, which drop sheer into the green water. Red and threatening, the grandiose headland rises a stark 70 m (230 ft) out of the water, overshadowing the tiny boats. The same launches also make trips up the Rance estuary to Dinan. Further information can be obtained from the tourist offices in Saint-Malo (tel. 99 56 64 48) and Dinard (tel. 99 46 94 12).

EATING AND DRINKING

Armor and Argoat – coast and interior – combine to provide the natural ingredients required to cook a wide range of gourmet dishes. The sea and rivers yield an unequaled variety of fresh- and salt-water fish, shellfish and crustaceans. The Breton hinterland, for its part, produces over half of France's pigs, 45% of its chickens and 20% of its dairy cows. Many Breton dishes and specialties are nowadays almost universally known. Lovers of good food are familiar with *sauce à l'amoricaine, homard Mélanie* (lobster dish named after a famous cook from Riec-sur-Belon), *Paris-Brest* (a delicious gâteau), *petit beurre nantais* biscuits, or the lacy pancakes known as *crêpes dentelles,* to name only a few of the gastronomic delights of Brittany.

Above: Gastronomic symbol of Brittany, a Léon artichoke. Right: Crêpe dentelle, a fine-as-lace pancake.

214

Traditional Breton Cookery

Together with milk and eggs, flour was for centuries the mainstay of Breton cookery. All types of grain were transformed into flour: wheat, oats, rye and buckwheat. Mills, whether water- or wind-powered, worked day and night to produce the precious foodstuff. Oat meal gruel, or *iod*, is still the cornerstone of the traditional household economy. Like its Scottish cousin, porridge, it has remained, through centuries of hardship, the staple food of rural folk, and can still be sampled in country inns. Breton butter is justly famous. In a land of animal husbandry and dairy farming, butter is king, and the sea air gives it an inimitable salty savor. Without forgetting the part played by lard, salted fat or oil, it is fair to say that the base of the vast majority of Breton recipes is Brittany's delicious, creamy, unforgettable butter.

Pancakes in various forms (*crêpes* and *galettes*) are fundamental. Although the term "galette" is more generally used in the east, whereas the term "crêpe" is more common in the western part of Brittany, both are traditionally composed of buckwheat flour and prepared in the same way. They are usually cooked in a *pillig,* or pan, using a *rozell,* or spatula, to spread the mixture, and an *askelleden,* or slice, to turn the pancake at the half-way stage. Originally, pancakes were eaten with hot sausages and eggs, or consumed on their own with a knob of butter. Since wheat flour has been introduced, pancakes have also become a wonderful dessert. Making pancakes was, and still is, a most demanding task. It is said that the cook would unfailingly cross herself before setting to work, hoping to be blessed with the necessary patience to achieve perfection.

In Brittany, a soup is not just a broth containing more or less fat, but a thick preparation containing many ingredients such as fish, meat, shellfish, vegetables,

bread or pancakes. The best known are onion soup; bean soup, also called *potage à la bretonne*; and cabbage soup. One of the most famous is fish soup, or *contriade,* which may include conger eel, hake, whiting, gilt-head, and several other species.

Farz (of which there are many varieties) is another pillar of traditional Breton cuisine. The celebrated *kig ha farz,* which may be served as an entrée, main course or side dish, combines buckwheat flour, meat, salt, sugar, prunes or raisins! When prepared with white flour, milk and eggs, on the other hand, *farz* becomes a succulent dessert. It is then known as *gwiniz du.*

The Breton Vegetable Garden

Since the mid-19th century, Brittany has gone in for market gardening in a big way. Exporting to the rest of France and abroad, the Breton *départements* now account for half of the artichokes, a third of the cauliflowers, and a quarter of the peas and green beans produced in France, as well as quantities of carrots, cabbages, onions, tomatoes and spinach. The star of the show is undoubtedly the Léon artichoke, more commonly known as the *gros-camus,* grown mainly around Roscoff and Saint-Pol-de-Léon. When picked young, it can be eaten cooked or raw, with a sprinkling of salt or pepper, or dipped in vinaigrette. When fully grown, it can be stuffed and fried or grilled, and served with a cream or *bechamel* sauce. Artichoke fritters are known as *biguezennou.* Cabbages are another important crop. Grown mainly in the coastal area around Lorient, large quantities are exported to Germany as a basis for the *sauerkraut* enjoyed by the inhabitants of Munich or Frankfurt. The potato, introduced to Belle-Île in the 18th century, was long regarded with suspicion. Accused of spreading cholera, it did not find favor with the Bretons until a hundred years later. The "little truffle" has since become the faithful partner of many a Breton recipe.

Salt-cured meats

The pig, whose meat holds pride of place on the Breton table, is served up in a number of guises: bacon, fresh or smoked sausage, black pudding, *andouille*, pâté, and so on. Breton tradition in this field is best illustrated by the way andouille is prepared at Guéméné-sur-Scorff. Real Breton *andouille* – as opposed to the factory-produced substitutes which go by the same name – is now something of an endangered species, such is the care and effort required in its preparation. The home-produced article is made with the large intestine of the pig, which is first steeped in salt for a month. After a thorough rinsing, the entrails are cut up into 40 cm (16 in) lengths then threaded on a string, one after the other, beginning with the smallest. The *andouille* can then be hung up in the chimney (or nowadays in a special smoke-house) to be smoked for three months, and is finally cooked for three hours at 90 degrees with a handful of hay. After all these operations, the *andouille* can be eaten cold, as an appetizer, or hot with potato purée. It is quite delicious.

Whilst on the subject of meat, let us not forget the famous *pré-salé* mutton from the salt meadows of Mont-Saint-Michel bay and the island of Ouessant. Also justly celebrated is the small Janzé chicken. The *challan,* a duck from the Nantes region, is delicious when prepared with muscadet.

Treasures of the Breton Seaboard

Every inlet, every tidal river, every estuary has its little harbor. The fishermen of Brittany have sailed all the seas of Europe – from the Bay of Biscay to the shores of Greenland – to bring home sardines, anchovies, herring, cod, conger eel and dozens of other species. Today, Lorient, Concarneau, Le Guilvinec and Douarnanez are major fishing ports, supplying the markets with the seas' harvest. The "cod" – in fact a haddock – on which the prosperity of Paimpol and Saint-Malo was once built is still a local specialty, available dried or salted. Each town has its own way of preparing it: with a cream sauce and potatoes, with leeks, or with the famous *beurre blanc* (white butter). Other types of fish also enjoy a reputation for quality: sardines from the bay of Audierne, tuna from Concarneau, brill, hake, sole (cooked with Muscadet), plaice, John Dory, skate, gurnard, and many more.

Fresh-water fish are also to be had: eel from the Brière marshes (locally known as *pimpeneau*), shad, pike, trout, and salmon, which is making a return to Brittany's rivers. Two hundred years ago, 4500 tonnes of salmon were taken each year, in the happy days when servants had to beg their masters not to serve them salmon more than twice a week! Things have changed quite a lot since those far-off days.

Brittany's oysters have been renowned since classical times. The most highly prized are those from Belon, Cancale and Prat-ar-Koum. They are raised in beds extending over 6500 hectares, which gives Brittany first place among European oyster producers. Crustaceans are also caught in great numbers: lobster (including the sought-after blue variety, which can be grilled or sautéd *à la crème*), crayfish (of which the red kind is best), various species of crab and shrimp, scallops, and many other excellent varieties besides.

Desserts and Drinks

"Butter with everything" is an appropriate slogan for Breton sweets and puddings. Butter, in generous measure is a prime ingredient of most traditional recipes, whether it be the *gâteau breton,* a

Right: The joys of going to market.

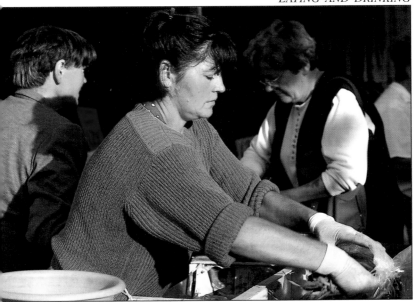

speciality of southern Brittany, from Lorient to Brest, the *quatre-quarts*, the *gâteau de Pont-l'Abbé,* the sweet-chestnut cake made at Rieux and the famous *kouign-amann* from Douarnanez. The delicious *kouign-amann* is said to have been invented by a baker's wife, who accidentally placed her butter on a lump of dough, then sugared it rather than let it go to waste. Not too thick, baked to a golden brown in the oven, it has a caramelized surface and gives off an unmistakable buttery aroma! Many cakes and biscuits can be bought in tins. The *Traou-Mad* (good thing) of Pont-Aven, Pleyben galettes and Quimper's famous *crêpes dentelles* make delicious presents to take home for friends and family.

Nor is Brittany lacking in beverages. Cider has been around for 1500 years and is a suitable accompaniment to nearly every dish. Most drinkers choose the sweet variety, but true connoisseurs prefer it dry. The locals stick to rough farm cider, which is drunk from the bowl or *cul de fût.* The most prestigious ciders come from Fouesnant and Beg-Meil. From the cider apple is also derived *lambrig* or *louarn ham,* a kind of brandy When added to one's coffee, it gives what is known in the Ille-et-Vilaine dialect as a *mic.* Brittany also produces perry, and *chouchen*, a type of mead with an alcoholic content of 16 to 18 degrees, for which Rosporden enjoys a very justifiable fame.

Muscadet or *gros plant* is the vine generally grown in the Nantes region. It was introduced from Burgundy around 1600 to replace earlier types of grape. Three vintages are officially recognized, of which Muscadet de Sèvre-et-Maine is the most delicate, while its counterpart from the Coteaux de la Loire is more fruity. This lively dry wine consorts well with oysters, shellfish and fish of every kind. It is used to give an aroma to sauces, meat dishes and marinades, and may be drunk on its own or with biscuits. Wines from the Coteaux d'Ancenis, both red and rosé, are light and easy, and should be drunk young.

217

BRETON TRADITIONS

The Breton flag – *Gwen ha du* – was designed in 1923 by the architect Morven Marchal (1900-63) and first flew officially in 1925, over the Brittany pavilion at the exhibition of decorative arts in Paris. It consists of nine bands, five black and four white. The black bands stand for the five ancient bishoprics of upper Brittany: Dol, Nantes, Rennes, Saint-Brieuc and Saint-Malo, while the white bands represent the lower Brittany bishoprics of Cornouaille, Léon, Trégor and the Vannetais. The upper left-hand corner of the flag is quartered with ermine on a white ground.

This flag replaced the former black cross on a white ground, assigned to Brittany by Pope Gregory VII in 1188, on the eve of the Third Crusade. This ensign was flown on Breton ships throughout the Middle Ages and can be seen on

many nautical maps dating from the 15th and 16th centuries. The white flag dotted with black ermines, which for centuries distinguished the Dukes of Brittany, first appeared in the 13th century, during the reign of Pierre Mauclerc, or his father John I.

The ermine or stoat, a small mammal of the weasel family, was used in heraldry from early times, portrayed either realistically (the ermine passant) or in a stylized form (what was inspired no doubt by its fur). The device is roughly cross-shaped with three (and sometimes five) points at the base. Its use spread to many European countries. Adopted in Brittany by the Monfort line of dukes, it eventually came to be accepted as the paramount symbol of the province. It features on the arms of many Breton towns and is now much used in sophisticated advertising and packaging.

The decorative *Triskell* motif (from the Greek triskelês, meaning "three-legged") did not reappear in Brittany until the 1920s, though it was widely used by the

Above: The traditional way of drying garlic.

ncient Celts. It is found on many items of Iron Age jewelery (550 to 50 B.C.), when Celtic civilization extended over most of Europe. The *triskell* continued to be used in the Middle Ages, in Ireland. It does not have any occult significance but, like the wheel or the swastika, may be a symbol of the sun, or of perpetual motion. Nowadays widely adopted as a decorative motif in the six Celtic countries, the triskell serves as a kind of label for all things Celtic and is a widely recognized symbol among Celtic scholars.

Breton Language

Twenty-five centuries ago, Celtic was spoken exclusively over two thirds of Europe. Only two groups of Celtic languages have survived to the present day: the Goidelic group, which includes Irish, Scottish Gaelic and Manx, and the Brythonic group, consisting of Welsh, Cornish and Breton. Breton itself breaks down into four dialects, spoken in the regions of Léon, Cornouaille, Trégor and the Vannetais.

As it evolves, language reflects the history and mentality of a civilization. The proper and place names that have come down to us are evidence of the customs and values of the early Bretons. It is possible, for instance, to discern the importance of hunting: names such as Alan or Alain refer to the stag or fox, considered noble animals, just as the old Breton term *arth-mael*, or "bear-prince", has evolved into the name Armel or Arzel. The power of Celtic Brittany rested on its warriors: a fact reflected in the forenames Tanguy and Jézéquel, and the family name Giquel. Proper names such as Cavanec or Cavaloc derive from the old Breton word for horse, an animal of vital importance in Celtic society. Pronunciation and spelling have changed over the centuries. In 1821, Le Gonidec published a Celto-Breton dictionary, whose prescriptions were accepted as the norm until 1939. Today, the faculties of literature at Rennes and Brest are attempting to standardize spelling on phonetic lines, with one letter or group of letters always representing a given sound, and vice-versa.

The 20th century has witnessed a resurgence of the Breton language. Banned in schools, the mother tongue of the Breton people, alone capable of expressing Breton thought and feeling, was no longer being passed down from one generation to the next. The dreaded clog, hung from the neck of a pupil who would not refrain from speaking Breton in class, was the badge of a whole era. It symbolized a long-standing campaign.

Writing to the Minister of Education in 1831, the Prefect for Finistère declared: *We must, by all possible means, work for the impoverishment and corruption of the Breton language, until the people are unable to communicate with one another from one town to the next.* Times have changed for the better. In 1977, a group of parents and sympathizers opened the first *Diwan* school – a term signifying the moment when a young shoot breaks through the ground.

The movement, which claims to be independent of any party political ties, is secular, and schooling is given free of charge. The accent is on the richness of a bilingual education. Diwan is now educating 620 children in 21 nursery and primary schools and one secondary establishment. Until the State agreed to pay the salaries of the 52 teachers, a great wave of sympathy swept Brittany, inspiring petitions and fund-raising efforts. At most *festnoz*, the admission charge was raised by one franc to support the Diwan.

A publishing house, *An Here*, has been set up to produce children's books and magazines in Breton, and has also completed the first ever dictionary in Breton alone. According to recent estimates, some 600,000 people, mainly in lower Brittany, have a command of the

old Breton language. This indicates the strength of the movement and the way people's thinking has developed.

Many elected politicians are beginning to think that, with European unity the order of the day, the cultural dynamism of a region is the best guarantee of its economic progress.

Oral Culture, Music and Song

Apart from the great success of Pierre-Jakez Hélias's novel, *Le cheval d'orgueil* (The Horse of Pride), Breton literature has not as yet made much impression. On the other hand, Brittany is a region with a strong oral tradition, and the Breton language is more widely spoken and sung than it is read. In the Middle Ages, the most popular literary genre was the *lai,* a sung poem similar to the Irish *laodh* or

Above: A gathering of bagpipers, at Gourin (Morbihan). Right: Local girl, at Pont-Aven (Finistère).

the German *lied.* It was performed to the strains of the harp and the *hrotta* (a small version of the violin), or accompanied by other instruments such as the hurdy-gurdy. However, not until the end of the 18th century and the counter-revolutionary Chouan wars, which inspired many great songs, did the oral tradition really develop and spread. The Abbé Cadic was its chief publisher. In the 19th century, the Breton protagonist of the Romantic Movement was Hersart de la Ville-marqué, who collected and published an anthology of popular authentic Celtic folk songs entitled *Barzaz Breiz* (Songs of Brittany).

It is therefore no surprise to discover that singers and musicians are today the spokespeople of this oral tradition, the storehouse of authentic Breton culture. For instance, the compositions of Alan Stivell, the best known of Breton musicians, combine age-old themes with modern musical arrangements, creating the synthesis of past and present that must characterize any living tradition. Less amous is the bard and harpist Myrdhin, vho, with great feeling, gives new vigor ɔ the eternal poetry of the Arthurian egends. A whole succession of instrunental and vocal groups have followed ₁ the footsteps of the *Diaouled ar Menez* (Devils of the Mountains), a group who vere outstanding in energizing Celtic festivals. Some have lacked staying power, ɔut others, solidly rooted in their native ɔil, continue to play an important role in ɩe cultural life of their region: *Tri Yann* (The Three Johns) in the Gallo country, *)ir ha Tan* (Steel and Fire) in the Vanietais, *Kanfarted Rostren* (The Lads of Rostrenen) in central Brittany, *Sonerien)u* (The Black Players) in the Bigouden ɔountry, and so on. It is a growing tradition of great vigor.

The range of Breton songs, constantly ɩpdated in line with current tastes, denonstrates the strength of poetic feeling ₔmong Celtic people. One of its most inɩeresting manifestations is the k*an-hadiskan,* a dance to a song for two alternatɩng voices. In this case, a human voice ₐccompaniment is preferred to the more ɩsual bagpipes. To keep time without beɔoming exhausted, the singers alternate at ɩe end of each musical phrase. Conɩisting of 80 to 100 couplets, these comɔositions put considerable emphasis on ɩe lyrics, harking back to the learned 3reton lays of the Middle Ages. The two ɔest-known types of song are the *gwerz* ₐnd the *son.* The *gwerz,* or lament, is ɔomposed in a minor key, and may reɔount a tragic event, or regret at the death ɔf a famous person. The *son,* on the other ɩand, is sung to a cheerful tune and is ɔoncerned with daily life and its pleasɩres. This duality can fairly be said to ɩum up the two sides of the Breton ₑemperament.

Contemporary poetry, especially when ɩet to music, makes a major contribution ɩo the spread of oral culture. Its four chief ₑxponents are Yann-Ber Calloc'h, Anjela Duval, Maodez Glanndour and Youenn

Gwernik. In his recordings, the last of these four brings together the written and the spoken word, thereby renewing the authentic ancient verbal tradition of the Celtic bards.

Breton Costume

Traditional Breton costume, nowadays less and less worn, is not in fact of very long standing: It certainly originated no earlier than the 16th century. Its rise and fall have taken less than four centuries. The Breton writer, Pierre-Jakes Hélias, has set it in its proper context: *Local costume – highly decorative, original and striking – is a typical feature of peasant civilizations. I hope this will not offend those who would like to trace it back to the distant past, thereby lending an aura of nobility to Celtic culture.*

By wearing original costume and headgear, men and women proclaimed their membership of a well-defined group. Confusion with a neighboring group was to be avoided at all costs. Proud of their

identity, the Breton peasants eventually created 70 different styles of dress, each corresponding to a particular clan, family unit or ethnic group. In referring to any such group, a characteristic aspect of dress was always used. For instance, the term for her head dress identified a *chikoloden, borleden* or *bigouden* woman. Where men were concerned, a *glazig* (cornflower blue) or *melenig* (pale yellow) was identified to the initiated observer by the predominant color of his costume.

As well as signaling membership of a group, costume also served to define the individual wearer. In addition to the person's geographical origins, it was possible to discern his or her occupation, marital status and wealth. A rich woman might wear a number of skirts, one over the other; a wealthy man several waistcoats of different lengths and colors.

Above: Breton wearing traditional dress.
Right: A procession at the pardon de Plouguerneau (Finistère).

Pieces of braid and the quantity of velvet were a sure guide to the social standing of individuals.

Nowadays, it is the costumes of the Cornouaille region that are best known. Until the turn of the century, there was a veritable guild of *bigouden* embroiderers who, knowing exactly the social status of their customers, assigned to each his or her proper social station by the quantity of braid they employed on an item of clothing. They used a number of motifs of which the most striking was the prestigious peacock feather. Others included the chain of life, the planet, the fish bone and the ram's horn. It took roughly three months to sew a complete wedding outfit for one couple.

The female headdress soon ceased to be a protective covering, becoming rather a coquettish piece of ornamentation. The cornets and collarets of the Fouesnant area; the lobster tails of the Paimpol coast; the megalithic contours and impish peaks of the Tréguier country were expressive of the quirks and temperament of each region, revealing its character and spirit. For instance, the restrained headgear of the Léon area – bespeaking the piety of the local women – contrasts with the exuberant creations of southern Cornouaille, where the women are more liable to kick over the traces and love change for its own sake. The most extreme expression of the southern temperament is seen in the headdress of the Bigouden country. Over the years from 1880 to 1950, it grew to a height of 32 cm (12.5 in). At Pouldreuzic, it is nicknamed the *pike* ("what a point!"), an amazing development in such a wind-swept area. Another striking example is the airy Fouesnant headdress, which has four curving wings of fine lace. A blue or pink ribbon surrounds the central bonnet, its two ends floating out behind. The wearer's face is framed in a high frilled collar. A Breton woman's head gear may equally bespeak tragedy. For instance,

e black linen *chipillien* worn by the women of the Île de Sein when in mourning has not changed in any respect since the lethal epidemic which decimated the local population during the last century.

Pardons and Pilgrimages

A *pardon* is a specifically Breton institution: a festival devoted to the patron saint of a local or regional sanctuary. Certain pardons have a very high reputation and, as well as pilgrims, they attract large numbers of tourists in search of local color. Others are unknown outside their local parish or small village. In the past, the great day was the local saint's feast day; nowadays, the event is generally held on the nearest Sunday. The liturgy would begin the day before. At midmorning on the actual day, there was a solemn mass, celebrated by a bishop whom they wished to honour. This was followed by a time of relaxation and entertainment. After vespers, the procession would set off, each parish having brought its cross and banners, the bearers in festive dress.

Latin litanies and Breton hymns alternated as the procession moved on. Before starting for home, the faithful were permitted to indulge in more worldy amusements. Pardons were therefore a meeting point of the sacred and profane, a manifestation of attachment to one's parish and local area, loved, celebrated and venerated by the Breton people.

On 19 May, **Tréguier** is the setting for a great pardon in honor of Saint Yves Héloury, who was both priest and lawyer. Having been the seat of a bishopric for almost ten centuries, the town boasts a fine cathedral in red granite. Beside the tomb of Saint Yves rest the mortal remains of Duke John V of Brittany, who insisted on being buried close to the man whom, ever since his death, the Bretons have considered their patron saint. According to the popular hymn: *Nann, n'eus ket e Breizh; Nann, n'eus ket unan. Nann, n'eus ket ur sant-Evel sant Erwan!* (There is no saint in Brittany to compare with Saint Yves). Yves Héloury was not canonized until 50 years after his death, in 1347.

At **Rumengol**, Trinity Sunday is the day of the pardon of Notre-Dame-de-tout-Remède (Our Lady of all Remedies), which is held on the summit of the **Menez-Hom**. Originally this was the chief place of pilgrimage for the sick and crippled.

At **Locronan** , on the second Sunday in July, the *Troménie de saint Ronan* is celebrated. A short pilgrimage takes place each year, commemorating the walk which – barefoot and on an empty stomach – Saint Ronan would take each morning. Every six years, there is a major pilgrimage – *la grande Troménie* -across 13 km (8 mi) of open countryside. The last took place in 1989. The itinerary follows the boundaries of the saint's territory, and probably corresponds to an older route of religious significance to the pre-Christian Celts. Dozens of flower-decked shrines mark the way, and there is a riot of magnificent costumes and parish banners.

The *pardon* of **Saint Anne**, Brittany's greatest religious festival, takes place on 26 July at **Auray**. Drawing 20,000 pilgrims and 800,000 visitors, it is almost a Breton version of Lourdes. Pilgrims come from far and wide to call on Saint Anne, who appeared here to Yves Nicolazic in 1623. The mother of the Virgin asked him to erect a chapel in her honor, on the precise spot where he had discovered a statue of the saint. Considered the female patron of Bretons, Saint Anne is even said to have been born in Brittany. As a widow, she made her way to Palestine, where she bore a child, Mary, the mother of Jesus. It is highly likely that devotion to Saint Anne, originating in the East, has here become mixed with the

worship of Ana, the mother of all the Celtic gods.

The *pardon* of **Sainte-Anne-la-Palud** is held on the last Sunday in August. According to legend, Jesus came to bid farewell to his grandmother before his passion, and opened up a miraculous spring. After the death of the saint, fishermen dragged up a statue in their nets. Recognizing her features, they built a chapel in her honor close to the spring. This is one of the most ancient Breton *pardons,* taking place in a magnificent setting overlooking the bay of Douarnanez.

Josselin celebrates its *pardon* on 8 September. In the 4th century, a ploughman discovered a statue in a bramble bush and took it home with him. Next morning, the statue had disappeared and he found it again on the original spot. This phenomenon was repeated several times, and the man eventually understood that the Virgin wanted to be venerated in this place with the title of Notre-Dame-du-Roncier (Our Lady of the Bramble Bush).

Also on 8 September, there is a *pardon* at **Le Folgoët.** The story goes that a simpleton, Saluan, nicknamed *ar fol coat* (the idiot of the wood), used to roam the area repeating the *Ave Maria*. On his death, in 1350, a lily bearing the inscription *Ave Maria,* grew up on his grave. Jean de Monfort accordingly had a chapel built to the Virgin of the idiot of the wood.

Breton Homes

Its features governed very much by local topography, climate and custom, the basic structure of the Breton house depends on whether its location is coastal or inland. On the one hand, there is the fisherman or sailor's cottage; on the other the peasant dwelling, surrounded by fields and woods, and often deliberately sited out of the way. With the spread of

Right: Stone-built house, in the Armorique regional park.

modern building methods, the traditional Breton house is tending to disappear, especially in the Côtes-d'Armor and Ille-et-Vilaine *départements*, where outside influence is most pronounced. The old styles of dwelling are most likely to be found in the Morbihan and in Finistère.

In the Morbihan, the builder can count on a milder climate and less violent winds than his neighbors to the west. As a result, the houses tend to be higher roofed, and their more curved lines contrast with the melancholy, austere spirit which tends to prevail in Finistère. This is particularly evident if one studies the thatched roofs: the thatch flows smoothly and harmoniously round dormer windows and loft doors. The loft is reached by a massive, sturdy stone staircase which is built against the outside wall of the house.

In Finistère, dwellings have to contend with two enemies: wind and rain. Their defense against the elements consists of appropriate external and internal arrangements. The orientation of the house is the main consideration, since wind and rain make their fiercest assaults from the west. The façade is therefore south-facing, and doors and windows are small and few. In towns and villages, the houses tend to be terraced, the terraces running east-west. Dwellings are invariably low, and rarely of more than one story. The walls are built of local materials, mainly granite, which varies in color from region to region. Construction methods also vary, featuring horizontal courses of irregular blocks, square blocks, or carefully cut blocks evenly laid, all following the traditions of centuries.

This latter technique is found only in aristocratic houses and the big 17th-and 18th-century farms. On the coast, walls are often white-washed, the bare granite appearing only in the uprights and lintels of doors and windows. The end walls surmounted by the two chimneys are a characteristic feature of houses in Finistère, which have absolutely no irregularities, being based purely and simply on a rectangular plan.

LIFE AT SEA

Many a Breton's destiny has been intimately linked with seas and oceans, whether he set sail as an adventurer in search of gold and glory, as a sailor to take part in foreign wars for colonial supremacy, or as a fisherman to exploit the seemingly inexhaustible resources of the deep.

Explorers and Colonists

From the 15th to the 18th centuries, the previously mysterious planet began to deliver up its secrets: New continents and new sources of wealth cast their spell upon seafarers, among them Bretons famous or obscure.

Whalers crossed the Atlantic in pursuit of their quarry, discovering Greenland and Newfoundland. Then, in the 16th century, sailors from Saint-Pol reached

Above: Ships' graveyard, Camaret-sur-Mer (Finistère).

226

Brazil, where they challenged the Portuguese monopoly.

But the most celebrated 16th-century Breton navigator, known to every French schoolchild, was undoubtedly **Jacques Cartier** (1491-1557). His manor house of Limoëlou, situated at Rothéneuf near Saint-Malo, contains a memorial to his discovery of Canada. In 1534, 1535 and 1541, this great explorer sailed up the Saint Lawrence in search of gold and diamonds, which were then thought to be readily available throughout the New World. Francis I, disappointed by the more down-to-earth French discoveries, eventually encouraged his sailors in piracy, which he had condemned in 1519 Since a colony with substantial gold deposits was not to be had, French explorers might as well take it from the most abundant available source: Spanish and Portuguese galleons bearing precious cargoes from South America.

A century later, Breton sailors were abroad on every ocean, as France and the rest of Europe strove to extend or strengthen their colonies and their empire.

In 1698, the Saint Malo captain **Gouin de Beauchesne** rounded the dreaded Cape Horn, aiming to reach the western seabord of South America and take on precious metals in Chile and Peru. Off the coast of Argentina, he landed on some islands discovered in 1592, and baptized them the *Iles Malouines* (in honor of Saint Malo). The islands were settled by the French and sold to the Spanish in 1766. In 1833, they were occupied by the British, who called them the Falklands.

Another sea dog from Saint Malo, **Bertrand François Mahé de la Bourdonnais** (1699-1753), having entered the service of the *Compagnie des Indes* (the French India Company), in 1735 became governor general of the Mascarenes. These Indian Ocean islands, which included Réunion, supplied France and Brittany with sugar cane, and in the mid-19th century assured the prosperity of the Nantes refineries.

In the Indian Ocean again, **Yves Joseph de Kerguelen-Trémarec** (1734-97), a native of Quimper, discovered the islands which bear his name in 1772.

Opportunist Pirates

From time immemorial, **piracy** seems to have offered an alternative life-style to seafaring peoples, from Brittany to the China Seas. In the West, it was practiced as early as the 8th century B.C. This form of brigandage developed spontaneously on all the great sea routes: easy access to great wealth has always excited human greed.

In the Middle Ages, sea-going trade developed mainly in the Channel and along the coasts of the Bay of Biscay. For small isolated ports, and impoverished islands such as **Batz, Groix and Ouessant**, pillaging ships that had been forced onto the rocks or attacking a vessel that had strayed off course was often a way of

ensuring the community's survival. The Bordeaux wines carried by English ships or the salt taken on board by the Dutch in the ports of the Retz country were like manna from heaven, immediately resold through contraband networks. For the English, the greatest robbers of all were the sailors of Saint Malo, who recovered by piracy what they had just sold for coin of the realm! More frequent encounters in the 13th and 14th centuries between whaling vessels in the Channel and out in the Atlantic led to new temptations. Quarter was rarely given, and if seafaring was synonymous with adventure, it was also the source of danger, violence and untold savagery.

Nation states tried in vain to tackle the problem. Finally, they resolved to legalize the practice, themselves taking a share in the profits. So a new form of pirate appeared, the mercenary, otherwise known as a privateer. In time of war, attacks on enemy merchant shipping became common practice. The vague regulations governing it were easily bent to serve respective private interests: Attacks on Spanish treasure ships were too profitable for those in authority not to turn a blind eye, at least once in a while.

The great age of the **privateers** began in the 16th century, and with it the heyday of piracy and buccaneering. There was also a form of small-time piracy, concentrating on estuaries and off-shore islands and linked with the no less traditional activity of coastal smuggling.

This was absolutely true of the lord of **Coëtlestremeur** and his crew, who began their careers locally in the **Léon** area. They later joined forces with Norman pirates and sought their fortune off the Spanish coast. They ended their days on the gallows in 1556: a not infrequent end for members of their trade.

The crews were often a mixed bag: As well as professional sailors, they included many renegades from both town and country, merchants, peasants and ar-

tisans, all forced into the sea-going life by poverty. Whatever their origins, they did not fail to terrorize their victims, Spanish or Portuguese. Pirate or privateer? The distinction was a very fine one. National governments looking for daring sailors willing to run great risks were not too particular about engaging former pirates of proven ability to serve as privateers. On the other hand, the lust for gold was often enough to transform a privateer into an out-and-out pirate.

Life at sea was dangerous in the extreme, and conditions on board spartan to say the least. Crew members were often reduced to eating *hard ship's biscuit, an apology for butter, and a bit of bacon or fish,* a diet that was liable to continue for months on end. Often poorly armed, pirates set more store by their cunning and courage: cunning in approaching their prey without causing alarm (they

Above: Deep-sea fisherman – heir to a proud tradition. Right: Lighthouse on the headland of Saint-Mathieu (Finistère).

would fly a friendly flag, or dress up as peaceable seafarers), and courage when it came to grappling and fighting at close quarters!

The West Indies, through which the treasure-laden Spanish galleons had to run on their homeward journey, quickly became the favored haunt of the buccaneers: a string of islands and islets where the smallest inlet might conceal a privateer (or pirate) lurking in ambush. The most famous, Turtle Island, became the setting for many a novel. Here was born the legend of pirate and privateer complete with barrels of rum, blood-spattered pieces of eight, and distant turquoise horizons. The great Breton privateers were seen as very romantic figures by some novelists.

The 18th century, golden age of sailing ships, saw a general strengthening of national navies, which sounded the death-knell of piracy. Privateering, on the other hand, continued until the turn of the 19th century. Three great Breton sailors cast their shadows over this period: René

Duguay-Trouin, Jacques Cassard and Robert Surcouf.

René Duguay-Trouin (1673-1736), the son of a rich Saint Malo ship owner, enlisted at the age of sixteen as a privateer. At 24, he was already in command of a frigate and earned a great reputation for courage and strategic sense in attacking English and Dutch vessels in the Atlantic, the Channel and the North Sea. During the War of the Spanish Succession (1701-14), he was appointed head of a squadron and ennobled by Louis XIV. He then embarked on a Brazilian adventure with a fleet fitted out by the ship owners of Saint Malo. The capture of Rio de Janeiro in 1711 was a highly profitable conclusion: 350 merchantmen captured or destroyed, for the loss of only three ships. In 1726 he was promoted to lieutenant general.

Jacques Cassard (1679-1740), a native of Nantes, first went to sea at the age of twelve. He began his life as a privateer in the Channel, then switched to the Mediterranean (from 1708 to 1710), where he fought alongside the Barbary pirates (Louis XIV had signed a treaty with the Dey of Algiers whereby Muslim pirate galleys and French privateers combined to harry the English). In 1710, he enlisted in the royal navy and became the scourge of the seas, plundering ports in the English West Indies, the Cape Verde islands, Dutch Guyana and Curaçao.

Robert Surcouf (1773-1827), another product of Saint Malo, began as a cabin boy, aged thirteen. During the stormy years of the Revolution, having risen to the rank of captain, he was involved in the highly lucrative slave trade, carrying "ebony" from the African coasts to the island of Bourbon (now Réunion). During the Coalition wars, he returned to privateering, attacking British ships in the Indian Ocean. His fame soon obscured even that of his illustrious predecessor, Duguay-Trouin. Returning to Saint Malo in 1801, he went into early retirement,

living off the enormous booty he had stashed away. But idleness did not agree with him for long, and he was again harrassing English shipping by 1807.

Fishermen Past and Present

In the past, Brittany's deep-sea fishermen have been engaged in two epic pursuits: whaling, and later cod fishing off Iceland.

Following the example of the Basques, the Bretons ventured into northern latitudes as early as the 15th century in the hunt for whales. For two hundred years, they quartered the seas between Newfoundland and Greenland, demonstrating remarkable courage and resilience. According to the historian Jules Michelet: *Whaling was not then the safe mechanized slaughter it has since become: the harpoon was hand-thrown at close quarters, with considerable risk to life and limb. Relatively few whales were killed, but the chase demanded infinitely more in seamanship, patience, discernment and*

229

courage. The outcome was less oil but more glory. In its approach to the task, each nationality displayed its especial virtues. The Bretons were renowned for their endurance and quiet determination, though at times of danger they were capable of sublime eccentricity. Whaling in northern waters declined in the 17th century, and mariners turned their attentions to the southern oceans, where first the Dutch then, in the 19th century, the Americans held a near monopoly.

More important to Brittany was the era of the *terra-neuvas* (Newfoundlanders) and "Islandais" (Icelanders), who fished for cod in distant waters. The activity began towards the end of the 15th century, flourished off Newfoundland in the 17th, and reached its height in the 19th in the waters around Iceland. It brought prosperity to the ports of the north Brittany coast, from Saint-Malo to Paimpol.

Above: Fishing nets at Guénolé harbor.
Right: Worker harvesting salt on the Guérande peninsula.

When Pierre Loti published his novel *Pêcheur d'Islande* (The Fisherman of Iceland) in 1886, he was recording for posterity a way of life already doomed to extinction. The fishing fleets would leave Brittany in early March and not return until August, when they would *return to to the Gascony coast where their catch would fetch a good price, and visit the sandy islands to buy salt for next year's voyage.* All in all, the fishermen were lucky to spend six months of the year at home with their families, which is why they were known as Icelanders or New-foundlanders. Each year the sea would send a number of ships to a watery grave and, near Paimpol, the chapel of Perros-Hamon, known as the chapel of the ship-wrecked, stands beside the Widows' Cross (*Croix des Veuves*).

The work was rough, long and ex-hausting; conditions on board ship primi-tive in the extreme: Below deck, the sailors' accommodation consisted of a "low chamber" with a single opening *cut in the ceiling and covered by a wooden hatch.* This cramped area was occupied by a *massive table*, round which the sailors had to *slide themseves to sit on narrow boxes fixed to the oak walls.* On either side, *the niche-like bunks seemed to have been cut into the timbers of the ship's hull. The woodwork was rough-hewn and clumsy, impregnated with the smell of unwashed bodies and of salt.* Up on deck, when the ship struck a shoal of cod, the work continued day and night without a pause. Teams of fishermen worked in shifts, some hauling in the long lines of *heavy, steel-gray fish,* others gutting the cod with widebladed knives and salting them as they went.

Nowadays, while inshore fishing has remained largely a matter of human skill and strength, harvesting the ocean deeps has been mostly mechanized. Factory ships drag an enormous conical net in their wake, which sweeps up all in its path. This trawling technique is highly

destructive of the marine environment, since it makes no distinction between the cod and thousands of other species. Once hauled aboard, the fish are washed and cleaned on automated production lines. For tuna, a seine netting technique is used: the boat encircles the shoal of fish by playing out a floating net, whose bottom is pulled tight to imprison the catch. The tuna are then hauled out with large landing nets and almost immediately frozen. Seine netting is also practiced in sardine fishing.

In modern times, a plethora of regulations have been introduced to prevent over-fishing and conserve fish stocks. This is true, for instance, of scallop fishing: In the bay of Saint-Brieuc, the prime French breeding ground of this species, fishing is authorized only three times a week, in the period between November and March. Each outing is limited to three quarters of an hour, the time it takes to set up and dismantle the *dragues*: steel-mesh nets which are stretched between upright stakes.

The Extraction of Salt

The Bretons have been extracting salt from sea water since Roman times. The industry is esablished on the southern shores of the peninsula: in the eastern part of the Golfe du Morbihan (between Sarzeau and Séné), west of the Brière marshes (between Quimiac and Pont d'Armes) and, first and foremost, on the Guérande peninsula (between Le Croisic and Guérande itself). The basic principles are simplicity itself, since the aim is to exploit the natural forces of wind and sun in the evaporation of sea water. The first task is to find a suitable natural site: a tidal meadow, or *baule,* flooded by the sea at high tide. In such locations, crystalizing pans for the various stages of the process are dug out of the clay, together with channels (*étiers*) to allow the influx of sea water.

During high tides, sea water is channeled into extensive *vasières*, or ponds in which the mud can precipitate, where it heats up and the salt concentrates as a re-

from each sink-hole, in thirty or forty successive harvests, and between 70 and 90 kilos (150-200 lb) of fine salt. The rest of the year is spent in repairing salt-pans and inlet channels, which are constantly being eroded by natural forces.

The salt workers of Guérande have declined in numbers over the years, and the 10,000 tonnes of salt they produce annually are but a drop in the ocean compared with the vast quantities produced by the southern French *Salines du Midi* (1.5 mio tonnes in 1982). Nevertheless, the Breton attachment to tradition is a guarantee of superior quality: Unrefined and rich in trace elements, their salt is much sought after in many quarters, particularly by the health conscious.

Oyster Farming

For many centuries, Breton oyster beds were able to meet the demands made upon them. The bay of Cancale, whose supplies seemed virtually inexhaustible, was exploited by the Normans and the English, as well as by local fishermen. In the mid-18th century, there was at last growing concern that this precious natural resource was being depleted. A royal edict, issued in 1759, simply forbade oyster fishing between April and October, the breeding season of the shellfish.

Even so, stocks continued to diminish, and more active attempts were made to safeguard the mollusc's future. How dear the delicious oyster was to 19th-century gastronomes is shown by the fact that one of Paris's most celebrated restaurants was called *Les Rochers de Cancale*. It is referred to several times in Honoré de Balzac's chronicle of Parisian life and society, *La Comédie Humaine*.

In the years 1826 to 1858, ways were found of gathering the seed oysters, or spats, using a sort of wooden plank strategically placed in the sea. The technique was widely adopted and cultivation of the wild oyster began. In the Gulf of

sult of evaporation. Water enters these reservoirs at a temperature of 18°C and is released when it reaches 22°C. The brine then runs gently down into a second storage basin, the *corbier*, where evaporation and precipitation are allowed to continue until the solution reaches a concentration of 250 grams of salt per litre of water. The last stage is the salt-pans proper (*salines*), a network of small rectangular basins, where the brine settles into sink-holes or *oeillets*. At the end of this drawn-out process, the salt separates off and crystalizes.

All is now ready for the salt "harvest", which in Brittany normally begins in mid-June. The finest crystals are scraped off the surface, while tens of kilos of coarser salt are extracted from the bottom of the sink-holes. By the end of the season, in September, almost a tonne and a half of coarse salt will have been taken

Above: Salt worker driving water from a sink hole, where the brine precipitates. Right: Farming oysters, Cancale.

Morbihan, at Auray and Locmariaquer, it was Napoleon III's cousin, Elisa Bacciochi, who around 1875 encouraged the spread of oyster growing. The Cancalais soon followed her example, and it worked. Fifty years later, farming techniques were also introduced in the Côtes-d'Armor region, around Lézardrieux and Paimpol.

Infinite care is lavished on the young oysters. The larvae are given tiles on which to attach themselves and develop during their first nine months of life. In the spring, the spats are separated from these first supports and "sown" at high tide in special oyster beds. There, the seed oysters attach themselves to metal netting fixed to stakes, which are known as *clas*. It takes a further three or four years for the oysters to reach maturity. Throughout this time, they have to be separated one from another each time a storm throws them together *en masse*. When harvested, they are washed, sorted, purified in tanks of clean sea water, washed and checked again, and at last packed in hampers, ready for their final journey to the table.

Nowadays, the Cancale oyster beds cover 400 hectares (988 acres) and produce 3000 tonnes of oysters a year. A good half of these are eaten during the Christmas and New Year celebrations.

Tradition and the Modern World

A list of Breton industries dependent on the sea would not be complete without a word for the *goémoniers*, or gatherers of seaweed, who harvest both coastal algae, such as the *Fucus* varieties, and deep-sea kelp of the *Laminaria* family. These are used as fertilizer, and are also processed by chemical companies for the valuable iodine and alginates that they contain.

Algae also enrich the waters in which they grow. With the invigorating sea air, they form the basis of thalassotherapy, whose health-giving benefits can be enjoyed at at least ten centers around the coast of Brittany.

233

BRITTANY'S NATURAL HISTORY

Brittany is a peninsula stretching 200 km (124 mi) from east to west between the Atlantic and the English Channel: a projecting mass of granite and schist, 35,311 square kilometers (13,634 sq mi) in area, its coasts constantly lapped by the tides. Though the landscape varies considerably from locality to locality, there is an underlying unity determined by a number of common factors: the nature of the soil, the effects of erosion over thousands of years, a temperate maritime climate, and the dominating influence of the sea on three sides of the peninsula.

An Ancient Land

Geologically speaking, Brittany is one of the most ancient land masses in Europe, since it had already emerged from the sea some four million years ago.

Above: The imposing cliffs of the Pointe du Raz (Finistère).

The rocks of the Armorican shelf are therefore very old. Over two thirds of the peninsula dark-colored schists predominate. Some are hard and may be used for roofing, such as the fine **Sizun** slates, others are soft, for instance the clays and kaolins that have given rise to Brittany's ceramics industry. Granite accounts for the other third of the land mass. The gray and pink granites of **Trégor** are magnificent building materials and give Breton architecture its character. **Kersanton** granite is an ideal stone for carving and has been used all over Brittany.

The relief of the peninsula is determined by two ranges of hills orientated east-west. In the north, they run parallel with the Channel coast from **Méné** heath (south-east of Saint-Brieuc) to the **Monts d'Arrée,** whose highest point, **Tuchenn-Gador,** is 384 m (1260 ft) above sea level. To the south, the second range – the **Black Mountains** – runs parallel with the Atlantic coast from **Guerlédan** lake to the majestic **Ménez Hom** (330 m or 1083 ft), which bars the way to the **Cro-**

zon peninsula. The land rises from south to north, and from east to west. This means that the eastern half of the province, known as Upper Brittany (Haute Bretagne), is actually lower-lying than Lower Brittany (Basse Bretagne) to the west. This paradox is due to the fact that, for the ancient Celts, the prime point of the compass was not north but east – in honor of the rising sun. Hence the term Haute Bretagne (Upper or High Brittany) has nothing to do with the relief of the area, but signifies its important easterly location.

A Coastline of Contrasts

Brittany faces the sea on three sides, giving the province a coastline (without counting the islands) 3000 km (1864 mi) long: as much as the rest of France put together. Its amazing indentations are explained by the fact that, some 5500 years before our era, there was a general rise in sea level, which completely transformed the landscape: Deep gulfs appeared, and river valleys became winding estuaries.

These narrow drowned valleys, in which the tides ebb and flow, are known as *abers* in the **Léon** area (**Aber-Wrach, Aber-Benoît, Aber-Idult**) and elsewhere as *sters* or *rivers* -the same word as in English – (the **Odet** between **Bénodet** and **Quimper**, or the **Auray** flowing into the Gulf of Morbihan). The effects of the tide are felt as much as 10 or 15 km (6-9 mi) inland, reaching towns such as Auray, **Hennebont**, Quimper, **Châteaulin** and **Dinan.** In former times, the tidal nature of these inlets made it possible to install mills worked by sea power (*milin-mor* or *meil-mor*), which have now become the object of conservation efforts. These were the ancestors of the modern **Rance** hydro-electric scheme and dam. As a landscape feature, these *abers*, their banks studded with countless châteaux and manor houses, are a priceless scenic asset and tourist attraction.

A further attraction of the Breton coastline is its many bays (at **Mont-Saint-Michel, Saint-Brieuc, Douarnanez** or **Audierne,** for example), while a most remarkable feature is the Gulf of Morbihan. This inland sea is dotted with over 300 islands, on one of which – the island of **Gavrinis –** menhirs now standing in the water indicate to what extent the sea must have risen over the last 5000 years. The many off-shore islands, once integral parts of the mainland, are further evidence of the same steady reclamation of the land.

Bays and gulfs may be fringed with marshland where the sea has deposited its silt, as for instance at **Dol.** Some of these areas have been reclaimed for agriculture by building dikes and flood ponds. Similarly, the marshlands bordering the **Loire** have been transformed into meadows. The vast **Brière** marshes, on the other hand, have remained a wilderness. On the **Guérande** peninsula, a remarkable complex of salt-pans has been in use since the Middle Ages, providing one of the oldest sources of wealth for Brittany.

Elsewhere, the coast is rocky. The highest cliffs are to be found in the north (72 m or 236 ft at **Cap Fréhel**) and on the Crozon peninsula (100 m or 328 ft the **Cap de la Chèvre**). In other places, the cliffs are less dramatic, rising to 10 or 20 m (33-66 ft) and interspersed with sandy coves and beaches, as on the Côte de Granit Rose (Pink Granite Coast) around **Perros-Guirec.** Long beaches of fine sand, popular with tourists and holiday makers, are common on the Atlantic coast, from the island of **Tudy** to **Beg-Meil,** between **Lorient** and **Quiberon,** and at **La Baule.**

The coastline is constantly evolving. Watching the fury of the waves at the **la Torche headland**, not far from the celebrated **Tronoën calvary** on the **Penmarc'h peninsula,** or the naked power of the sea at the **pointe du Raz,** it is easy to understand how, from a geological per-

spective, change is occurring at an alarmingly rapid rate. It is tempting to define Brittany as a country that the sea has not yet managed to wipe out completely. Meanwhile, the wounds and lacerations inflicted during the titanic conflict of land and elements lie open to view.

An Oceanic Climate

It is often said that Brittany suffers from a harsh, inhospitable climate – a judgment which has no foundation in fact. Of course, Brittany's weather can hardly be compared with that of the South of France, where Mediterranean conditions prevail. Rather, Brittany enjoys a maritime climate, dominated by the Atlantic weather systems of wind and tide.

One of the most positive features of this climate is its general mildness. Varia-

Above: The Trévezel outcrop, in the Amorique regional park. Right: Breton fauna, from a gastronome's point of view.

tions between day and night-time temperatures, and also from one season to the next, are far less pronounced than further inland. The ocean, bearing the relatively warmer waters of the Gulf Stream, warms up more slowly than the land masses it meets, but the cooling process is also correspondingly slower. The moderating influence of the sea is felt particularly in winter, when, at least in coastal areas, frost and snow are extremely rare. The average January temperature on the island of **Ouessant** is 8 degrees Centigrade (46°F) and 7 degrees Centigrade (45°F) in **Brest** and **Quimper**: very similar to readings at Nice on the Côte d'Azur.

Mild winters, then, are one of the features of Brittany, against which must be balanced temperate – though by no means cool – summers. The average July temperature is 17.3°C (63°F) in Quimper, 18.5°C (65°F) in **Saint-Malo**. These figures are distinctly lower than readings taken in the south of the province. At **La Baule,** on the Breton Riviera, the average s 19.5°C (67°F), while at **Le Croisic** the sun's power is sufficiently intense to permit the extraction of salt from sea water. It is common for Brittany to enjoy a stable period of fine weather in July and August, unlike the British Isles where weather is far less predictable.

Having said this, it is rain rather than low temperatures for which Brittany most often stands accused. Again, the charge is unjust: Annual rainfall at Carnac (732 mm or 29 in) or Dinard (698 mm or 27.5 in) is actually lower than in Bordeaux (947 mm or 37 in) or Nice (868 mm or 34 in). It is true, of course, that Brittany, while not experiencing heavy rainfall, is generally damp. Unlike the Mediterranean area, it rains off and on throughout the year, often in the form of drizzle or Scotch mist. As a result, rain may be officially recorded on 150 to 200 days a year, but this figure hardly reflects the reality, since days of significantly heavy rainfall are far fewer. What statistics cannot show is that the weather changes very quickly, especially in summer, when it is common for a brief shower to be followed by a long period of warm sunshine.

Vegetation

Coastal Brittany (Armor) is frequently contrasted with its forest hinterland (Argoat), though little of the primeval forest that once covered much of the interior now remains. The surviving woodland is somewhat patchy. The main forests are to be found in the Morbihan (the Forêt de Lanoucé north of Josselin, and those of Quénécan and Lanvaux north of Vannes), in Ille-et-Vilaine (Rennes and Paimpont), and in the Loire-Atlantique (Forêt du Gâvre). Mankind must bear responsibility for the present situation. For centuries, they cut timber for house building and furniture, for fuel, and above all for ships. Even so, the original woodlands were probably far more restricted than legends of the ancient forest of Brocéliande would lead us to believe. The surviving woodland consists mainly of oak and beech, and there are plenty of coppiced areas planted with smaller species such as holly, aspen and mountain ash.

Hedged fields (*bocage*) cover much of the countryside. This is not so much to create windbreaks or dry out boggy soil, but rather reflects the system of land tenure. The right to enclose a plot of land was a mark of ownership. *Bocage* is not therefore a natural form of vegetation, but the result of farming methods and human intervention on the landscape during feudal times.

More natural, though by no means unique to Brittany, are the vast heathlands which cover much of the interior and, in some places, extend as far as the coast. The characteristic plants of this secondary vegetation, which has replaced the original forest cover, are broom and heather. The different seasons are marked by the bright yellows of gorse and broom, and the pink of the heather. Some heath areas are now officially protected, as much for their flora as their fauna, since they constitute ecological environments of special interest. Other specialized environments are the peat bogs of the Grande Brière, which harbor many rare marshland plants of special interest to botanists and photographers.

The coastal vegetation is quite different, reflecting three different types of habitat. Cliffs and rocks are home to the sea pink or thrift, white-flowering sea campion and the golden-yellow horned poppy. Along the dunes grow sea bindweed, sea spurge, dwarf thistle, sea stock, salad burnet and everlasting. Finally, mudbanks and saltmarshes support glassworts, sea aster and lilac-tinted sea-lavender.

Wildlife

As everywhere in Europe, wild animals are on the decline. Packs of wolves are now but a distant folk memory. A hundred or so were left in 1850, but the clearing of heathland and systematic use of poisons ensured that none survived into the 20th century. The roe deer is the animal most typical of Brittany, thriving in woodland and finding cover on gorse-clad heaths. Sightings of wild boar, fox and badger are becoming less and less frequent, as these creatures are relentlessly hunted. Smaller predators still flourish on the hillsides: weasel, pine marten, stone marten, and Brittany's emblem, the elegant stoat or ermine which wears a white coat in winter.

Efforts have been made to reintroduce certain endangered species: the beaver in the **Monts d'Arrée**, bats in the **Châteaulin valle**y (where a reserve has been established to protect 15 of Europe's 30 species), and the salmon. These extraordinary fish, which migrate to feed-

Right: A flight of gulls, on Brittany's northwest coast.

ing grounds off Greenland and return two years later to spawn in their native rivers, abounded until the last century. According to official statistics, 4000 were then caught every year. By the late 1970s, the number recorded as caught had dropped to just 150. Now, hundreds of rivers have been cleaned of pollution, and organizations have been set up to re-establish this valuable natural food resource.

One of Brittany's great natural assets is the abundance and variety of its wild birds, which can be observed in 35 sanctuaries created and maintained by the SEPNB (*Société d'Etude et de Protection de la Nature en Bretagne*). Founded in 1958 by a small group of enthusiasts, this association runs many social and educational activities, and publishes a bulletin (*Pen ar Bed)* avidly read by all those concerned with the environment in the west of France. Bird watchers from all over Europe visit Brittany when rare sightings are officially reported .

Inland, it is possible to observe whimbrel, buzzard, harrier, pipit and a wide variety of song birds. On the coast, one encounters gulls of various kinds, cormorant and, less frequently, puffin, guillemot and razorbill. Puffins, especially, are becoming a rarity.

The waters of southern Brittany are a haven for seasonal visitors such as the leatherback turtle, the largest of all marine reptiles. Weighing up to 800 kilos (1764 lb), in some years this giant creature travels from the coast of Guyana to Europe, making landfall anywhere between Portugal and Norway. Another large visitor is the basking shark, which may measure 13 m (43 ft) and weigh up to 5 tonnes. From March to the end of May, this harmless beast is still hunted by **Concarneau** trawlers off the **Glénan islands,** the Île de Groix and **Belle-Île.** Its liver yields a vitamin-rich oil, while its flesh is fed to poultry. Finally, near Ouessant is the main breeding ground of the gray seal. Three m (7 ft) in length and

weighing almost 300 kilos (661 lb), this seal can descend to depths of more than 100 m (328 ft) and remain under water for over fifteen minutes while hunting for various species of fish.

Sites of Special Interest

In the Côtes-d'Armor département, the **Sept-Iles** archipelago off Perros-Guirec is home to a vast colony of sea birds: some 10,000 pairs representing fifteen different species, which nest on Rouzic Island. The pink sandstone cliffs of **Cap Fréhel**, backed by 300 hectares (741 acres) of wild heathland, are another sanctuary for thousands of cliff-nesting sea birds which offer a magnificent, if noisy, sight to bird watchers.

In Finistère, the **Parc Naturel Régional d'Armorique** (tel. 98 21 90 69) extends over 110,000 hectares (272,000 acres), taking in 38 local authority areas. The park staff make visitors more aware of their environment by organizing nature walks along the sea shore or inland.

At the **Domaine du Menez-Meur** hides have been set up to enable visitors to watch the wildlife. The **Maison de la Baie d'Audierne** (tel. 98 82 61 76), where the reserve consists of 600 hectares (1483 acres) of pools, marshland and dunes, stages a program of activities of botanical and ornithological interest. Further south, the **Cap-Sizun-Goulien bird sanctuary** (tel. 98 70 13 53), located in a magnificent setting of high cliffs and heathland, is an ideal place for rambles and nature walks. The walks vary in length but it is a good idea to wear stout shoes or boots.

The **Gulf of Morbihan**, a veritable inland sea of 12,000 hectares (48 sq. miles), is a haven for many species of migratory bird, while the **Koh Kastell reserve on Belle-Île-en-Mer** (tel. 97 31 81 93) is home to one of the finest colonies of sea birds in all of Brittany.

In the Loire-Atlantique, the **Grande Brière regional park** authority (tel. 40 88 42 72) runs tours of its vast (7000 hectare or 27 sq. mile) marshland wilderness.

Nelles Maps ...the maps that get you going.

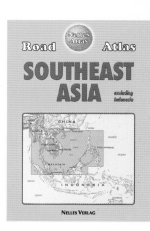

- Afghanistan
- Australia
- Bangkok
- Burma
- Caribbean Islands 1 /
  Bermuda, Bahamas,
  Greater Antilles
- Caribbean Islands 2 /
  Lesser Antilles
- China 1 /
  North-Eastern China
- China 2 /
  Northern China
- China 3 /
  Central China
- China 4 /
  Southern China
- Crete
- Egypt
- Hawaiian Islands
- Hawaiian Islands 1 / Kauai
- Hawaiian Islands 2 /
  Honolulu, Oahu

Nelles Maps

- Hawaiian Islands 3 /
  Maui, Molokai, Lanai
- Hawaiian Islands 4 / Hawaii
- Himalaya
- Hong Kong
- Indian Subcontinent
- India 1 / Northern India
- India 2 / Western India
- India 3 / Eastern India
- India 4 / Southern India
- India 5 / North-Eastern India
- Indonesia
- Indonesia 1 / Sumatra
- Indonesia 2 /
  Java + Nusa Tenggara
- Indonesia 3 / Bali
- Indonesia 4 / Kalimantan
- Indonesia 5 / Java + Bali
- Indonesia 6 / Sulawesi

- Indonesia 7 /
  Irian Jaya + Maluku
- Jakarta
- Japan
- Kenya
- Korea
- Malaysia
- West Malaysia
- Manila
- Mexico
- Nepal
- New Zealand
- Pakistan
- Philippines
- Singapore
- South East Asia
- Sri Lanka
- Taiwan
- Thailand
- Vietnam, Laos
  Cambodia

GUIDELINES

PREPARATION

Entry Requirements

All nationalities need a valid passport and some also require a visa to enter France. Visas are not required by citizens of the European Community (EC), Andorra, Monaco, Switzerland, United States and Canada. Three types of visa are currently issued:

- a transit visa, valid for 3 days
- a short stay visa, valid for 90 days after date of issue, good for multiple entries, and
- a *visa de circulation*, allowing multiple stays of ninety days over three years with a maximum of 180 days in any one-year period.

After a three-month period EC nationals are officially supposed to apply for a *carte de séjour*, however as EC-passports are rarely stamped, it will only be in a working situation that this will be enforced. Applications have to be made to the *Préfecture* in the *département* where you are resident.

Climate

Brittany has a distinctly maritime climate with fairly stable patterns. Summer is invariably reliable, beginning around mid-June and often lasting until mid-October. Sea temperatures during summer are consistently warm on the south coast, less so on the north coast. Winter is seldom severe, but in the west and along the coast it can be damp and very misty.

French Government Tourist Offices

These can help tourists plan their holidays but they do not book tours or hotel rooms.

Australia: Kindersley House, 33 Bligh Street, Sydney, NSW 2000, Tel: (612) 233 3277. **Belgium**: 21 Av. de la Toison d'Or, 1060 Brussels Tel: 513 0762. **Canada**: 1981 Avenue McGill College, Suite 490, Montreal, Que. H3A 2W9, Tel: (514) 288 4264. 1 Dundas Street West, Suite 2405, Box 8, Toronto, Ontario M5G 1Z3, Tel: (416) 593 4723. **Denmark**: NY Ostergarde 33, 1101 Kobenhavn, Tel: 3311 4641. **Great Britain**: 178 Piccadilly, London W1V 0AL, Tel: (071) 491 7622. **Hong Kong**: c/o Air France, Alexandra House, 21st Floor, Chater Road, Hong Kong, Tel: (852) 5-22131/35. **Ireland**: 35 Lower Abbey Street, Dublin, Tel: 771871. **Netherlands**: Prinsengracht 670, 1017 KX Amsterdam, Tel: (20) 620 3141. **Spain**: Gran via 59, 28013 Madrid, Tel: 541 8808. **Switzerland**: Löwenstrasse 59, 8023 Zürich, Tel: 212 1644. **USA**: 610 Fifth Avenue, Suite 222, New York, NY 10020-2452, Tel: (212) 757 1125. 645 North Michigan Avenue, Suite 630, Chicago, IL 60611-2836, Tel: (312) 337 6301. 2305 Cedar Springs Boulevard, Dallas, Texas 75201, Tel: (214) 720 4010. 9454 Wilshire Boulevard, Beverley Hills, California 90212-2967, Tel: (213) 272 2661.

French Embassies Overseas

Before arrival, visas and specific enquiries can be obtained through the French embassies and/or consulates in your home country.

TRAVELING TO BRITTANY

By Air

Nantes, and to a lesser extent Brest, Quimper and Rennes are the only airports in the region offering international connections. Brit'Air has scheduled services from Brest, Quimper and Rennes to London-Gatwick.

Most international flights will necessitate changing at Paris to one of the domestic carriers serving Brittany, with domestic airports in Dinard, Lorient, Saint Brieuc and Vannes. There are flight connections from Brittany to major French towns such as Lyon, Marseille, Bordeaux, Nice, Toulouse and Strasbourg.

By Sea

Brittany Ferries, Wharf Road, Portsmouth PO2 8RW, Tel: 0705 827702 and Millbay Docks, Plymouth PL1 3EW, Tel: 0752 2211312. Portsmouth-Caen (6 hours); Portsmouth-St. Malo (9 hours); Plymouth-Roscoff (6 hours); Poole-Cherbourg (4 hrs 30 mins).

Condor, New Jetty, P.O. Box 10, St. Peter Port, Guernsey, Tel: 0481 726121. Jersey-St. Malo (1 hr 10 mins); Guernsey-St. Malo (1 hr 45 mins); Sark-St Malo (1 hr 55 mins).

P & O European Ferries, Channel House, Channel View Road, Dover CT16 3BR, Tel: 0304 203388. Portsmouth-Cherbourg (4 hrs 45 mins).

Sealink Stena Line, Charter House, Park Street, Ashford TN24 8EX, Tel: 0233 647047. Southampton-Cherbourg (5 hours).

By Train

Travelers from Paris can choose between the TGV (high-speed train), a night train with couchette, and ordinary services. Trains coming from the North and East enter Brittany via Le Mans and Rennes; those from the South generally pass through Nantes. A coastal line from Normandy enters Brittany at Dol.

The advent of the TGV Atlantique train has considerably reduced journey times from Paris. Seats must be reserved on these trains, and at certain peak times a supplement is obligatory, costing between 32F and 120F, depending on the day, traveling time and class. For destinations not served by TGV, travelers will have to change trains. For instance, passengers for Saint-Malo change at Rennes, and for Quimper at Brest or Lorient.

The Paris terminus for trains to and from Brittany is the Gare Montparnasse. Information, Tel: (1) 45 82 50 50, reservations, Tel: (1) 45 65 60 60, and Minitel 3615, code SNCF.

Tourists planning to travel extensively in Brittany should invest in a *France Va-*
cances pass (unlimited travel for any four days during a period of 15 days or any 9 days in a month), which must be purchased outside of France. Once in France, discounts are available for couples with the *Carte Couple*, for families with a *Carte Kiwi*, for senior citizens with a *Carte Vermeille*, and for the under-26s with a *Carte Jeune*, and for anyone traveling on *Période Bleu* days.

By Car

It takes 3 hours to reach Brittany by the *autoroute l'Océane* (A11 motorway), which divides at Le Mans, with branches to Rennes (A81) or Nantes (A11). A 24-hour information centre gives details of hold-ups, road works and alternative routes, Tel: (1) 48 58 33 33 (Paris), or Minitel 3615, code ROUTES.

Along the French autoroutes you will find a service station every 40 km open 24 hours a day, a rest area *aire de repos* every 10 km and a free emergency telephone every 2 km.

If possible avoid traveling on the last weekend of July, the first and last weekend of August and the holiday weekends closest to July 14 and August 15.

TRAVELING IN BRITTANY

By Train and Bus

Since 1986, the SNCF (national railway company), in partnership with local and regional authorities, has made efforts to develop its Brittany network. As well as TGV and Corail express trains, there are TER (regional express) services giving access to the main towns, with connecting TER coach services to less important destinations. These connections are particularly useful for touring inland Brittany, the Crozon peninsula and the Cornouaille region. Information/reservations: Minitel 3616, code TERINFO.

SNCF rail services in Brittany, information (I) and reservations (R):

Côtes-d'Armor: Saint-Brieuc, Tel: (I) 96 94 50 50, (R) 96 01 61 64. **Northern Finistère**: Brest, Tel: (I) 98 80 50 50, (R) 98 31 51 64. **Southern Finistère**: Quimper, Tel: (I) 98 90 50 50, (R) 98 90 26 21. **Ille-et-Vilaine**: Rennes, Tel: (I) 99 65 50 50, (R) 99 65 18 65. **Morbihan**: Vannes, Tel: (I) 97 42 50 50 / (R) 97 42 50 10. Nantes, Tel: (I) 40 08 50 50 / (R) 40 08 60 60. Timetables and information regarding the TER bus and train services are published twice yearly in the *Guide Régional des Transports*, which is available at train stations and tourist offices.

By Sea

There are five main ferry companies operating year-round sailings to the Breton islands. Certain services (shown with an asterisk) run only in summer (from June to September).

Île de Batz from Roscoff (15 min): *Cie Finisterienne d'Aconnage*, Tel: 98 61 76 66. *Vedettes Blanches*, Tel: 98 61 76 98.

Belle-Île from Quiberon (40 min, cars): *Companie Morbihannaise de Navigation*, Tel: 97 21 03 97. From Vannes, Port-Navalo* (1h): *NAVIX-Bretagne*, Tel: 97 63 79 99.

Île de Bréhat from the Pointe de l'Arcouest (10min): *Vedettes de Bréhat*, Tel: 96 20 03 47.

Glénan archipelago from Bénodet or Loctudy* (April to September, 1h30): *Vedettes Aigrettes*, Tel: 98 57 00 58. From Concarneau* (1h10): *Vedettes Glenn*, Tel: 98 97 10 31. Hydrofoil (35 min), Tel: 98 50 72 12.

Île de Groix from Lorient (45 min, cars): *Companie Morbihannaise de Navigation*, Tel: 97 21 03 97.

Île d'Houat and **Île de Hoëdic from Quiberon** (1h15 + 30min): *Companie Morbihannaise de Navigation*, Tel: 97 21 03 97. From Port Navalo*: *Vedettes Panoramiques*, Tel: 97 53 70 25.

Île de Molène and **Île d'Ouessant** from Le Conquet (30min): *Service Maritime Départemental*, Tel: 98 80 24 68. It is sometimes possible to sail from Brest via Le Conquet (+1h).

Île de Sein from Audierne (1h10): *Service Maritime Départemental*, Tel: 98 70 02 38.

Le Fret from Brest: *S.A. Vedettes Armoricaines*, Tel: 98 44 44 04.

By Plane

Local air connections: Brest–Île d'Ouessant: Finist'Air, Tel: 98 84 64 87. Lorient–Quiberon-Belle-Île: Finist'Air, Tel: 97 31 41 14. Lorient–Groix: Heli-Bretagne, Tel: 97 86 03 66.

By Car

Rental Cars: Internationally recognized agencies such as Avis, Budget, Hertz and Europcar along with a large number of local agencies can be found at airports, SNCF stations or through enquiry at the local tourist office. When renting a car, a substantial deposit is usually required unless you hold a credit card. It may prove cheaper to bring your own car from Northern Europe or Britain than to hire one for more than a couple of days.

Major roads, (*routes nationales*, abbreviated to N or RN) are always of the highest standard, conditions on secondary roads, (*routes départmentales or D*) vary but are usually still good. *Dual carriageways connect Rennes with Brest along the north coast and Nantes with Quimper along the south coast.*

Driving is on the right with overtaking on the left. Remember: Unless there are signs to the contrary, you must always give way to traffic coming from your right, even when it is coming from a minor road. All passengers, both in the front and back seats, must wear seat belts. Children under 10 years old are required to ride in the back seat. You are also required to carry a hazard warning triangle and headlights must be dipped towards the right.

Avoid leaving your car in an area

marked *Zone Piétonne* (pedestrian precinct), *Stationnement Gênant* (parking obstructive) or *Stationnement Interdit* (parking prohibited). Cars with foreign number plates are rarely stolen, but radios, tapedecks and luggage are always tempting targets.

Constantly updated information regarding congestion, road works and alternative routes in the whole of France: Tel: (1) 48 58 33 33.

Speed limits, unless otherwise posted and *on dry roads:*
- 130 km/h on toll motorways.
- 110 km/h on dual carriageways and motorways without tolls.
- 90 km/h on other roads.
- 50 km/h in towns. Town name sign starts the limit, a bar through the town name marks the end of the restriction.

On wet roads:
- 110 km/h on toll motorways.
- 100 km/h on dual carriageways and non-toll motorways.
- 80 km/h on other roads. *Rappel* means a continuation of the restriction.

PRACTICAL TIPS

Accommodation

All types and categories of accommodation are available throughout Brittany. During the summer, visitors would do well to make advance bookings. The peak period lasts from 15 July to 15 August. Some tourist offices are willing, for a small fee, to find you suitable accommodation and make reservations.

Hotels are officially classified: from 4-star (luxury) to 1-star (plain but comfortable). All hotels will provide a continental breakfast. Charges vary according to the grade of the hotel and the time of year, being at highest from mid-June to mid-September. In many hotels 15% is added to the bill for service – whether provided or not – , and when the bill is marked *service et taxes compris* no additional gratuity is expected.

Luxurious accommodation is offered by the *Châteaux hôtels indépendants et Hostelleries d'atmosphères*, information B.P.12, 41700 Cour Cheverney; or *Bienvenue au château* (with 15 châteaux offering bed-and-breakfast accommodation), free brochure from the Brittany CRT (Comité régional de tourisme) at Rennes, Tel: 99501115, or from the Maison de Bretagne in Paris, Tel: 4538 7315.

Less expensive are the *Logis de France*, with a membership of 300 hotels and restaurants throughout Brittany. Information: Fédération es Logis de France, 83 avenue d'Italie, 75013 Paris, Tel: 45 84 70 00 or 4 quai A. Thomas, 35260 Cancale, el: 99 89 60 16. The Association *Destination Bretagne*, offers 2- and 3-star hotels, with special rates for out-of-season bookings. Information: Balmoral Hotel, 35800 Dinard, Tel: 99 46 16 97.

If you are travelling to Saint-Malo, Rennes or Nantes, the SNCF offers a combined train ticket and hotel accommodation at reduced rates. Information and bookings can be made at all train stations, or by Minitel 3615, code TH.

Contact the government service *Fédération national des Gîtes de France*, for bed-and-breakfast accommodation (the *chambres d'hôtes*), rental houses, camp sites or self-catering accommodation in the vicinity of a farm or village (*gîte rural*). Information: 35 rue Godot-de-Mauroy, 75009 Paris, Tel: 47 42 20 20.

The association *Bienvenue à la Ferme* (Welcome to the Farm) provides farmhouse accommodation or camping facilities. Information: The Agriculture and Tourism department of the Chambre d'Agriculture, 9 avenue Georges-V, 75008 Paris, Tel: (1) 47 23 55 40.

The *Fédération française de Camping-Caravaning*, 78 rue de Rivoli, 75004 Paris, Tel: 42 72 84 08, publishes an official guide to French camp sites. It also provides a Minitel service: 3615, code FFCC. For practical information of all kinds, get in touch with the Camping Club de France, 218 bd. Saint-Germain, 75007 Paris, Tel: (1) 45 48 30 03.

Camping in places other then authorized camp sites is tolerated in some areas, but strictly forbidden in all nature reserves and regional parks.

Currency and Exchange

Banking hours can be unpredictable but generally they are from 8 or 9 am to 4 or 5 pm, with or without a lunchbreak around 12 noon until 2 pm. Some branches open Saturdays and close Mondays. Bureaux de Change at the international airports operate a daily service from 6 am to 11 pm. Rates of Exchange and commission can vary from bank to bank, even more so with the Bureau de Change. *Banque Nationale de Paris* and *Credit Lyonnais* usually take the least commission and offer the best rates.

Travelers' cheques remain one of the safest ways to carry around money. An alternative are Eurocheques for those with a European bank account. Credit cards (*Carte Bancaire*), particularly Visa, are known as *Carte Bleue*, and are probably the safest and best way of settling bills. Access, Mastercard and American Express are accepted, but less frequently.

Electricity

Virtually without exception all of France uses 220v (50-cycle) with double or triple round-pin wall sockets.

Emergencies and Problems

There are three emergency phone numbers:

15 - SAMU (ambulance service)

17 - Police

18 - Fire brigade

In case of theft or loss, contact the nearest police station, the *Gendarmerie* or *Commissariat de Police*. For loss or theft of credit cards, you should immediately notify the police station and the credit institute that has issued the card.

Carte Bleue (Barclaycard, Visa), Tel: (1) 42 77 11 90. Eurocard (Mastercard, Access), Tel: (1) 45 67 84 84. American Express, Tel: (1) 47 77 72 00. Diner's Club, Tel: (1) 47 62 75 00.

Health

While the French health service is efficient and reliable, it can be expensive if you are hospitalized, unless you are covered by a travel insurance or member of an EC state. All pharmacies (designated by a green cross) are obliged to give first aid on request, – for which you will be charged unless you are a minor, – and to provide you with the address of a doctor or a dentist. In urgent cases you can contact *SOS Médecins* in most major towns. In the event of a pharmacy being closed, a list of alternatives, including those with night service (*pharmacie de garde*) will be displayed in the window and in the local newspaper.

Post and Telecommunication

Post offices, indicated by the sign PTT or *Bureau de Poste* are open from 8 am to 7 pm on weekdays, and until 12 noon on Saturdays for both postal and banking services. Correspondence marked *poste restante* may be addressed to any post office and will be handed out on proof of identity. Postage stamps (*timbres*) are also sold in most tobacconists.

The simplest method of making telephone calls is with a *télécarte* telephone card giving credits of 50 or 120 units, available from post offices, tobacconists, and newspaper kiosks. All calls within France outside of Paris require no prefix. Calling from Paris dial 16 before the required number, and to ring Paris from the provinces dial 16 first, then 1.

Restaurants

The conventional eating times in France are earlier than in many other countries. Most people lunch between 12 noon and 1 pm (hence the remarkably traffic-free roads) and many hotels will expect their guests to arrive by 7.30 pm should they wish to dine. Tipping is not obligatory, but if the service has been good it is accepted practise to round off the bill with and extra 5 to 10%.

In many provincial towns the main meal of the day is at noon, and any specialities that may have been available are unlikely to be on the evening menu; nor are these specialities cooked every day, or prepared at a moments notice.

Bars and **Cafés** serve snacks including sandwiches, tea, coffee, soft drinks, beer, wine and spirits.

Bistros offer simple meals like omelettes, steak and chips, dishes of the day (*plat du jour*) or house specialities.

Brasseries serve hot meals throughout the day in a café-style ambience, quality of food and prices are similar to those in restaurants, but the service is faster.

Rôtisseries specialize in grilled meat.

In the country, **Auberges**, **Hostelleries** and **Relais de campagne** all serve full meals at defined hours. It pays to ask for recommendations from locals, regard long menus with suspicion and to think twice if you're paying only 50F for a regional speciality like *cotriade* (a northern version of *bouillabaisse*).

Shopping

VAT or TVA (*taxe sur la valeur ajoutée*) in France runs at a standard 18.6% and rising to 22% for luxury items. Goods purchased by non-French residents, over a certain value (often 1000F) can have the TVA refunded directly at the point of purchase, or by leaving the *ventes en détaxe* form with the customs at departure for a refund at home.

Shopping hours can vary considerably. Grocers, bakeries and butchers generally open 7 or 8.30 am to 12 noon, and 2 pm until 6.30 or 7.30 pm Monday to Saturday and occasionally Sunday morning. Bakeries often operate a rota system, so that at least one is open in the neighborhood every day. Department stores and supermarkets generally open from 9 or 9.30 am to 7 or 7.30 pm without a break, Tuesday to Saturday. Most close Monday morning or the whole day but many open Sunday morning in the high season.

Tipping

However anachronistic this practice might appear, it is the difference between a minimal and a living wage for a diminishing number of services. Hotel porters will expect 5 to 10F per item, chamber maids 50 to 100F per week, hairdressers, tour guides and taxi drivers around 10%, waiters in cafés and bars a small tip.

Time

France follows Central European Time (GMT + 1) and from the last Sunday in March to the last Sunday in September, clocks are put one hour ahead (GMT + 2) for daylight saving.

Tourist Information

Each region and department has its own tourist office (*Comité régional du tourisme*), and in addition each town of any importance and many smaller places with specific sights of interest have a local SI (*Syndicat d'Initiative*) or an *Office du tourisme*. If not, the town hall (*Mairie*) will give information.

Opening hours vary, but during summer most of them will be open every day (except Sunday) from 9 am to 12 noon or 1 pm, and 1 or 2 pm until 6 or 6.30 pm. From late October to early April many small-town offices will be closed, or open only for a couple of hours daily.

For advance information, reservations and itineraries, contact the enthusiastic and efficient **Maison de la Bretagne**, Centre Commercial Maine-Montparnasse, B.P. 1006, 75737 Paris Cedex 15, Tel: (1) 43 38 73 15.

SPORTS AND LEISURE

Sailing

With nearly 1700km of coastline, Brittany offers an enormous range of water-based sports: As well as yachting and dinghy-sailing, scuba diving, and windsurfing, there are facilities for water-skiing, sand-yachting and sea-kayaking. There are many sailing schools, which hire out sailing boats and run courses for beginners and more experienced yachtsmen. Before putting to sea, do not forget to listen to the weather reports and find out the times of tides (Minitel 3615, code Shom).

Some useful addresses:

Ille-et-Vilaine: Comité départemental de Voile, 2 allée Port-Louis, 35000 Rennes, Tel: 99 36 04 16. **Côtes-d'Armor**: Direction départementale de la Jeunesse et Sports, 4 boulevard Charnet, BP 32, 22000 Saint-Brieuc, Tel: 96 94 02 24. **Finistère**: Comité départemental de Voile, Port du Moulin blanc, 292000 Brest, Tel: 98 41 50 03. Nautisme en Finistère, 11 rue Théodore-Le-Hars, BP 91, 29103, Quimper cedex, Tel: 98 52 04 80. **Morbihan**: Comité départemental de Voile, Port-en-Dro, 56340 Carnac, Tel: 97 52 10 98. Ecole nationale de Voile, Beg Rohu, Tel: 97 50 27 02.

Loire-Atlantique: Comité départemental de Voile, S.N.O. Port Breton, 44470 Carquefou, Tel: 40 50 81 51.

Diving

Brittany has many sub-aqua clubs, offering courses for beginners and more advanced underwater exploration. Information: Maison de Bretagne, or Comité Bretagne " Pays de la Loire de la Fédération Française d'Etudes et Sports Sous-Marins, 78 rue Ferdinand Buisson, 44600 St.-Nazaire, Tel: 40 70 79 20.

Inland Waterways

Brittany is an ideal place for pleasure boating, which is also a relaxed way of discovering the charms of the inland country. The main waterways are:

The Channel-Atlantic link (*liaison Manche-Océan*), connects St.-Malo and Arzal via Dinan, Rennes, Redon and La Roche-Bernard, using the Ille-et-Rance canal and the river Vilaine (238 km, 64 locks). The Loire-Atlantique and Morbihan section of the Nantes-Brest canal connects Nantes and Pontivy via Redon, Malestroit and Josselin (205 km, 105 locks). The Blavet waterway runs between Pontivy and Lorient (72 km, 28 locks). The Finistère section of the Nantes-Brest canal connects Carhaix-Plouguer and Port-Launay, via Châteauneuf-du-Faou, Pleyben and Châteaulin (104 km, 35 locks).

Detailed information on boat hire and routes: Comité de Promotion des Canaux Bretons et des Voies Navigables de l'Ouest-Bretagne, 12 rue de Jemmapes, 44000 Nantes, Tel: 40 47 42 94.

Horse Riding

Information can be obtained from the Fédération des Randonneurs équestres de France, 16 rue des Apennins, 75017 Paris, Tel: (1) 42 26 23 23 or, more locally, from the Association régionale du tourisme équestre en Bretagne, 1 rue Gambetta, 56300 Pontivy. A full list of equestrian centres is available from the Ligue équestre de Bretagne, 16 rue Georges Collier, 56103 Lorient cedex. Some useful addresses:

Ille-et-Vilaine: Comité départemental des Sports équestres, 1 place Pasteur, 35000 Rennes, Tel: 99 36 46 54. **Côtes-d'Armor**: Comité départemental du Tourisme équestre, La Villa Banuel, Saint-Alban, 22400 Lamballe, Tel: 96 72 28 13. **Finistère**: Comité départemental des Sports équestres, 4 rue de la Gare, 29120 Pont l'Abbé, Tel: 98 87 02 62. **Morbihan**: Comité départemental du Tourisme équestre, Pen-er-Men, 56610 Arradon, Tel: 97 26 02 07. **Loire-Atlantique**: Comité départemental du Tourisme équestre, Le Châtelier, 44117 Saint-André-des-Eaux, Tel: 40 01 29 49.

Golf

Brittany has thirty or so golf clubs, 21 of which subscribe to the *Charte des golfs touristiques*. Many of these clubs offer reduced rates for a weekend or a full week, including green fee and accommodation, with or without breakfast and evening meal. Additional information from the Comité régional du tourisme or the Maison de Bretagne.

Golf clubs that can be recommended are: **Ille-et-Vilaine**: Dol-de-Bretagne, golf des Ormes, Tel: 99 48 40 27. Miniac-Morvan, golf de Saint-Malo/Le Tronchet, Tel: 99 58 96 69. Rennes/Le Rheu, golf de la Freslonnière, Tel: 99 60 84 09. St.-Briac, golf de Dinard, Tel: 99 88 32 07. Vitré, golf des Rochers-Sévigné, Tel: 99 96 52 52. **Côtes-d'Armor**: Fréhel, golf des Sables-d'Or-les-Pins, Tel: 96 41 91 20. Pléhédel, golf du Boisgélen, Tel: 96 22 31 24. Pleumeur-Bodou, golf Saint-Samson, Tel: 96 23 87 34. Saint-Cast-le-Guildo, golf de Pen-Guen, Tel: 96 41 91 20. Saint-Quay-Portrieux, golf des Ajoncs d'Or, Tel: 96 71 90 74. **Finistère**: Bénodet-Clohars Fouesnant, golf de l'Odet, Tel: 98 54 87 88. La Forêt Fouesnant, golf de Cornouaille, Tel: 98 56 97 09. Landerneau Saint-Urbain, golf d'Iroise, Tel: 98 85 16 17.

Morbihan: Belle-Île-en-Mer, golf de Sauzon, Tel: 97 31 64 65. Saint-Gildas-du-Rhuys, golf du Kerver, Tel: 97 45 30 09. Ploërmel, gold de Saint-Laurent, Tel: 97 56 85 18. **Loire-Atlantique**: St-André-des-Eaux, golf de la Baule, Tel: 40 60 46 18. Vigneux-de-Bretagne, golf de Nantes, Tel: 40 63 25 82. Le Cellier, golf de l'Île d'Or, Tel: 40 98 58 00. Missilac, golf de la Bretesche, Tel: 40 88 30 03.

Rambling

Ramblers can obtain information from the Association Bretonne de randonnées et itinéraires, 9 rue des Porte-Mor-delaises, 35000 Rennes, Tel: 99 31 59 44, which also supplies useful guide books and maps, lists of overnight shelters and camp sites. Information: Minitel service 3615, code Rando.

Please note: walkers need to be properly equipped, with comfortable clothes affording protection from wind and rain, and suitable walking shoes. They should carry a map (1:25,000 scale), water container, pen knife, and high-energy foods.

Tours

The Comité Régional du Tourisme gives information on thematic tours featuring less-known aspects of Brittany: *Route des peintres en Cornouaille*, featuring painters, information from the Finistère local tourist board (CDT) or from the Cornouaille tourism group (GIT), BP 410, 29330 Quimper cedex, Tel: 98 44 17 45). *Route des phares et balises*, featuring lighthouses, information from the Finistère CDT or the Brest GIT, Tel: 98 44 17 45. *Circuit Villes d'Art*, featuring towns of artistic interest, information from the CRT or the Maison de Bretagne. *Route des enclos paroissiaux,* featuring parish churches and associated monuments, information from the Finistère CDT, Tel: 98 53 09 00. *Voyages en Trégor*, featuring the Trégor district, information from the Côtes-d'Armor CDT, Tel: 96 62 72 00. *Circuits des Petites cités de caractère*, featuring smaller centres of distinctive character, information from the CRT or the Maison de Bretagne.

Organized Holidays

Loisirs Accueil promotes inexpensive holidays organized around a particular activity or pursuit – sports, cultural visits etc. Prices include transport and accommodation. Information at Fédération Nationale des Service de Réservation, Loisirs Accueil, 2 rue de Linois, 75015 Paris, Tel: (1) 40 59 44 12.

LOCAL EVENTS AND FESTIVALS

Châteauneuf-du-Faou: Festival international des Danses et Traditions populaires (dance and folk traditions), 15 August, Tel: 98 81 83 90. **Concarneau**: Fête des Filets bleus (Blue Nets Festival), 3rd Sunday in August, Tel: 98 97 01 44. **Dinan**: Festival international de musique et Concours de la Harpe celtique (music festival and Celtic harp competition), end of July, Tel: 96 39 75 40. **Dinard**: Festival du Film britannique (British Film Festival), early October, Tel: 99 46 94 12. **Fougères**: Festival du Livre vivant (Living Book Festival) in July, Tel: 99 94 12 20. **Guingamp**: Festival des Danses bretonnes (Breton Dance Festival), mid-August. Festival du Film anglais (English Film Festival), end of August, Tel: 96 43 73 89. **Lannion**: Festival d'Orgue et de Musique (Organ and Music Festival), July-August. Festival photographique du Trégor (Photography Festival), end of August, Tel: 96 46 41 00. **Lanvellec**: Rencontre internationale de Musique ancienne (ancient music), October, Tel: 96 35 18 82. **Lorient**: Festival du Théâtre (Theatre Festival), second half of July. Festival Interceltique (Pan-Celtic Festival), first half of August, Tel: 97 21 07 84. **Monterfil**: Fête de la Musique gallège (Gallo Music Festival), end of June, Tel: 99 07 90 47. **Nantes**: Festival international d'été (Spring Festival), July, Tel: 40 69 74 14. **Paimpol**: Fête des Terres-Neuvas et des Islandais (a festival celebrating the port's deep-sea fishing traditions), 3rd Sunday in July, Tel: 96 20 83 16. **Perros-Guirec**: Festival de Musique de chambre (Chamber Music Festival), April, Tel: 96 23 21 15. **Quimper**: Festival de Cornouaille, last week of July, Tel: 98 53 04 05. **Redon**: Fête de la Batellerie (in celebration of canals and canal transport), July). Festival de l'Abbaye (Abbey Festival), mid-July to mid-August, Tel: 99 71 06 04. **Rennes**: Transmusicales, first week in December, Tel: 99 30 38 01.

Festival des Tombées de la nuit (cultural festival), first week in July, Tel: 99 79 01 98. **Saint-Malo**: Festival de Musique sacrée (Sacred music), mid-July to mid-August. Festival du Jazz, first weekend in August, Tel: 99 56 64 48.

BRETON GLOSSARY

Breton belongs to the Brythonic branch of Celtic languages and is closely related to Welsh and Cornish. Over the centuries French influence led to a decline in the speaking of Breton. It is only very recently (since the 1970s) that the language has begun to be taught and passed on once again. Currently, 600,000 people speak Breton, mainly in Finistère, the Côtes-d'Armor and the Morbihan.

aber	estuary
aod (aot)	coast, shore
arvor (armor)	coastline
avon (aven)	river
beg (bec)	peak, summit
bihan (bian)	small
bran	hill
bras (braz)	big
dol	table
du	black
enez (inis)	island
geun (yeun, yun)	marsh
goaz	current, incoming tide
gorre	top
gwenn (guen)	white, sacred
gwern (guern)	marsh
gwig (guic, gui..-vic)	village
hent	road, way
hir	long
hroek (wrach)	witch
-ig (-ic)	diminutive ending
iliz	church
kastell	castle
ker (car)	town, village, hamlet
koad, koed, (-hoat, -hoët)	wood
kozk (koh, coz)	old
lann	hermitage, monastery
lech	flat stone
lenn (len)	lake, pond

loc'h . . . . lagoon, tidal pool
milin (meil) . . . . mill
menez (mane, mine) . . . . . mountain
meur . . . . big, important
mor (moor) . . . . the sea
nevez (neue, neve) . . . . new
penn . . . . . head, extremity, summit
plou (plo, plu, pleu, ple) . . . . . parish
pors . . . . port
roc'h (roh) . . . . rock
ster . . . . river
ti (ty) . . . . house
traezh (trez, treas) . . . . beach
treizh (treiz, treh, trech, tre) . . passage
uhel (huel, ihuel) . . . . . . top, most

Everyday Expressions

demat . . . . good day
kenavo . . . . good bye
trugarez . . . . thank you
yec'hed mat! . . . . your health!
d'ur wech all . . . . . . see you soon
kreiz'Ker . . . . town centre
fest-noz . . . . festival
breizh (abr. BZH) . . . . Brittany

AUTHORS

Françoise Leymarie-Legars has known the Côtes d'Armor region since childhood, taught by her Breton grandmother. Now a journalist specializing in tourism, and married to a Breton, she has undertaken a number of major assigments as a reporter, in France and worldwide.

Catherine Bray studied various subjects at university (art history, philosophy and modern literature), but always dreamed of travelling afar. Her passion for books led her to travel literature and publishing. This is how she comes to be responsible for coordinating the Nelles guides to Provence-Côte d'Azur and Brittany. She also writes articles on subjects in her field.

Isabelle du Boucher originates from the Basque country but lived in Brest for about ten years. In Brittany, she dis-

covered an attachment to local values and traditions similar in intensity to that of her native region. She is especially interested in Breton costume, history and legend, and also writes on cookery.

Sophie Bogrow contributes to the travel magazine *Grands Reportages, le magazine de l'aventure et du voyage,* and is responsible for the section on France. In this capacity, she has several times visited Brittany and Provence, and has come under their spell.

PHOTOGRAPHERS

Archiv für Kunst und Geschichte, Berlin 23l, 23r, 28l, 28r, 34l, 34r, 36, 37, 38, 39, 42l, 42r, 43.

Berbalk, G. 8/9, 10/11, 134, 223.

Pansegrau, E. 54, 154r, 206, 209, 212, 221.

Poblete, J. 12, 14, 18, 21, 22, 24, 26, 27, 31, 33, 48/49, 52, 55, 57, 59, 60, 61, 62, 67, 69, 74, 84, 85, 86, 92, 98, 106, 107, 114, 119, 120, 121, 123, 124l, 129, 130, 131, 137, 139, 143, 147, 148, 150, 154l, 155, 164, 168, 169, 173, 174, 175, 180, 182, 186, 192/193, 194, 197, 200, 204/205, 210, 217, 218, 220, 222, 226, 229, 231, 232, 233.

Radkai, M. and K. cover, 16, 17, 29, 32, 41, 44, 46/47, 53, 64, 78, 80, 89, 90, 97, 99, 100, 101, 104, 105, 108, 112/113, 118, 124r, 125, 128, 136, 142, 144, 151, 156, 158, 170, 176, 178, 179, 188, 189, 208, 213, 214, 215, 225, 228, 234, 236, 237, back cover.

Stadler, H. 1, 19, 65, 66, 72/73, 81, 88, 96, 103, 135, 162/163, 230, 239.

Teufelhart, R. 202/203.